RAILWAYS OF THE WORLD

5 Railways of Asia and the Far East

RAILWAYS OF THE WORLD

1 Southern Africa
2 Australia
3 Canada
4 Western Europe
5 Asia and the Far East
6 United States of America

Great Indian Peninsula Railway: a Neilson built class 'V39' waits with a local train outside Victoria Station, Bombay in 1904

RAILWAYS OF THE WORLD

5 *Railways of Asia and the Far East*

O. S. NOCK

B.SC., C.ENG., F.I.C.E., F.I.MECH.E.
HONORARY FELLOW AND PAST PRESIDENT,
INSTITUTION OF RAILWAY SIGNAL ENGINEERS

WITH 88 PHOTOGRAPHS
AND 42 MAPS AND DIAGRAMS

ADAM AND CHARLES BLACK · LONDON

FIRST PUBLISHED 1978
A. & C. BLACK LIMITED
35 BEDFORD ROW, LONDON WC1R 4JH

ISBN 0 7136 1855 8

British Library Cataloguing in Publication Data

Nock, Oswald Stevens
Railways of the world.
5: Railways of Asia and the Far East.
1. Railroads
I. Title
385 HE1021

ISBN 0-7136-1855-8

Text set in 11/13pt VIP Bembo, printed by photolithography, and bound in Great Britain at The Pitman Press, Bath

Contents

Illustrations

MAPS AND DIAGRAMS

Acknowledgements

The author and publishers thank the following for permission to use photographs:

P.S.A. Berridge, Esq., for 2a, 5a, 5b, 5c, 12a, 12b, 12c.
Beyer, Peacock & Co. Ltd., for 19b.
Caprotti Valve Gears Ltd., for 10a.
GEC Traction Ltd., for 16a, 29a.
Indian Railways, for 2c, 2d, 3c, 4c, 7b, 11a, 13c, 14a, 14b, 14c, 16d.
Japanese National Railways, for 21, 31a, 31b, 32b.
Malayan Railways, for 20a.
L. Marshall, Esq., for 6a, 6b, 6c, 6d, 7a, 10c, 15a, 15b, 15c.
National Portrait Gallery, for 1.
O. S. Nock, Esq., for 2b, 4b, 9a, 9b, 10b, 11b, 11c, 13a, 13b, 16b, 16c, 17c, 18a, 18b, 18c, 20b, 22a, 22b, 22c, 23a, 23b, 24a, 24b, 24c, 25a, 25b, 26a, 26b, 27a, 27b, 28c, 29b, 29c, 30b, 32a.
North British Locomotive Co. Ltd., for 3a, 3b, 3d, 8a, 8b, 8c, 8d, 19a, 19c, 19d.
North British Loco. Records, courtesy of Mitchell Library, Glasgow, for 7c.
Thailand, Royal State Railways of, for 17a, 17b.
H. Uematsu, for 28a, 28b, 30a.

The coloured frontispiece is from a painting by Jack Hill.

The maps and line diagrams were drawn by Mrs. C. Boyer of Corsham from data in the author's collection.

Preface

After the end of the Second World War the newly formed United Nations Organisation set up an Economic Commission for Asia and the Far East (E.C.A.F.E.) with its headquarters at Bangkok. Its main purpose was to assist the countries of that huge region whose economies, lands and industrial plants had been disrupted and ravaged by the war. Backed by the Great Powers of the world in varying degrees of enthusiasm and help, the attentions of E.C.A.F.E. were mainly concentrated upon the lands bordering upon the oceans of the south-east and the Pacific. Geographically the term 'Asia and the Far East' was a misnomer, because the activities of E.C.A.F.E. covered a mere fraction of the vast area embodied in this all-embracing name.

It is the same with this book. 'Asia and the Far East' is a euphonious title under which to group together a series of railways large and small that I have visited and been able to study in some depth; but like E.C.A.F.E. itself it does not cover all Asia, nor all the Far East—very far from it. There is nothing about the railways of China, or the Soviet Union, nor yet of Hong Kong, Indonesia, Taiwan or Manchukuo. Even so, with India and Japan alone I have a vast enough canvas on which to work, and I have included also the two countries in which I first met the railways of South-East Asia; Malaya and Thailand.

The first railways in India date from 1853, and with them will always be associated, and held in high honour, the name of the Marquis of Dalhousie, Governor-General from 1848 to 1856. It was natural that the development of Indian railways in the nineteenth century was wholly under British influence; but equally it was British influence and engineering acumen that launched the Imperial Government Railways of Japan, while in later years British enterprise played no small part in the development of the Siamese railway. To an English writer there is a natural pride in being able to chronicle these historic events; but it is with the most wholehearted praise that

I record subsequent developments—how the Indian Railways, for example, have progressed since Independence, and the success of the astonishing Shinkansen project of the Japanese National Railways.

Now that the book is finished and I am arranging the pictures, maps and diagrams, I am feeling rather overwhelmed with a sense of gratitude for all the help I received while on my travels. In the ordinary way it would have been no small undertaking for a stranger, however enthusiastic, however experienced in railway engineering, to embark on journeys of several weeks' duration in strange lands; but with the generous help of so many people, whom I am now proud to regard as personal friends, it was all made so easy. In Japan I certainly had a good start, with two pen friends who had been kind enough to write to me earlier about matters covered in some of my earlier books—H. Uematsu in Tokyo and Y. Kawakami in Akita. That they both had a command of English was encouraging to me! But when the time came for me to begin planning my visit to Japan, the Tourist Organisation in London, Japan Air Lines, and above all, the International Department of the Japanese National Railways in Tokyo just could not do enough. Mr. Makoto Iwamatsu, the Director of the International Department, and his staff, not only arranged my itinerary and saw that I had an English speaking guide everywhere I went, but also made my hotel reservations. Of this there is a story to tell, because in Japan one's age must also be declared when registering. My guides must have looked over my shoulder when I was signing up, because afterwards, in deference to my three score years and nine, I was scarcely allowed to carry a briefcase, let alone any luggage!

In India I have professional associations extending back for fifty years, but apart from touching down at Calcutta's Dum Dum airport briefly on my way to Bangkok in 1964, I had not set foot in the country until 1975. But again I was launched to a flying start. My old friend and Westinghouse colleague, Jack Brown, resident in India for many years, arranged for me an entrée at the highest levels of the Railway Board. There Mr. M. Menezes, then Director of Railway Planning, later General Manager of the South Eastern Railway, and now Member (Engineering) Indian Railways Board, and Mr. R. N. Seth, Joint Director, Corporate Planning, arranged a splendid tour for me. At each centre where I called I was most warmly and enthusiastically received. It was a special pleasure and privilege to meet Mr. M. N. Bery, then Chairman of the Railway Board, and now retired, and equally that he should have taken the chair when I gave a talk to senior railway officers in New Delhi. Many others who helped me on my way are mentioned in the text. Home again, I am very grateful to Mrs. C. Boyer, of Corsham, for her care and skill in producing the maps and diagrams.

O. S. NOCK

Silver Cedars
High Bannerdown
Batheaston
Bath

December 1976

Part One

India

CHAPTER ONE

Introduction–the Indian railway scene

A visitor from the West, standing for the first time at any one of the great railway stations of India, whether it be on the platforms, in the concourse, or even in the street outside, could well be excused for being momentarily dumbfounded. My own introduction was at Delhi, at the main station within the precincts of the Old City, but by use of the word 'precincts' I do not wish to convey any sense of the calm of a cathedral close. An Italian engineer, writing to a close friend of mine to thank him for some kindnesses ended his letter: 'Yours with deep commotion' (!), though commotion is a mild word to describe the scene of fevered animation that follows the arrival of a long distance Indian express train. Hundreds upon hundreds of passengers of many castes and creeds, and of all ages, many of them carrying large amounts of luggage and bedding on their backs or on their heads, disgorge in a torrent upon the forecourt. But all this is nothing to the situation on the carriageway alongside, where a wild mêlée of three-wheeler taxis, bicycle-hauled rickshaws, battered old 'Ambassadors', and horse-drawn carts jostle for position and patrons.

The confusion is more apparent than real, however, for in a surprisingly short time, all the arrivals are spirited away—nothing less than six in a horse-drawn cart, and goodness knows how many inside an 'Ambassador'. How the various forms of transport get away with their loads, weaving indiscriminately in and out with hairbreadth clearances is a minor miracle; but this is a book about railways, not road transport, or else whole chapters could be written about the rush hour traffic in the city streets of India! Having overcome one's astonishment at this maelstrom of vehicles and people, one is naturally curious about the inside of the station, and there again in the concourse the scene is equally strange to Western eyes. Scattered in squatting groups all over the spacious marble floor are passengers patiently waiting for the departure of their trains. Whole families, many of them fast asleep amid piles of luggage and bedding, pay no attention to the milling crowds around them, quite content to wait thus for many hours before train time. Others whose departure times are nearer at hand press around the luggage weighing machines, because all luggage must be weighed in India. This is indeed a necessary provision, because some families tend to travel with little short of the proverbial 'kitchen sink'.

The process of entering the trains is orderly and well-disciplined, and for the most astonishing spectacle of the whole station one must go to the platform ends. Here more groups of squatters are ensconced; and down on the ballast between the tracks, groups of men and women are camped out for the day as it were, and children, often of quite tender years, run across the tracks, happily and unconcerned, even though a large 'Pacific' engine may be bearing down upon them! The crews move their locomotives with much whistling, very slowly about the yards, but the children seem to have developed a kind of sixth sense. It was cool when I first went to Delhi, and some ballast picnic parties had lighted small fires to keep themselves tolerably warm. Of the more orthodox type of train spotters, there were none.

But to see Indian railway stations at their most spectacular one must visit big city stations like Churchgate or Victoria Terminus in Bombay, or Howrah in Calcutta, at the height of the suburban rush in the morning. This takes place later than in European and American countries, because most offices do not open until ten. Later in this book I shall discuss the purely railway problems that concern this time of the day, but here I must convey my astonishment at the sight of these trains, because one has got to live with them in India! It is not enough that the insides of these spacious multiple unit coaches should be literally *packed* with passengers. Where other suburban trains have sliding doors that close, the Indian ones are open, and round each opening is a cluster of people hanging on by their very eyebrows, with their bodies extending far beyond the outer profiles of the coach. On the older multiple unit trains that have footboards, one often sees men standing *between* the doors, hanging on to the cantrail above!

One of these trains approaching presents an almost unbelievable sight, with a white 'cluster' bulging out from every door on both sides. The only clusters that are not white are those of the women-only sections, where gay coloured draperies are flying in the wind created by the train's movement. As the train comes to rest people literally pour out, from both sides, and while most will surge towards the normal exit others will rush across tracks to some way out of their own, often in the face of another incoming train. At Howrah, the great terminus across the Hooghly River opposite Calcutta, I have seen three such trains arrive almost simultaneously, and disgorge about eight thousand passengers. And so far as hanging on is concerned, I think the palm must go to the intrepid man who found a foothold, but no hand grip, so hooked his umbrella round a distant roof-rail! There are of course some, even today, who ride on the roofs.

I rode into Bombay one evening in the driver's cab of one of these trains, just as the suburban rush outward from the city was working up to its height. Our own train gradually packed up at each intermediate station until it was virtually 'bulging at the seams', as the saying goes; but it was the outward bound traffic that held me spellbound, and at times made me catch my breath. Train after train came towards us with the characteristic clusters of white-clad commuters hanging on round each open door. Fortunately the tracks have been laid with ample space between, so that there is no risk of these human 'bulges' being swept off as two trains pass, or when the train passes beneath a bridge. Incredibly risky as it looks to a visitor, I was told that casualties are astonishingly few. Most of these hangers-on seemed cheerful enough, and when I photographed some of the trains there were frequent waves and shouts of amusement.

It was, however, not the hangers-on, of both sexes, whose attitudes and intrepidity made my heart occasionally miss a beat. Our own train into Bombay that evening was one that passed some suburban stations without stopping. We would be approaching, at about 40 m.p.h. when an outgoing train on the adjacent track would draw in, and stop. Instantly a torrent of people would pour out, from *both sides*, some surging along the platform, but nearly as many jumping down on the opposite side and racing across our own track, despite continuous whistling. Of course the motormen of the electric trains are familiar enough with this kind of thing, and our man had slowed down a little in preparation. It was like driving down a street crowded with pedestrians. There was another hazard too. Indian station platforms are built in the British style, high enough for one to step level into the carriages, so that any one on the track has to climb up to get clear of an approaching train; but these agile commuters, men and women alike, seemed as adept at this as in hanging on round the open doors of the carriages.

It is, of course, only around the larger cities that there is such a tremendous intensity of passenger traffic, and such emphasis on speed and punctuality. As will be told later in this book, the engineering techniques used to ensure safety and reliability in working are of a very high order; but the problem of the peak hours, that is present in every city throughout the world, is exceptionally severe in India because of the high density of population in Calcutta, Bombay and Madras, all of which have highly developed electric commuter train services. On the long distance trains there is not the same sense of urgency, and the groups of sleeping passengers that surprise the European visitor entering the concourse of an Indian station for the first time are probably catching a train one or two *days* later. An English traveller, at the turn of the century, wrote:

In India no one undertakes a railway journey rashly or in a hurry. If the intending traveller be a first- or second-class passenger he probably begins proceedings by writing to the stationmaster on the subject the day previous. If he propose to join the train at an intermediate station this course is enjoined by the company's regulations. Some two or three hours before the time of departure he sends off his 'boy', or native servant, in charge of the *saman*, or luggage. Half an hour before he will arrive himself, see his luggage safely through the excess department, purchase his dinner ticket and breakfast ticket, and then during the last quarter of an hour he will probably be engaged in an argument with his fellow-passengers as to the amount of *saman* he may bring in the carriage.

If the traveller be a native, however, and intends to travel third-class, he will probably arrive at the station some hours before it is necessary, and, with his family, he will proceed to camp out on the station platform; and, if he be a Brahmin, his *saman* will include all the food and water he intends to consume on the journey, carried in brass vessels.

Nowadays it would seem that preparations for a journey have to be made much earlier than was necessary three-quarters of a century ago.

As in all countries with a high density of population the passenger traffic problem in India, severe though it is nation-wide, is secondary to that of freight; and unlike the situation that prevails in Europe and North America there is no appreciable alternative to the railway for freight haulage. One does not need to travel further in India than the major cities, and their respective airports, to realise how little modern road transport facilities are available; the prevalence of bicycles, rickshaws and bullock carts in a city street, is interspersed with the occasional camel or elephant carrying goods. In visiting some of the major centres of railway freight traffic I was therefore not surprised at the great diversity of goods carried, as well as its massive tonnage. Although the Indian railways originally adopted much of contemporary British practice, and with it standardisation of the vacuum automatic brake, it was fortunate that certain severe physical conditions virtually compelled the fitting of continuous brakes to freight trains from early days, and that the anachronism of the British loose-coupled goods train disappeared from the Indian railways. Development had scarcely begun when the first of all Indian railways, the Great Indian Peninsula Railway, was faced with climbing over the Western Ghats, and eventually did so on gradients of fearsome length and severity, where there were eventually as serious problems in getting the trains down safely as in providing the tractive power to haul them up. At the present time, however, I found many Indian railway officers wishing that when standardisation of continuous brakes took place the air rather than the vacuum had been chosen.

In alluding to a contentious subject, however, I am passing beyond the Indian railway scene and moving towards practical operating problems of today, and there is one other field of activity that must be looked at purely in its superficial sense before I pass on to detailed history and development—the proliferation of rail gauges. To the lover of quaint and historic locomotives the narrower gauges of India provide a constant delight, but I must be careful at the outset to explain the correct terminologies. I shall detail later how the Indian 'standard' gauge first came to be fixed at 5 ft. 6 in. in 1851, and how, some fifteen years later, authorisation of the metre gauge came about. Today the 5 ft. 6 in. is known as the 'broad gauge', while the term 'narrow gauge' is reserved for those lines built on gauges still narrower than one metre. Some English writers of the late nineteenth century, striving more for dramatic effect than actuality, referred to a 'Battle of the Gauges' in India. They endeavoured to draw comparisons between the situation in respect of the broad and metre gauge systems in India, and the major confrontation that took place in Great Britain in the 1840s, when standard gauge interests fought successfully to stem the advance of Brunel's 7 ft. 0 in. gauge on the Great Western and its associated companies in the West of England and South Wales. While there was some sparring for position in the south between the Madras, the Southern Mahratta, and the South Indian Railways, as will be told in detail later, it was quietly incidental compared to what had happened in England some fifty years earlier.

The 'gauge battle' in India was between the broad and the metre gauges, and today one metre gauge line has developed its traffic to such an extent that it is being converted to broad gauge. Of the narrow gauge lines, one could write whole chapters on the fascination they provide for those who love railways for their own sake. Darjeeling; Kalka-Simla; Ooty—their fame is legendary, and remote as they are, they still provide an essential role in the transportation system of India as a whole. I did not have an opportunity to visit all of them personally; but enjoying the friendship of those who have been and taken many photographs, it is not difficult to sense the unique atmosphere that makes railway enthusiasts worship at these shrines. Even today on the narrow gauge lines the trains travel very slowly; but then nobody is in the slightest hurry, and life jogs quietly along.

A final impression of the Indian railway scene is of the solidarity of the stations and of the fixed equipment. It is not only that the platforms are high; the buildings are massive and in some cases look as though they had been built to withstand a siege. I am not now referring to the great city stations, many of which are truly masterpieces of contemporary oriental architecture, but of numerous country stations. It must not be forgotten that many of the earlier railways of India were built when the country was recovering from a time of grievous internal disturbance, and strategic considerations in respect of both local as well as foreign interference loomed large in the planning and equipment of the railways. Consequently the stations were built so that they could be readily adapted as defence strong points, just as the ornamental approaches to certain important bridges, notably at Cawnpore (now Kanpur) and Benares (now Varanasi) could quickly be fortified. Happily the occasion never arose for this to be done.

CHAPTER TWO

Gateway of India—Development in the twenty years 1845–1865

The geographical situation of Bombay with its magnificent natural harbour made it an obvious point of entry to India, when the activities of the East India Company and British interests were centred in Calcutta. In the 1830s the mails from England were carried by ships of the East India Company, between Suez and Bombay, and it was a monopoly that was most jealously guarded. It was natural enough to bring the mails ashore at the 'Gateway of India'; but the service was slow and unreliable, and once ashore the subsequent distribution was unutterably bad. When the famous Peninsular Steam Navigation Company added 'Oriental' to its name in 1840 and became the P. & O., the East India Company offered them a 'bonus', for five years, if a service was introduced between Suez, Madras and Calcutta, leaving the East India with its monopoly to Bombay. This the P. & O. undertook, with such success that mail carried by their ships round the south of India reached Calcutta more quickly than when carried by the armed vessels of the East India Company, and subsequent land transport from Bombay.

It was the general dissatisfaction with existing inland transport facilities that led to the first proposals for railways in India, and appropriately enough they began in Bombay in the year 1843. An Inland Railway Association was formed in January 1845, and simultaneously plans were announced for a Bombay Great Eastern Railway which, despite its rather grandiose title, proposed no more than a line to Thana, a distance of only 20 miles. In the meantime business interests in England had also been studying the possibilities of railway development in India, and early in the same year the first step towards the organisation of a company entitled the Great Indian Peninsular Railway was taken in London. This was the result of three years of careful research among the records of India House in Westminster, on the part of one John Chapman, and contact with the Honourable Court of Directors of the East India Company. By August 1845 matters had progressed to the extent of Chapman setting out for Bombay to investigate on the site, and with his arrival local interests that formed the Inland Railway Association felt that their main purpose had been fulfilled, by the launching of the Great Indian Peninsula Railway, and threw the whole weight of their influence and enthusiasm behind John Chapman.

While preliminary surveys were being made in India, however, the financial situation of railways in England was in great confusion. The year 1845 was that of the Mania, when the prospects of getting rich quickly lured vast numbers of investors, of high and lowly estate, to buy railway shares. Many of the schemes put forward at the time were unblushingly spurious, and countless people were ruined. The inevitable recession slowed down the progress of genuine projects, of which the G.I.P.R. was one, and it was not until August 1849 that the Act of Incorporation of the company was passed by the British Parliament, and a contract signed between the newly incorporated railway company and the East India Company. But although it transpired that the G.I.P.R. was the first Indian railway to be opened to the public, it was not the first company to be formed—if not actually incorporated. It was perhaps natural that much interest should have been shown in Calcutta, the headquarters of the East India Company, and plans for an East Indian Railway were put forward in 1844. As with the G.I.P.R. the principal investment had to come from London, and for the same reasons the proposals hung fire for several years, amid disagreements, doubts, and plain opposition.

The appointment of the Marquis of Dalhousie as Governor-General in 1848, was in many ways a turning point in Anglo-Indian history, particularly in respect of transport and the development of natural resources. He had already held high Government office at home, and as Vice-President of the Board of Trade during the Government of Sir Robert Peel, had become keenly aware of railway engineering and operating matters at the time of the Royal Commission on Railway Gauges. He was familiar with the views of the great men of the day—Robert Stephenson, Joseph Locke, Brunel and others; and he combined with his great abilities as an administrator a far-sighted outlook, deep personal sincerity and altruism. His arrival in India in 1848 was fortunate beyond measure for the development of Indian railways. The relation then existing between the East India Company and the Government of India was such that the Company held wide powers and territorial control, and the Governor-General had not a great deal more than a co-ordinating role between the Company and the Native States. So far as the early railways were concerned, it was the Company that authorised their construction, though it is amusing to find in many of the old records that directly some awkward question of principle arose, the Honourable Court of Directors stepped smartly to one side, and said that it should be a Government decision!

In this role, and in the detailed and expert attention he gave to it, Lord Dalhousie can well be called both the father and architect of the Indian railway system. While the railway company had not been formally incorporated nor contracts signed when Dalhousie arrived in India, the promoters of the G.I.P.R. were quite clear in their aims—of pressing eastwards from Bombay—if not so clear as to how they were going to mount the Western Ghats and reach the Deccan. His principal concern was with the proposed East Indian Railway, expressed in a lengthy memorandum, in his own handwriting, which I have had the opportunity of studying in the National Archives of India, in New Delhi. It was written on 4 July, 1850, at Chini, a mountain settlement some 70 miles to the north-east of Simla, on the Satlej River. A sum of £1m. sterling had been allocated to the project, and Lord Dalhousie's lengthy memorandum centres on his point 12:

> The object of that experiment is to prove not only that it is practicable to construct Railways in India as Engineering works, but that such Railways when constructed will as commercial undertakings afford a fair remunerative return on the money which has been expended in their construction; so that the public may thereby be encouraged to invest their capital in the construction of similar works in other parts of India.

Lord Dalhousie was quite scathing in his comments on certain features included in the report submitted to the Government, particularly in that the experimental railway should be constructed as a double-track line. The map included in the report by George Turnbull, engineer to the East Indian Railway Company, shows two alternative routes, one passing through Burdwan and the other heading towards Rajmahal. To spend the agreed allotment of capital on a double line railway, Lord Dalhousie comments: '. . . one terminus will be at the Capital but the other will be literally nowhere'. He then proceeded to give his own proposals as to how a line could be built from Howrah to the Raneegunge coal district, where there would be a potentially profitable traffic to be tapped at the end of the line. Then he takes up the question of the gauge:

The Court of Directors have recommended at the same time the use of the narrow gauge of 4 ft. 8½ in. for the railway about to be constructed. Although the letter of the Court recommends, but leaves to the Govt. of India to determine as to the gauge which should be adopted on this occasion, I consider the question to be one of such moment as to deserve careful consideration and an authoritative and conclusive decision by the highest authority connected with the Indian Empire; who alone can have access to that full in foundation and extended experience which would make such a decision really and satisfactorily conclusive.

The British legislature fell unconsciously and perhaps unavoidably into the mischievous error of permitting the introduction of two gauges into the United Kingdom. The numerous and grievous evils which arose from that permission are well known, and will long be felt throughout all England. The Govt. of India has in its power, and no doubt will carefully provide, that however widely the Railway system may be extended in this Empire in the time to come, these great evils shall be averted and that uniformity of gauge shall be rigidly enforced from the first. But I conceive that the Govt. should do more than this, and that now at the very outset of railway work it should not only determine that a uniform gauge shall be established in India, but that such uniform gauge shall be the one which science and experience may unite in selecting as the best.

At one time this question was much before me; and although I should not myself attempt to offer an opinion on so vexed a question, yet I may venture to form one on the recorded views of men competent in every way to judge.

The evidence which was given before the gauge commission in 1846 and the evidence which has been given from time to time before the Committee of Parliament backed as it has been by very high authority abroad, is I venture to think, sufficient to show that the narrow gauge of 4 ft. 8½ in. (a measurement adopted originally at haphazard and from the accident of local circumstances) is not the best gauge for the general purposes of a Railway; and that something intermediate between the narrow gauge of 4 ft. 8½ in. and broad gauge of 7 feet will give greater advantage than belong to the former, and will substantially command all the benefits which are secured by the latter.

He decided on 5 ft. 6 in. and instructions to that effect were conveyed to the Great Indian Peninsula Railway in January 1851, while his forthright observations about the proposed route of the East Indian Railway led to almost immediate acceptance of his alternatives, as evidenced in a memorandum addressed to the Government of Bengal in August 1850:

The Govt. of India having determined that the experimental line of Railway in Bengal shall be constructed from Howrah on the right bank of the Hooghly towards the coal-fields at or near to Raneegunge and that the line proceeding by Serampore, Chinsurah and Hooghly, shall be carried in the direction of Burdwan to such a point as may leave it open to the Govt. to select hereafter the further line direct to Mirzapore or to Rajmahal, without any sacrifice of railway already constructed, it has become necessary that steps should now be taken for placing the officers of the East Indian Railway Company in possession of the land required for the Railway and for this purpose some alteration in the law is required, which will be immediately made and promulgated.

In the meantime interest had shifted from Bengal to Bombay where the construction of the Great Indian Peninsula Railway was presenting many problems. The city of Bombay is built on a narrow island, some 10 miles long, and connected with the mainland by the Sion Causeway; and before the G.I.P.R. was off the island there were engineering difficulties in crossing the low, swampy flats and creeks. James J. Berkley was appointed Resident Engineer, and took up his work in Bombay in February 1850. He followed the precedent set in England by George Stephenson, when crossing Chat Moss, by 'floating' the line across the marshes upon large hurdles made out of mangrove bushes. On the mainland the route lay through a region of low, but rugged hills covered with thick jungle until the foot of the mountain range of the Western Ghats was attained. From the outset, despite the modest scope of the original proposals it was intended that the Great Indian Peninsula Railway, in emulation of its high-sounding title, should provide trunk routes across the peninsula to both Calcutta and to Madras, and this involved not one, but two crossings of the Ghats.

The situation was entirely different from that facing the East Indian Railway, which was projected through country so level that in one of his inimitable memoranda Lord Dalhousie said that the gradient should not exceed 1 in 2000. By contrast, an engineer later in the service of the G.I.P.R. described the Western Ghats as rising 'like a Titanic wall of sheer cliffs over 2000 ft. high with here and there a noble peak towering high above, like the keep of some gigantic castle'. After having described the Thul Ghat incline, by which the main line to Calcutta ascends the mountain face, he continues:

The Bhor Ghat, which is on the direct route to Madras, is an even finer piece of work, and its construction brought lasting fame to its designer, Mr. James Berkley, who, however, did not live to see it completed. In the 16 miles of its length, it rises 1821 ft. with the same maximum gradient as in the case of the Thul Ghat, viz., 1 in 37. It passes through 3985 lineal yards of tunnel and over 1330 lineal yards of viaduct. Its route lies through, probably, the finest scenery of its kind in India, including bold mountain scarp; towering peaks of bare, black rocks; deep canyons, down the sides of which, in the monsoon, fall silvery waterfalls and filmy cascades, marking the presence of roaring torrents and mountain streams; valleys, the slopes of which are clad with dense virgin forest, below which lie sweet, peaceful villages surrounded by fertile rice fields; while high up, among the peaks, gleam the white walls of many a neat bungalow, peeping out from groves of hardy trees, and marking where the hard-worked citizens of steamy Bombay have established retreats on the everlasting hills, where they can enjoy the cool, mountain breezes after the exhausting heat and toil of the busy city.

The line takes advantage of a great spur of the Western Ghats, enclosing the great gorge of the River Oolassa, and ascends its right flank for some distance, crossing several magnificent ravines. It then pierces through to the left flank, creeping along under the huge crags, which seem to literally overhang it, in a mere notch cut along the side of the precipice, which falls steeply down to the valley immediately below. Thence, it reaches the reversing station, at which the engines change their position to the other end of their trains, and once more curving along the steep hill side and passing through Khandalia Station, arrives at the Sanitorium of Lonavla, 80 miles from Bombay.

These are no fanciful word pictures. I have ridden up and down the formidable Bhor Ghat incline in the driver's cabs of electric and diesel locomotives and can testify to the sheer thrill of coming *down* the gradient on the leading unit of a triple-headed, 2000-ton freight train, when skilful control of the brakes was infinitely more important than development of high tractive power to lift a heavy train *up* the slope! But in referring to modern operation I have drawn more than a century ahead of my period, and I must go back to the days when the Ghat inclines were being built. That over the Bhor Ghat took 7½ years to build, and was opened to traffic in 1863. Ten years earlier, with the G.I.P.R. and the East Indian under construction, Lord Dalhousie once again applied himself to the question of railways in India, and in a monumental minute in his own immaculate handwriting, which when copied extended to *forty-eight pages* of closely typed foolscap(!), he laid down the principles on which the railway network for the whole of India should be built up. This was in April 1853. As to the need for railways in general he wrote:

Great tracts are teeming with produce they cannot dispose of. Others are scantily bearing what they would carry in abundance, if only it could be conveyed whither it is needed. England is calling aloud for the cotton which India does already produce in some degree, and would produce sufficient in quality and plentiful in quantity if only there were provided the fitting means of conveyance for it from distant plains to the several ports adapted for its shipment. Every increase of facilities for trade has been attended, as we have seen, with an increased demand for articles of European produce in the most distant markets of India; and we have yet to learn the extent of value of the interchange which may be established with people beyond our present frontier, and which is yearly and rapidly increasing.

Ships from every part of the world crowd our ports in search of produce which we have, or could obtain in the interior, but which at present we cannot profitably fetch to them; and new markets are opening to us on this side of the globe, under circumstances which defy the foresight of the wisest to estimate their probable value or calculate their future extent.

It needs but little reflection on such facts to lead us to the conclusion that the establishment of a system of railways in India, judiciously selected and formed, would surely and rapidly give rise within this empire to the same encouragement of enterprise, the same multiplication of produce, the same discovery of latent source, to the same increase of national wealth and to same similar progress in social improvement; that have marked the introduction of improved and extended communication in various Kingdoms of the Western world.

Lord Dalhousie then continued:

I apprehend that any attempt to lay down at this time a perfect and comprehensive system of Railways covering the surface of India, is premature and can lead to no practical result. I conceive that my present business is to advise the Honourable Court as to those great trunk lines which are of primary importance, not only as being most immediately required, but as forming the main channels which future lines shall be able to take advantage of, as the best and readiest means of communication with other portions of the Indian Empire.

That some such general outline of a system should be described at the commencement is of essential importance, in order that whatever capital may now be made available for the construction of railways in India may not be frittered away upon local and inconsiderable schemes, but may, as far as possible, be made to conduce schemes to the establishment of those great lines by which the general interests of India would best be served.

The main considerations which should determine the selection of a great Trunk line of railway in India must be 1st the extent of political and commercial advantages which it is calculated to afford: 2ndly the engineering facilities which it presents; and 3rd its adaptation to serve as a main channel for the reception of such subordinate lines as may hereafter be found necessary for special public purposes, or for affording the means of conveyance to particular districts.

Tried by these tests, I apprehend that the line from Calcutta by the valley of the Ganges to the North West Provinces which is referred to by the Honourable Court in the despatch 67–1852 will stand the first in order of importance and value, and ought to command the earliest and best, attention of the Government of India.

Following this he outlined the routes which eventually took shape as the Madras, to make an end-on junction somewhere with the G.I.P.R. and provide one main line right across India; the Bombay,

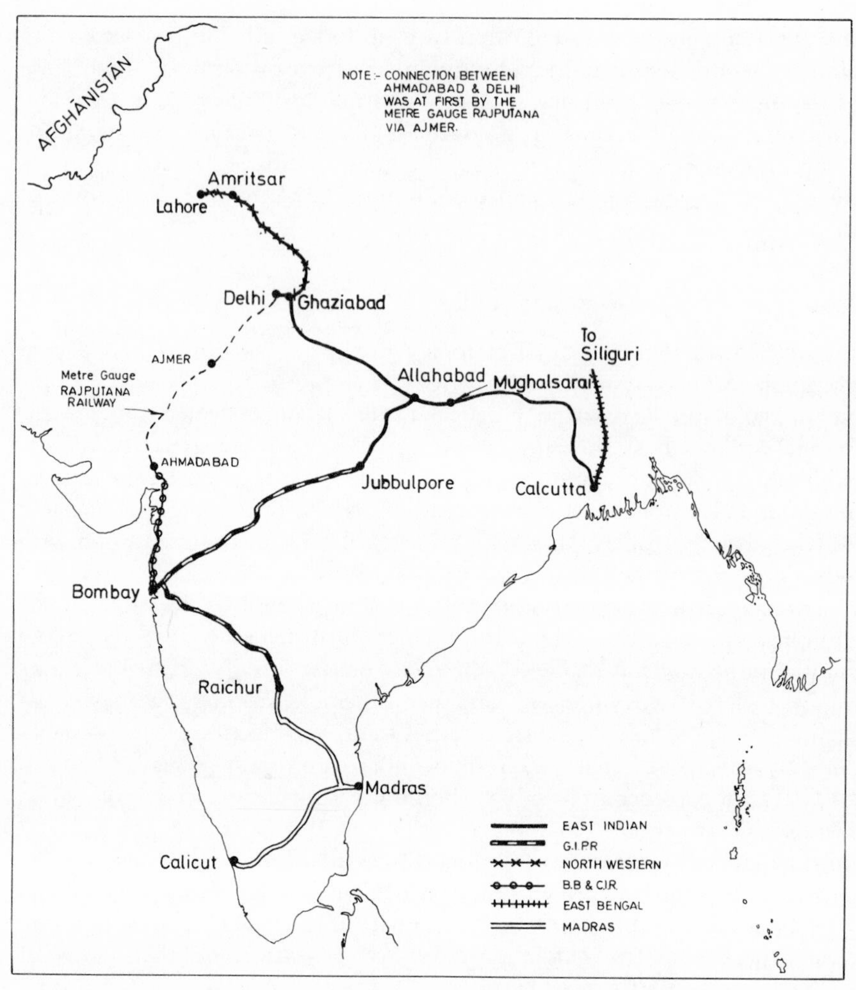

1. The Dalhousie Plan: the first main line network in India

Baroda, and Central India, to provide a direct line from the 'Gateway' (Bombay) to Delhi, and further connection to the highly strategic North West Frontier; and then also the South Indian, which he recommended should be prolonged by Salem, to Coimbatore, and through the gap in the ghats at Palgautcherry to the opposite coast. A branch should be thrown off to Bangalore, which Major Pears entertained a hope of being able to effect satisfactorily by way of a ghat beyond Vamimbady. A branch might be carried with advantage to the foot of the Neilgherries near to Ootacamund, and ultimately perhaps Cannanore might be included by means of a short extension.

It is very interesting to find, at so early a date in Indian railway history, that Lord Dalhousie made a most resolute stand against the Government building of railways. He wrote:

Railway works in India will probably consist for the most part of embankments and bridges of various descriptions. These are works with which the Engineers in the several armies of the Hon'ble Company are thoroughly conversant. There can be no doubt, therefore, that railways would be executed by the local governments with as full efficiency as by the Engineers of the private companies. Again the Engineers of the Government have had long practice in the construction of such works as form the component parts of a railway, though not in the formation of continuous railway lines. They are familiar with the people and their ways, acquainted with their language, inured to the climate, versed in the machinery of Agency, and on their guard against its abuses. Great works exist to testify to their professional ability and I am not aware of any well founded allegations of reckless or unthrifty expenditure in the execution of them.

Officers so highly qualified undoubtedly are likely to carry on the works of an extensive undertaking upon the plains of India, with greater economy and greater speed than can be possible now, or for some time to come, in the case of men freshly arrived from England, ignorant of every thing connected with this country, and sometimes not altogether inclined to learn. And although I have some hesitation in believing that the Government of India is any exception to the general rule which holds good elsewhere, that a government always works at greater expense than any body else; and although I am not prepared to say that during the five years I have passed in India the execution of the Grand Trunk road, or even of the Ganges Canal, (noble work though it be) has, in any respect, been characterized by speed, as compared with the execution of corresponding works in other countries, still I do not wish to dispute that railway works may be executed here with greater economy and speed by the Government than by Railway Companies.

But admitting unreservedly that Engineer Officers would make a railway as well, and admitting for the sake of argument that they would make it as cheaply and as quickly as private companies, I am still of opinion that the Government ought not to undertake the making of Railways.

The Government in these Presidencies is at present deficient in the Agency they would require for the purpose. The number of Engineer Officers is so wholly inadequate for the duties they have to perform, that other officers have been numerously employed in the Department of works. The Hon'ble Court has declared its readiness to augment the Corps of Engineers; but that measure would not for many years to come diminish the difficulty to which I have referred. Even if the duty of the Government Engineer on a railway were solely that of superintendence, a few would not suffice for the work. Many must be withdrawn from the duties on which they are now employed; and it is my opinion that this could not be done without detrimental to the general interests of the state. I think it far better that railway works should be entrusted to parties ready to execute them by professional Engineers than that public works in other parts of the country should be starved through the withdrawal of the Engineers for whom no adequate substitutes can be furnished; merely in order that the railway works may be executed at something less cost and in something less time than European Agency would spend upon them.

He added these trenchant paragraphs:

One of the greatest drawbacks to the advance of this country in material prosperity has been the total dependence upon the Government in which the community has placed itself, and its apparent utter helplessness to do anything for itself.

Until very recently the only regular carrier in the country has been the Government, and no man could make a journey but with Government establishments and by the Agency of a Government Officer.

Then, after many more pages of observation, which show clearly his grasp of railway matters generally, and his knowledge of Indian affairs, he concludes:

I have the honour respectfully to submit these several recommendations to the Honourable Court of Directors, and to express my earnest hope that it will resolve at once to engage in the introduction of a system of Railways into the Indian Empire; upon a scale commensurate with the magnitude of the interests that are involved, and with the vast and various benefits, political, commercial and social which that great measure of public improvement would unquestionably produce.

His term of office in India ended in 1856. The eight years of Government, during which he had done so much for the country and laid the foundations for much more, had told heavily upon his health, and back in his native Scotland he did not live long. In India for a time it seemed that his great plan for railway development might well be stillborn, for he had hardly departed before there came that series of tragic disturbances that in English history books are grouped under the name of the Indian Mutiny. This is no place to recall the events, still less to discuss their rights or wrongs. But one thing is certain: if construction of the railway network advocated by Lord Dalhousie had been more advanced at the time of that fatal parade at Meerut, in May 1857, the subsequent casualties and sufferings would have been minimal compared to what actually occurred. As it was, the great distances of India, the lack of efficient communications, and the stranglehold of officialdom, made it virtually impossible at first for the management of the East India Company in Calcutta to apprehend fully what was happening in Oudh and the Punjab. Such was the indignation in England when the full story became known that there was general resolve that the authority of the Company for Governmental responsibility, and defence, must speedily be ended, and in 1859 India was brought directly under the British Crown.

The building of railways was resumed, and by the end of 1865 the lines actually constructed can be seen on the map on page 16. At that time there were seven different railways, all state *owned*, but six were worked by companies operating under a system of Government guarantee. These were the G.I.P.R.; the East Indian; the Madras; the South Indian; the Bombay, Baroda, and Central India; and the Scinde, Punjab, and Delhi Railway. The last mentioned became a state *worked* line, in 1885, when it was amalgamated with certain others to become the North Western Railway. The remaining line was the Eastern Bengal, which ran due north from the Sealdah station in Calcutta, and eventually reached Siliguri, the starting point of the very famous Darjeeling Himalayan Railway. The Eastern Bengal has an interest of its own, quite distinct from that of the other pioneer railways of India, in that the consulting engineer was none other than Isambard Kingdom Brunel. His private sketch books,

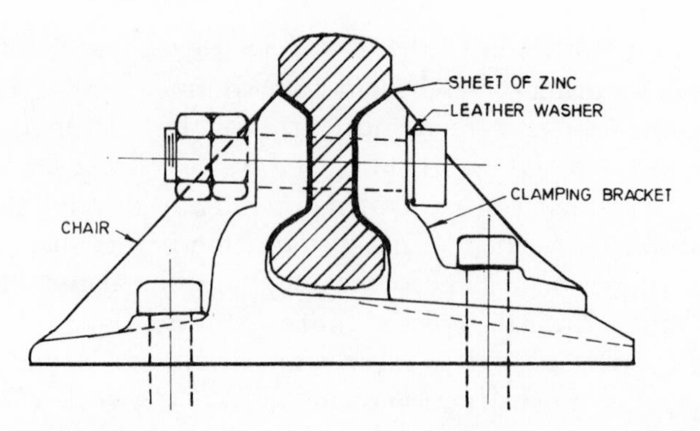

2. Brunel's bull head rail for the Eastern Bengal Railway

now in the library of the University of Bristol, include his proposals for the terminus station of Sealdah, in Calcutta; but even more interesting is the form of track he recommended.

In England in 1835 Joseph Locke had introduced the double-headed reversible type of rail. The idea was that when the top surface was worn, the rail was turned over, and what had been the under surface became uppermost. It was hoped that this would double the life of the rail. In practice, however, the constant passage of traffic led to some battering of the under surface, where it rested in the cast iron chairs, and rendered the under surface unfit for subsequent use as the running surface. The 'dumb-bell' section was so advantageous in other ways that it was developed into the bull-head section that became the British standard form of rail, from 1858 onwards. For the Eastern Bengal Railway Brunel modified the double-headed type of rail in a most ingenious way, to avoid the battering effect on the under side, and so make double life a reality. Instead of resting the under side of the rail directly on the chair, and using a wooden key to hold it tightly in position, he clamped it, as shown in the sketch, so that the bottom surface was clear. I have not been able to find out what mileage of the Eastern Bengal Railway was actually laid with this section. As far as the records show, Brunel did not visit India in person, but he was busy with the designs during the cruise to Egypt that preceded his final illness, in 1859. The first 70 miles of the line were opened in 1862.

CHAPTER THREE

Problems in construction

It is one thing to take a map of India, note the principal centres of trade and industry as they existed in Lord Dalhousie's governorship, and decide how they should be connected by railway; but as briefly mentioned in an earlier chapter, India set railway engineers a host of difficult problems before the G.I.P.R. had progressed far inland from the 'Gateway' or the East Indian had begun to extend far beyond the first experimental length out of Howrah. The great trunk line envisaged by Lord Dalhousie, from its terminus on the Hooghly opposite Calcutta, to the far north-west, had the apparent advantage of very easy gradients because its route was planned to follow the valley of the Ganga and then of the Yamuna to the very walls of Delhi. In 950 miles from Calcutta, indeed, the line rises less than 700 ft. It is however difficult perhaps for those who have not been in India to appreciate what the monsoon period can do. Referring particularly to the easternmost sections of the line, the wide expanse of level country is subject to excessive tropical rainfall. Inundations from the flood spill from the great channel of the Ganga, and other very large rivers are often spread as a vast sheet of water over miles of country.

One particular 'incident', though severe, can be regarded as characteristic of what can happen. It occurred over a seven-mile length of the original main line of the East Indian Railway above Sahebgunge, and was caused by continuous heavy rain throughout the district. At one station 11 in. of rain were recorded in 24 hours, and that kind of downpour went on for days. At that point, the railway—at about a distance of two miles—follows the south bank of the Ganga. The flood caused great damage, destroying many villages, and drowning upwards of one thousand people. On the railway the water lapped the banks, washed out all the ballast, and carried away one of the piers of a five-span girder bridge. Two of the girders were swept 300 yards downstream. Traffic was at first completely stopped, but after three days a steam ferry was brought into operation to transport passengers across the flooded area. For a full month afterwards passengers and luggage were conveyed across the breach in the line by boats.

Despite the natural policy of following the valleys of great rivers, even before the railway network of India had extended beyond the stage shown on the map on page 16, some immense works of bridge construction had been necessary. The first of these was commenced as early as 1856, about 50 miles west of Patna, near the town of Arrah, where the main line of the East Indian Railway had to cross the River Sone. This is no mere tributary of the Ganga. It has a vast catchment area in the high country of central India, and it is about two miles wide for upwards of one hundred miles in its lower reaches. At the peak of the monsoon period, its discharge is reputed to be about $1\frac{3}{4}$ million cubic yards per second, while for eight or nine months of the year it is no more than a meandering stream in the middle of a wide sandy waste. To carry the pioneer railway across such an area was a tremendous task for the early railway engineers. By the year 1856 much experience in bridging had been gained on the railways of Great Britain, but none in such fearsome extremes of climate. Everything depended upon the foundations. There was no question of providing high clearance for navigation, and fortunately below the seemingly limitless expanse of sand so evident in the dry season there was a stiff bed of yellow clay. Into this the piers were sunk to a depth of 32 ft. below low water mark. There were no less than 28 wrought iron decked spans 157 ft. long, resting at their ends on massive 18 ft. diameter circular towers—three in line, at the junction point of each span.

Construction was halted during the grave disturbances of 1857, and it was not until 1863 that the Sone bridge near Arrah was completed. In the meantime the work of extending the line had rapidly advanced, continuing on or near the right bank of the Ganga. At Mughal Sarai, now the site of a great mechanised marshalling yard, the railway is almost opposite to the world famous Pilgrim city of Varanasi, though in early days the Ganga was not crossed at this point, and the line continued on the right bank to Allahabad. This city stands at the confluence of the River Yamuna (Jumna) with the Ganga, and the former was crossed by the Naini Bridge, another large and impressive structure, opened to traffic in 1865. Still the railway continued to the north west, on negligible gradients, through Kanpur of tragic memories, to the junction of Ghaziabad, and the approach to Delhi. The former place was the furthest extent of the East Indian Railway by the end of 1865 (see map on page 16), and the entry to Delhi from Ghaziabad was over the tracks of the Scinde, Punjab and Delhi Railway.

The River Yamuna flows beside the walls of the old city of Delhi, and the railway came in over another very large bridge. The engineers of this line gained experience of Indian river crossings in dramatic style, within the first dozen years of railway building in India. As at the crossing of the Sone near Arrah, the piers were formed of circular wells, built of brick, but in the early stages little was known of the effects of scour—the washing away of the river bed around the piers. In some places the alluvial soil in the river beds was as much as 100 ft. deep, and it was found, from mishaps, that when flood water met an obstruction (like a bridge pier), it circled round and washed out the soil at the river bed. Then the pier would fall over, and the span supported by that pier would collapse into the flood waters. At the bridge on the approach to Delhi old city, the main stream left half the spans of the bridge high and dry and took an entirely new course *behind* the abutment of the bridge.

In the previous chapter I mentioned briefly the obstacle of the Western Ghats. It was a mountain barrier that had only one parallel at that time in the history of railway construction—the Semmering Pass in Austria. But the similarity was only that of a bewilderingly wild and tumbled mountain region. In both cases there was no defined way in which a railway could be taken to the crest of the range, and the confused welter of peaks, ravines, and gigantic outcrops of rock was made all the more baffling to the surveyors by the density of the forests that made any long sights of the country around impossible. In these days, when any similar project would be made so much easier with the aid of aerial surveys, it needs a mighty test of the imagination to picture what James J. Berkley and his men had to cope with. Lord Elphinstone, then Governor of Bombay, made a remarkable statement:

> I fear that whichever way the railroad is made we must be prepared for very numerous casualties. Every possible means must be taken to lessen the risk—but it would be idle to expect that we shall carry on a victorious campaign on the Danube without loss, or we should successfully overcome the physical difficulties which we have to confront in making railroads in such a country as India without heavy sacrifice of human life.

Disease claimed the greatest number of casualties. Even to those born and bred to the extremes of climate in that part of India—the heat, the tropical rains, scarcity of water in the dry season, attacks from wild animals and dangerous reptiles—such conditions took their toll, and after work had been resumed following the disturbances of 1857, a great epidemic of cholera occurred in the rainy season of 1859–60. So heavy was the death roll (some records say 30 per cent. of the entire work force), that large groups of men panicked and fled from the working areas, and construction came to a standstill. Berkley usually had about 40,000 men on the job, and it was a mammoth task to recruit a new force. The very nature of the engineering was enough to daunt some of the stoutest hearts, with stupendous earthworks, long tunnels, and high viaducts—all necessary to obtain a uniform inclined surface for the railway in this extraordinary countryside.

In broadest outline the railway had to be carried slantwise up the face of the escarpment, and that escarpment was a wild, disorderly welter of rocks, bluffs, and every conceivable kind of mountain configuration flung together in fantastic array. Berkley made history in railway alignment by introducing the zig-zag device of getting up the face of the escarpment. The ascent was made so far, and then on coming to the reversing station the direction of running was reversed and on restarting, the climb was continued in the opposite direction. Although Lord Dalhousie had been so outspoken against incurring expense by building double-tracked railways in India generally, the wisdom of the Great Indian Peninsula Railway in building the two lines over the Ghats as double-track routes was incalculable, in view of the way traffic developed. One of the most spectacular features of the Ghat inclines are the runaway 'catch' sidings. Where the ruling gradient is 1 in 37 the consequences of a breakaway, or of a train overpowering its locomotive due to inadequate brake power, could be a positively apocalyptic smash, and catch sidings were constructed, in each case leading far up the mountainside, into which a runaway could be diverted to run safely on the steep rising gradient of the siding until its momentum was exhausted.

The Bhor Ghat incline, the longer of the two, and that which lies on the main line from Bombay to Madras was completed in 1863. By the 1920s however the old alignment and the reversing station had proved to be such a bottleneck in the handling of ever increasing traffic, that a very difficult and costly re-alignment was undertaken to avoid the need for reversal. It involved the construction of three new tunnels, but from 1928 when the new route was brought into service it proved an immense boon in train working. However, the reversing station was not the only bottleneck on the Bombay–Madras main line. The original double-tracked route was laid with the track centres 12 ft. apart, providing a space of 6 ft. between the rails, in the centre. The later Indian standard is 15 ft. 6 in. to provide for wider rolling stock, and incidentally plenty of room for passengers to hang on to the outside of carriages! In view of the tremendous cuttings and tunnels on the Ghat sections, it can well be imagined what a task it was to widen the line. The work was begun in 1945, and took six years to complete.

The need for more railways in India, and the high cost of construction on the standard 5 ft. 6 in. gauge, led to some extensive rethinking on the subject of railway gauges. By the year 1870 railways on gauges narrower than the standard British 4 ft. 8½ in. were being successfully operated in several parts of the world, and in India a network of narrow gauge lines was being urgently considered, as feeder routes to the broad gauge main lines. There was general agreement that all these should be built to a standard gauge, but the engineers concerned could not agree on what the gauge should be. There was strong support for both the 3 ft. 6 in. and the 2 ft. 9 in. gauge. In 1870 there was no Honourable Court of the East

India Company to be satisfied; a straight decision was needed by the Government of India. Lord Mayo was then Governor-General and in a long memorandum dated December 30, 1870 he carefully weighed the arguments for and against the two proposed gauges, and headed tactfully towards a compromise, in which strategic considerations had some influence. He wrote:

On the Eastern Bengal Railway, the horseboxes are 8 feet in the clear, 7 feet in the interior, divided into three partitions, two of 2 feet 6 inches, and the middle one of 2 feet. This is, I think, too small.

The 3 feet 3 inches gauge would give, according to these proportions, a horsebox 6 feet 6 inches in the clear, and 5 feet 6 inches in the interior. This would give a space for two horses abreast of 2 feet 9 inches each (including the partition), which is precisely the space allowed on the horseboxes of the East Indian Railway.

If, however, a great number of horses have to be moved in a short time, horseboxes would be little used; and if a rapid transit is desired for military objects, the main portion of the troopers must always be carried in ordinary goods wagons.

Six feet in the interior of a vehicle will be sufficient to carry gun-carriages for the heaviest artillery whose wheels do not, in scarcely any case, exceed 5 feet 3½ inches.

He concluded:

According to the best consideration I can give to this extremely difficult question, I recommend the adoption of a 3 feet 3 inches gauge.

So India got the metre gauge, as a feeder system to the earlier standard 5 feet 6 in. broad gauge.

An extensive metre gauge network grew up to the west of the broad gauge Bombay, Baroda and Central India Railway, which had been the first link from the 'Gateway' towards the sensitive North West Frontier. It runs fairly near to the coast for the first 200 miles, and although the gradients are easy there are several major river crossings. The old bridge over the Bassein River, about 30 miles north of Bombay, is remarkable not only for its immense length of 1¼ miles across a tidal estuary, but for the shallow, relatively short main girders supported on a very large number of deep-well type of foundations. A train crossing the bridge appears to

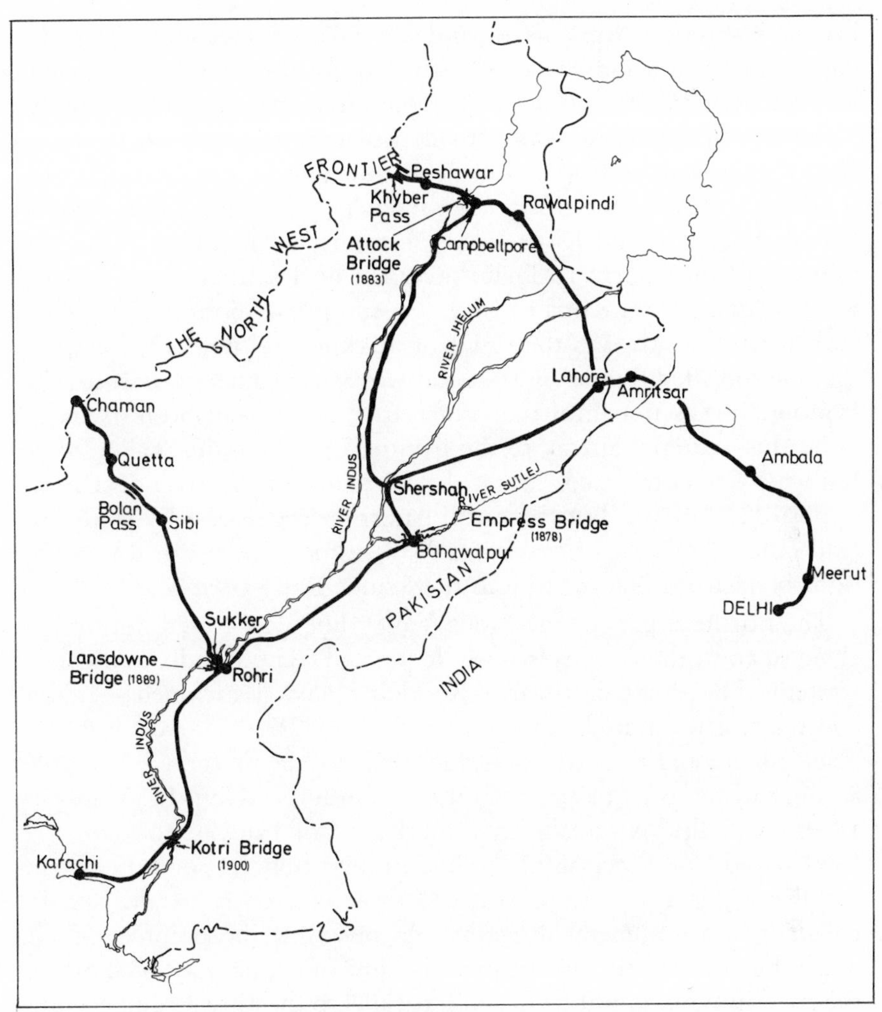

3. Railways to the North West Frontier

be running on no more than a platform supported on stilts! This fine bridge was brought into service as early as 1864.

I have referred to the North West Frontier as sensitive. It is really no exaggeration to say that in the latter part of the nineteenth century the history of the region was dominated by fear of a Russian invasion, through Afghanistan, and in 1876 orders were given for the construction of a railway to Quetta, purely for strategic purposes. One of the great difficulties in the region at that time was that the province of Baluchistan was virtually isolated, railway wise, from the rest of India by the Indus itself. The title Scinde, Punjab and Delhi Railway was something of a misnomer, because the Scinde section, between Karachi and Kotri was not connected to the rest and the journey from Karachi to Delhi included no less than 570 miles by river steamer, from Kotri to Multan. At a point about 200 miles up stream from Kotri was the town of Sukkur, and it was from there that the so-called Kandahar State Railway was planned to start for the frontier. It was not until two years after orders had been given to build the strategic railway to the frontier that the Indus Valley State Railway was completed, down the left bank of the river to Rohri, opposite to Sukkur; but there still had to be a crossing by water, to reach the other part of the Indus Valley line, which ran down the right bank from Sukkur to join the Scinde Railway at Kotri.

The northern part of the Indus Valley line was a vital link in the chain of communications from Calcutta and Central India to the new strategic line pointed towards Kandahar, and it included a major constructional feat in the crossing of the Sutlej River, at Adamwahan. The resident engineer was James R. Bell, and he presented a notable account of the job in a paper to the Institution of Civil Engineers in 1880. With the extraordinary experiences of bridge work on the Punjab and Delhi section of the line immediately in mind, he began by discarding any notions that the flow of a river would remain constant in any general direction. At one time, he pointed out, it might be directly athwart the intended line of the railway; at another, the river in flood might be flowing parallel to the railway and cutting across at a different place altogether. Instead of flowing beneath the prepared bridge, it would rise in such spate elsewhere as to breach the embankments. Another important lesson learned on the earlier bridges was the quite devastating effect of scour around the piers. At the Sutlej River the piers were made no less than 19 ft. in diameter outside, and the walls 5 ft. thick. They were sunk more than 100 ft. into the river bed, which was of sand, with layers of clay. When they were finished, hundreds of tons of stone were dumped around the piers, to give the scouring action something to work on, as it were. It became the accepted practice in such localities in India to dump train loads of stone around the piers after every major flood, to make up for the material washed away.

While the foundations were vital enough, the actual erection of the bridge in such a remote locality was a tremendous task. There were 16 spans in all, amounting to a total of 6700 tons of wrought ironwork, and it all had to be shipped out from England. Because of the limited port resources then existing in India, the Government insisted that the material should be landed at three different places, and the only ports that could then handle such cargoes were Calcutta, Bombay and Karachi, respectively 1500, 1800 and 600 miles from the site. Although Karachi was much the nearest transport thence by river steamer was much the most inefficient and expensive. There was no town anywhere near, and a work-camp similar to those in remoter parts of England and Scotland was set up. There however the similarity to a place like Blea Moor ended. At Adamwahan work was pushed ahead through the fearful summer heat and the season of torrential rain, and the casualty list was a bad one. Bell related that it was not unusual during the worst weather for three men out of four to be laid up with fever. When work was in full progress the inexperience of much of the labour in bridgework erection led to a wastage of rivets of up to 50 per cent.

The bridge was completed in 1878. It was designed for single line railway traffic, but it was very soon to be used in most unusual circumstances. Before that, however, had come one of those gestures from home which showed appreciation of the tremendous efforts being made to develop communications in India. In 1877 on the initiative of Benjamin Disraeli, Her Majesty Queen Victoria had been created Empress of India, and in 1878 she sent a telegram to the Government in Calcutta, congratulating them on the completion of the work and asking that the bridge might be named after her—'The Empress'. So it was, and this great pioneer work carried the traffic between Karachi, the Punjab, and Delhi until 1929, when it was reconstructed to carry a double line of railway. It was at the very outset of its life as a single-line bridge, in 1878, that the long anticipated war on the Afghan frontier broke out, and then the force that the indomitable Lord Roberts eventually led to Kandahar used it *as a road bridge*. Guns, camels, and cavalry passed over it, and there is a good story told of the first elephant who stepped on to it trying to shake the sleepers to make sure that the going was safe!

Although the Kandahar expeditionary force crossed the Sutlej River thus they were still on the wrong side of the Indus, and in 1878 little had been done to start work on the Kandahar State Railway. But the lack of good communication across the desert of the deadly Katchi plain, which in the campaign across the frontier caused more casualties than those actually suffered in battle, highlighted the desperately urgent need for the railway to Quetta. Once authority was roused the men actually on the job responded with a stupendous feat of railway construction in such conditions, and the 133½ miles of the line across the desert to Sibi were built in 101 days, and the line was opened thus far in January 1880. With the desert crossed the tremendous mountain ranges of the frontier lay ahead; but a general election in England and the return of a Liberal Government under W. E. Gladstone resulted in a less forthright policy towards the North West Frontier, and the advance of the Kandahar State Railway towards Quetta ground to a halt.

Before concluding this chapter on early railway construction, two more great bridges must be mentioned, one over the Ganga, and one over the Indus. I have described earlier how the main line of the East Indian Railway kept on the right bank of the Ganga, passing through Mughal Sarai, and continuing to Allahabad and Kanpur; but between the left bank of the Ganga and the Ghaghara River to the North lay the province of Oudh, and in 1864 the Oudh and Rohilkund Railway was projected, forming a shorter and more direct route to the North West than that of the East Indian. At the very beginning, however, the Ganga itself had to be crossed, to bring the new line from its junction with the East Indian near Mughal Sarai across to the pilgrim city of Varanasi. A feature of the great bridge constructed, and opened in 1887, was that it provided for both rail and road traffic, not in the improvised style of the Empress bridge but by design. On its opening by the Marquis of Dufferin and Ava, Viceroy of India, after whom it was named, it was described as 'in some respects the most perfect specimen of railway bridge engineering in India'.

The original Dufferin bridge, which was regirdered in 1947, was perhaps one of the least spectacular of all the great railway bridges of

India. The large girders over the river spans were of the compound 'triangular' type, presenting a completely rectangular assembly of ironwork as seen broadside, and wide enough inside as to carry both rail and cart traffic. At the Varanasi end there were fortified block houses. When I was in India in 1975, I crossed the present bridge on the roadway which is now carried at a higher level than the railway, and I had a splendid view up and down the great river, with a distant prospect of the world-famous riverside ghats of Varanasi itself with the skyline of turrets, minarets and temple buildings behind. The main girders of the modernised bridge are of the hog-backed type which, despite the contemporary eulogies of 1887, make it a more picturesque structure than the original. It is now known as the Malviya Bridge.

The second early bridge of immense significance was that over the Indus, from Rohri to Sukkur, which by connecting the two halves of the Indus Valley Railway completed the continuous line of railway communication between Calcutta and Karachi. At this location the river flows through two separate channels and it was that on the Rohri side that presented the greater problem. There the bedrock shelves out steeply from each shore, disappearing to leave a deep cleft in the middle filled with silt. It was thought unwise to attempt to build any intermediate piers, and so the channel had to be taken in a single stride. Sir Alexander Rendel, consulting engineer to the Government of India, designed a highly spectacular bridge of two anchored cantilevers carrying a suspended span of 200 ft. in the middle. The girder work was manufactured in London, and before shipment the whole of it was assembled in the contractor's yard, where its immense size towering 170 ft. into the sky, made a very striking sight. This procedure anticipated by nearly 50 years that adopted for the great Howrah road bridge over the Hooghly, at Calcutta, which was erected completely beside the LNER main line at Darlington, before shipment. The bridge over the Rohri channel, opened in March 1889, was named after Lord Lansdowne, then the Viceroy of India. This very striking bridge carried heavy main line traffic until 1962, when it was transferred to the new Ayub arch built by the Pakistan Western Railway.

CHAPTER FOUR

Running the trains—locomotives : carriages : wagons : signalling

In earlier days train operation in India was a leisurely business. It nevertheless began to supplant modes of transport that were incomparably slower and less efficient, and the spectacle of a mail train jogging along at 40 to 45 m.p.h. between stations would have been one of breathless haste around 1870 or 1880. With the exception of the Ghat sections of the G.I.P.R. most of the original main lines had been laid on easy gradients, though not quite so easy as the 1 in 2000 specified in Lord Dalhousie's famous minute of 1853! But from the twin circumstances of easy gradients and modest timetable requirements the earlier Indian locomotives, both for passenger and goods traffic, were small, and strongly influenced in details of design by contemporary practice in Great Britain. Down to the turn of the century the 4–4–0 was almost universal for mail and the more important passenger trains, and the 0–6–0 type for goods. The lead up to the 4–4–0 situation followed traditional British lines beginning with the 2–2–2 and the 2–4–0, and including the 0–4–2 for mixed traffic; and there was a time when there was some indecision as to whether inside or outside cylinders should be standardised.

Of these types it was perhaps those of the East Indian that were the most distinctive. A class of very pretty little 2–2–2 tank engines was introduced for the inception of the line in 1854; but with subsequent extensions westward greater fuel and water capacity was needed and they were converted into very elegant little 2–2–2 tender engines. Only in one respect could they be distinguished from locomotives on the home railways. At that time the drivers and most of the firemen were Europeans, and large canopied cabs were fitted to protect them from the heat of the midday sun. Engines of the East Indian Railway were painted what could well be described as 'Indian Red'—a rich colour, with a little more 'red' in it than the 'iron ore' shade of the Furness Railway at home. The G.I.P.R. and North Western—the latter formed by amalgamation in January 1886 of the various 'State' lines, in what is now Pakistan, with the Scinde, Punjab and Delhi Railway—used 2–4–0 locomotives for mail and passenger service, though with inside cylinders. Though not exclusively so, both these companies favoured stovepipe chimneys.

The East Indian continued to favour outside cylinders at first, and from 1866 purchased from England a number of 2–4–0s that were quite powerful for their day. They had inside frames throughout, and outside cylinders 16 in. diameter by 22 in. stroke. The canopied cab extended forward from the footplate, covered the entire length of the firebox, and continued until almost touching the steam dome. These engines were very much involved at the time of the great famine in Bengal, which reached its height in 1874. To get supplies through to the stricken areas the East Indian Railway had to run many more trains than normal, and a critical shortage of enginemen arose. Although the locomotives themselves could be double or treble shifted there were not the trained crews to man them. An appeal for help was made to England, and many drivers and firemen, mostly from the London and North Western, went out to India on short term engagements, with a promise of re-instatement to their former duties on return. It was treated like volunteering for military service abroad in a national emergency.

Mention of the L. & N.W.R. leads to the unofficial affiliations of Indian railways that developed as their traffics developed and their equipment increased. The North Western in many ways modelled its engineering practice on that of the L. & N.W.R. in England, even to the extent of adopting an almost identical style of lining out for its black engines. The East Indian on the other hand drew some of its mechanical engineering inspiration from the London, Brighton and South Coast Railway, not surprisingly in that its locomotive superintendent, A. W. Rendell, had been trained under William Stroudley. Rendell's earlier affiliations did not go to the extent of adopting the Brighton style of painting. 'Indian Red' remained the standard colour until the advent of the Indian Railways Conference Association engines of the 1920s. On the other hand the G.I.P.R. adopted a handsome livery of chocolate brown, which anticipated by many years the change on the London, Brighton and South Coast Railway from Stroudley's yellow to Marsh's dark umber—very similar to the basic colour of the G.I.P.R.

The Oudh and Rohilkund, mentioned in the previous chapter in connection with its great bridge over the Ganga near Varanasi, made Indian locomotive history in 1885 by purchase from Dübs & Co., Glasgow, of ten 2–4–0 express locomotives on the Webb 3-cylinder compound system. Until the previous year almost the entire traffic of the line had been worked by a stud of 0–6–0 engines introduced in 1871, and augmented up to the year 1878 until there were no fewer than 84 of them at work. Apart from these engines, there were only six rather extraordinary 0–8–0s, used during the constructional period. With the approaching completion of the Dufferin Bridge, locomotives that were more of an 'express passenger' category were needed. A word of praise must be reserved for the 0–6–0s, known as the 'B' class. They were an excellent type for the period. One of them has been preserved and restored to its original condition, and I had the pleasure of seeing and photographing it in the works at Lucknow, in 1975. It is a picturesque little thing, in a handsome purple-brown livery and polished brass dome mounted on the firebox, and very similar in general appearance to the first 0–6–0s of the Scinde Railway, though of less power. The comparative dimensions were:

Early Indian 0–6–0 tender engine

Railway	Scinde	O. & R.
Cylinders		
dia. in.	16	14
stroke in.	24	20
Coupled wheels		
dia. ft. in.	5–0	4–0

The first 2–4–0 express engines, received from Dübs & Co. in 1884, were very neat but quite conventional in design, with 17 in. by 24 in. inside cylinders, and 6 ft. diameter coupled wheels. Then in

1885 came the ten Webb compounds. They were smaller engines than any of the L. & N.W.R. classes, and had a volume ratio of low to high pressure cylinders of 2:1, as in the Crewe 'Experiment' class. The driving wheels were uncoupled, and as in England great difficulty was sometimes found in starting. They gave no satisfaction in India, and were completely outclassed by the ordinary simple 2–4–0s. In an attempt to cure the starting difficulties some of the compounds, if not all, were fitted with coupling rods; but this could not redeem their somewhat tarnished reputation. In the year of opening of the Dufferin Bridge the O. & R. took delivery from Neilson's of the first 2–6–0 freight engines. These were powerful units, and had 19 in. by 24 in. cylinders, inside, and the same neat appearance that characterised all engines on the line, with shapely tapering chimneys in the Stroudley style, copper capped, and a smart hemispherical-topped dome.

The era of the inside cylinder 4–4–0 on the Indian railways began in the 1890s. Among the first were those of A. W. Rendell on the East Indian, of which Neilson's and Dübs each supplied 25, in 1893–4. The placing of considerable orders simultaneously with these two famous Scottish works anticipated the action of the L.M.S. in 1927 when the order for 50 'Royal Scots' was divided between the same two factories, then the Hyde Park and Queens Park Works of the North British Locomotive Company. Rendell's 4–4–0 bore a very striking resemblance to the first 'Dunalastair' 4–4–0 of the Caledonian (see page 36).

The 'Dunalastairs' won worldwide fame for their boiler proportions in relation to cylinder volume; but their ratio in this respect had been anticipated three years earlier by Rendell's East Indian design, built in such close proximity to the Caledonian works at St. Rollox.

Rendell's 4–4–0s were neat and compact, rather than stylish in appearance; the palm in this latter respect must be awarded to S. J. Sargant's 'C/5' class on the G.I.P.R. These were really beautiful engines, and like those of William Adams on the London and South Western Railway showed how a stove-pipe chimney could be carried to perfection. They had the same basic dimensions as the 4–4–0s of the East Indian Railway, but the G.I.P.R. 'C/5' class had flowing curves and elegant proportions, and the company's coat of arms on

A 4–4–0 comparison

Railway	East Indian	Caledonian
Date introduced	1893	1896
Cylinders		
dia. in.	18	19¼
stroke in.	26	26
Coupled wheels		
dia. ft. in.	6–7	6–6
Heating surfaces sq. tubes	1131.7	1284.45
Firebox	109.9	112.62
Total	1240.7	1403.23
Boiler pressure lb. per sq. in.	160	160
Ratio:		
cylinder volume (cu. in.) to total heating surface (sq. ft.)	10.6	10.76

the leading coupled wheel splasher put the finishing touches on a nineteenth century masterpiece of locomotive design.

So far I have made no mention of the special engines used on the Ghat inclines of the G.I.P.R. In early days the ordinary types of locomotive, the small 2–4–0s and 0–6–0s did not work on the Ghat inclines at all. Engines were changed at the base stations, and trains taken up by massive 0–8–0 saddle tanks designed specially for the job and built by Kitsons of Leeds. With the years, progressively larger banking engines were introduced, and the larger main line engines worked through, with rear-end assistance up the Ghats.

The turn of the century saw the general introduction of larger engines on most of the broad gauge lines in India—'Atlantics' and 4–6–0s for passenger traffic and 2–8–0s for freight. There was the same apparent indecision as in England at the time as to whether the 'Atlantic' or the 4–6–0 was the most suitable type for express passenger work. The G.I.P.R. began with 4–6–0s in 1904, and followed this with a class of 40 'Atlantics' in 1907. These latter were powerful engines, with cylinders 21 in. diameter by 26 in. stroke, 6 ft. 6 in. coupled wheels, a total heating surface of 2037 sq. ft. and a grate area of 32 sq. ft. They had 8-wheeled bogie tenders, and departed from precedent in carrying the railway name in full, instead of just the initials. They were all named after men famous in the history and administration of India, beginning with 'Lord Clive', and then 'Warren Hastings'. The series also included military commanders—'Lord Roberts', 'Havelock' and 'Lord Kitchener'. The East Indian Railway was a little unfortunate in its introduction of large engines, in that the civil engineer refused to allow ten very fine 4–6–0s to run until the road had been strengthened. In 1906 therefore these engines were sold to the Oudh and Rohilkund Railway. They did so well there that 16 more of generally similar design were obtained from Great Britain.

So far no mention has yet been made, in any connection, of a railway that became one of the major broad gauge systems of India, the Bengal Nagpur Railway, and which with the G.I.P.R. made up one of the two great transcontinental routes between Bombay and Calcutta. The B.N.R. pursued a strikingly individual policy in its locomotive practice, and in 1908 delivery was taken of a batch of de Glehn 4-cylinder compound 'Atlantics'. Though having necessary Indian equipment such as cow-catchers and carefully ventilated and shaded cabs, these engines were closely similar in their general proportions to the de Glehn 'Atlantics' currently doing such excellent work on the Orleans and Northern Railways in France. Unlike the ill-starred Webb compounds on the Oudh and Rohilkund, the compound 'Atlantics' on the B.N.R. did such good work that the same system was adopted for some huge 'Pacifics' purchased from Scotland in the 1920s. The B.N.R. engines were among the most handsome in India. Their basic colour was a myrtle-green, not unlike that of the Great Central in England, but with black and white lining. On their cab sides they carried the striking coat of arms of the company, of which the central motif was a Bengal tiger.

* * * * * *

The earliest Indian railways had not been long in operation before passenger travel became very popular, and in providing for great numbers of third-class patrons there came the two problems of over-crowding and adequate ventilation. As early as 1863 the Bombay, Baroda and Central India Railway attempted to solve the first by building double-decker carriages, while ventilation was provided by having them completely open at the sides. It was necessary, however, to have sunshades to protect those near the openings from the direct rays of the sun, while second and first class vehicles had louvred shutters. From this there developed the deep, overhanging eaves that were characteristic of most Indian passenger carriages until well into the present century. The seating in second and third class carriages remained traditional to the layout shown in the sketch of the early double-decker, in that the seats were arranged longitudinally like an old-style English tramcar. On metre gauge lines there were just the two lines of seating, one under each window; with the extra width of the broad gauge there was an extra row of seats down the middle, usually with reversible backs. To meet the illiteracy of most third-class passengers the exteriors of the coaches were painted different colours, the usual ones being white for first class; green for second class; and red-brown for third class.

On the metre gauge, the make-up and equipment of the Southern Mahratta Railway mail trains running between Poona, Bangalore, Mysore and Nanjangudi, give a good impression of travel conditions at the turn of the century. The train was normally made up of seven vehicles, all bogie, and from the engine these were brake-third, third, third, first and second composite, part mail sorting van and part third, third, and brake-third. The third-class accommodation was divided into three categories and labelled accordingly: 'Native 3rd'; 'Native Female Third' and 'European 3rd'. The total capacity of the train was eight first-class passengers, 12 second class, and 400 third. Except for the composite carriage in the middle, which was painted

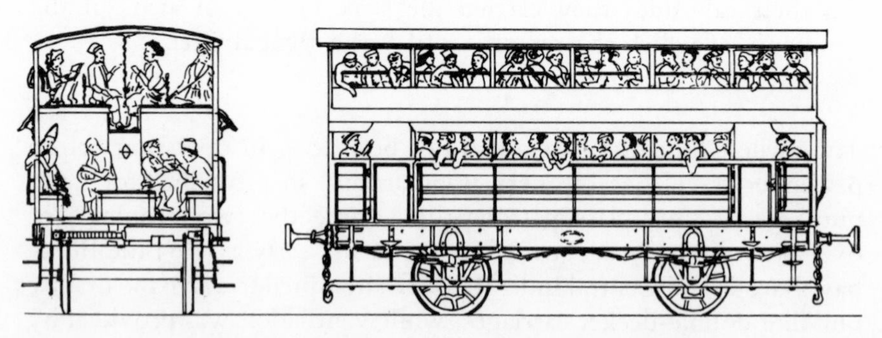

4. Early double-decker carriage, 1863, on the B.B. & C.I.R.

white, the coaches were painted a light brown, picked out with chocolate and white lining. These excellent trains were built at the Hubli Works of the Southern Mahratta Railway—a fine early example of indigenous manufacture of rolling stock. The trains were originally worked by small outside cylinder 4–4–0s, but the addition of dining cars to the load was accompanied by the importing of some handsome 4–6–0 locomotives, with 15 in. by 20 in. cylinders, and 4 ft. 9 in. diameter coupled wheels.

On the broad gauge lines some very fine trains were put into service in the early 1900s. Some of these were jointly operated, such as the mail trains between Calcutta and Bombay, and Calcutta and Madras, but there was also the handsome Darjeeling Mail, of the Eastern Bengal Railway, running north from Calcutta to the interchange station between the broad and metre gauge, at the Damukdeah Ghat, when the route crosses the Ganga. A notable development on the G.I.P.R. at that time was the abandonment of the exterior sunshades, using instead a layer of non-heat-conducting fabric between the inner and outer lining of the roof and sides. At the same time that very enterprising railway abandoned the use of distinctive colours for the three classes of carriages; all new stock, irrespective of class, was painted a rich red-brown for lower panels and cream for the upper, with umber mouldings lined in cream. These changes were due to Mr. A. M. Bell, the carriage and wagon superintendent. The first-class accommodation on Indian express trains was as luxurious as could be contrived, with numerous facilities for lessening the tedium and fatigue of long journeys in great heat.

* * * * * *

During the nineteenth century Indian railways were operated with a minimum of signalling. Speeds were low, there were few trains, and there was no standardised code of regulations. Thanks to the foresight of Lord Dalhousie, the country in general had the electric telegraph, and on most routes this was the only means of communication. While railway officers were well aware of contemporary developments in signalling in Great Britain the equipment was expensive, and not infrequently the civil engineers in India were not sure what they wanted. It was a time when much inventing of new systems took place—efforts quite unconnected with one another—and to appreciate how reliable arrangements came to be evolved the layout of an Indian wayside station must be studied. With few and isolated exceptions the entire main line network of the 1880–1890 period was single tracked. An intermediate station of the so-called 'third class' would have 'down' and 'up' loop lines on either side of the main. The last named would be used in either direction, as required, and the points giving entry to the loops would be about 500 yards away on either side of the central point. A 'second class' station would be similar, but have more extensive loop and siding accommodation. The Indian development arose from two major considerations, not then existing in Great Britain: first that all train movements had to be under the personal supervision of the station master, who remained at his central post; secondly, that the points were beyond the limit for manual operation from a locking frame, by rodding. Yet the safeguards of interlocking were needed.

Two distinct systems were developed, one by two engineers of the North Western Railway, G. H. List and A. Morse, and the other by Charles Hodgson, chief engineer of Saxby and Farmer Ltd. The heart of both systems was an interlocking key box in the station master's office—the withdrawal of a key from this instrument to set up a particular train movement locked in all the other keys. List and

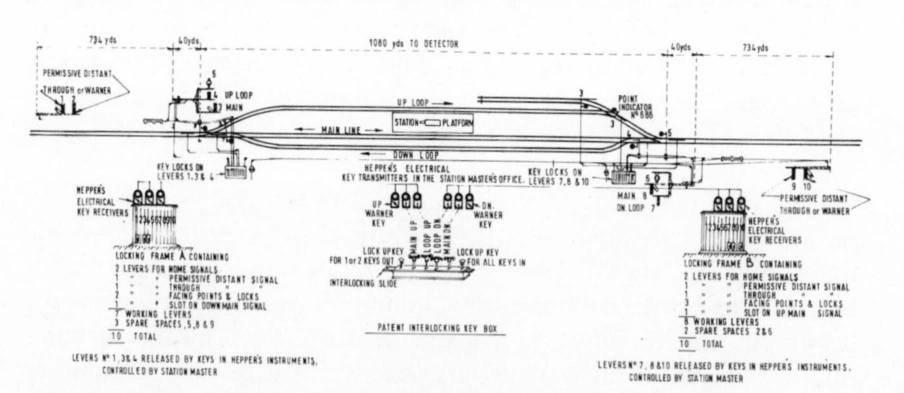

5. Layout of 'second class' station, as equipped with signalling on Hodgson's system

Morse had a small lever frame adjacent to the station master's office, from which the signals giving entrance to the station were operated. The points 500 yards away, were operated by hand levers electrically released by instruments connected with the central interlocking key box. The electric key release and transmitting instruments were the invention of Major H. A. L. Hepper, Signal Engineer of the North Western Railway, and later as Sir Lawless Hepper, General Manager of the G.I.P.R. Not until the points were correctly set could the appropriate signal be lowered to allow a train to enter the station on the main line, or proceed into a loop. Hodgson had no lever frame in the centre of the station, but had instead a fully interlocked frame of 7 working levers adjacent to the points, from which the signals were also operated. The integrity of the working was ensured by electric release locks connected to the interlocking key box in the station master's office.

These systems proved reasonably efficient for small stations with simple layouts. The train service of those days was light and the speeds low, crossings were not frequent and the wages of pointsmen very small. The necessity for employing several pointsmen and the delays when trains were crossed, due to men having to walk about with keys—especially at stations where succession locking was provided—mattered little in the majority of cases. The type of key used was not, however, proof against being tampered with. Many stories have been told of the ingenuity displayed by the staff to 'defeat' the locking or save themselves a little trouble. To mention one instance: there was a case of a station master who had a duplicate set of keys made by the local blacksmith to save himself from walking down to the ›ints!

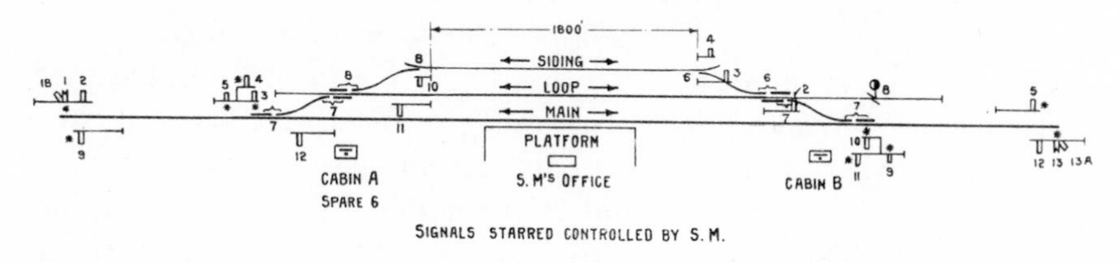

6. Arrangement of full cabin interlocking on the G.I.P.R.

The foundations of more modern practice were laid in 1903 after the G.I.P.R. had appointed I. W. Stokes, from the Great Western Railway, as Signal Engineer. He was not the first specialist officer to be so appointed in India, because S. T. Dutton had joined the East Indian in a similar capacity in 1899. But Stokes, by the very magnitude of the task set to him, broke new ground. In 1903, on the main line between Bombay and Delhi for example, out of 958 route miles, 605 miles were then single line and only 12 crossing stations had any form of interlocking. Eventually after much discussion a scheme of full cabin interlocking put forward by Stokes, and strongly backed by the General Manager F. T. Rickards, and the Managing Director in London, Colonel Firebrace, was accepted. The basis of this is shown in the accompanying diagram, and it consisted of separate, fully interlocked cabins at each end of the station, with control of the signals (asterisked) in the hands of the station master.

While it was essential to exercise correct interlocking control over train movement in the approach to stations, it was even more vital to regulate running on the intervening single line sections, and for this a unique combined token and block instrument was developed from a device invented by a certain Mr. Neale, on the North Western Railway. In broad principle it was similar to single-line staff or tablet instruments in use on British single-line railways; but the Neale's token instrument used a 1¾ in. diameter steel ball as the token. Many electrical safeguards were incorporated to prevent inadvertent misuse, and that perennial headache with single-line working—giving the driver a token for the wrong section. As recently as the 1930s there was a constant call for additional safety devices, with the design of which I was personally associated. The balls were carried in pouches, like the tablets on certain British railways, and on some railways the balls were provided with various shaped spigot holes, so that they could only be inserted into the correct instruments. In the 1920s a tablet version of the Neale's instrument had been designed, and on some Indian railways it was the practice to use ball and tablet instruments alternately along the line, so that at a crossing station a driver would hand in a ball, and receive a tablet for the next section, or vice versa. The chance of a driver accepting a wrong token became almost minimal by this practice.

7. The fortified approach to Kanpur (Cawnpore) bridge, when signalling and interlocking was first installed

Another feature of earlier Indian signalling was the procedure adopted on certain major bridges that were used by both railway and road traffic. An interesting example, complicated by the accommodation also of a metre gauge line, was that of the Oudh and Rohilkund Railway over the Ganga at Kanpur. Before a train was allowed to enter upon the bridge the level crossing gates on the Kanpur side had to be closed to hold back any road traffic. Then the bridgeman took the staff key over to the farther side clearing the road of traffic as he went, and closing the gates on the far side before the block instrument in the signal cabin could be released and 'line clear' sent to the cabin on the Kanpur side and the signals lowered for the train to go through. As Figure 7 shows there were fortified block houses on either side of the bridge.

CHAPTER FIVE

The hill railways—Darjeeling : Kalka : Simla

The climate of India in its extremes of heat and humidity is something that only Europeans with the toughest of constitutions can withstand; and those residents whose occupations allowed them to escape from the fierce summer heat of the plains made for the hill stations in the Himalayas. Thence, indeed, was transferred the seat of Imperial Government, and the high command of the Indian Army. Even when communications were quite primitive the Governor-General occasionally took refuge there in the summer, and Lord Dalhousie's historic minute of 1853 on railway planning was penned at Chini. By the latter part of the nineteenth century the practice of railway engineering had eliminated all ideas that trains could not climb steep gradients, and in the 1880s construction began of the daring and spectacular 2 ft. gauge line from Siliguri up to Darjeeling, the nearest of the summer hill stations to Calcutta, and a centre of tea growing. I do not think it would be wide of the mark to call the Darjeeling Himalayan Railway the Valhalla of all railway enthusiasts. *The Railway Magazine*, going strong after more than three-quarters of a century of continuous publication was not six months old before it carried an article describing the Darjeeling line, and the steam locomotives of which the line took delivery in 1889, together with those of the same design received later, are still handling the entire traffic today!

That alone would be a well-nigh irresistible force drawing enthusiasts from all over the world, except that Siliguri is not the most accessible place in India. However, the railway is also a top tourist attraction, and at least one traveller to Darjeeling by road found delight in counting the number of level crossings. She lost count when only half way up, having counted sixty-five! Despite its inaccessibility, and the permit restrictions that sometimes affect travellers of today, it is one of the most fully documented railways. The engineers resorted to spiral locations, 'Z' type reversals, and long gradients of 1 in 20 to get up to an altitude of 7407 ft. at Ghum; and the remarkable point is that at no part of the line was it found necessary to resort to a central rack—the Darjeeling is entirely an adhesion line. It was incorporated under the Indian Companies Acts, in 1879, and first opened for traffic in 1884, though the present class of 0-4-0 saddle tank engines did not arrive until five years later. For many years the line was extremely profitable, and between 1896 and 1911 the dividends paid varied between 11 and 16 per cent.—happy days! Business considerations apart, and indeed apart from technical matters, the utter fascination of the Darjeeling Himalayan Railway lies in the sublime mountain scenery.

In early days the mail train used to leave Siliguri at 8.25 a.m. and travellers frequently had the strange experience of climbing through cloud and early morning mist, and in the chill of the air a feeling of being poised between two cloud worlds. That early contributor to *The Railway Magazine* wrote:

> And now we approach the culminating wonder of the line. At one place we have been able to count three lines of rail below us which we have traversed, and to see three more above us, up which we are going to climb, making in all seven lines of track (counting the one we are on) visible at one time, nearly parallel with each other at gradually rising heights on the mountain side. But now the wheels groan with the lateral pressure caused by a tremendous series of curves, and for a few breathless seconds the train seems transformed into a veritable snake, as we pass 'Agony Point', and in so doing traverse two *complete* circles of such incredibly small diameter that the train, if at rest, would stretch round more than half of the circumference of one of them. They are placed spirally above each other, and form the exact figure of an eight, whose two loops have been bent till they are in the same vertical line.

And what of the little engines that take the trains up this line? The 'B' class, of which by 1927 there were 30, were first supplied by Sharp, Stewart & Co. in 1889. Down to 1903 that firm were the only suppliers, and after that, following the great amalgamation of locomotive firms in Glasgow, further 0–4–0 saddle tanks for Darjeeling continued to be built at the Atlas Works, but under the name of North British Locomotive Company. During the First World War three were built by the Baldwin Locomotive Works in Philadelphia, and three more were built locally after the war. The last nine came from the North British in 1925–7. All had cylinders 11 in. diameter by 14 in. stroke, coupled wheels 2 ft. 2 in. diameter, and carried a boiler pressure of 140 lb. per sq. in. The total weight of these sturdy little things in working order is only 14 tons. And the backcloth against which they worked, quoting again from *The Railway Magazine* of 1897—a description that cannot be bettered:

> The snowy peaks of Kinchin Junga and of Mount Everest are visible on a very clear day; but from the brilliant whiteness of their summits, and the grey colouring of the mists which usually envelop their middle heights, they appear as though they were but fantastically-shaped snow clouds poised in the ether.

On a January night, with Mr. Keswani, Chief Engineer of the Northern Railway, I set off from Delhi on the Kalka Mail, and in the comfort of an officers' saloon I slept well. We travelled over the tracks of the one-time Delhi–Umballa–Kalka Railway. It was not a rapid journey, and at Ambala, where we intersected the main line of the old North Western Railway to the cities of the Punjab, our 'WP' class 'Pacific' gave place to a diesel, and we came to Kalka soon after daybreak. We were bound for Simla, by the thrilling 2 ft. 6 in. gauge mountain railway, and changed into diesel railcar No. 10, a smart little 110 horsepower job, built in England by Gardners, in 1928, but with an engine by General Motors. I was accorded the privilege of a front seat, a place enjoyed by successive Viceroys of India when on their way to Simla, and so had an unrivalled view of the line ahead and of the tremendous mountain scenery. The line was constructed in 1903, and it climbs from an altitude of 2154 ft. at Kalka, to 6819 ft. at Simla. The straight-line distance between the two termini is about 30 miles, but such is the nature of the intervening country that the distance by rail is just double!

The geology of the area is highly erratic. The formation consists of a heterogeneous mass of boulders, clay containing small quantities of sand and other debris, while in other locations it is a solid rocky mass. There is frequent trouble during the monsoon season from slips and subsidences, and these sometimes occur without any preliminary warning because of the peculiar geology and the unpredictable hydrology in the area. Wherever possible the vulnerable places are protected by massive retaining walls, and these have stood the test of time, but as we began to mount the hillsides I soon realised why the engineers refer to the geology of the area as 'erratic'. I have travelled through many confused and tumbled mountain countrysides, but nothing to compare with this. There are 919 curves on the line, and indeed only about 30 per cent. of the total mileage is on straight-track. The sharpest curve has a radius of only 120 ft. Check rails are fitted on curves with a radius of less than 160 ft., but although there is necessarily very heavy wear on the outer rails of such curves, no lubrication is done because of the risk of wheel slip. The steepest gradient is 1 in 33 uncompensated, which when compensated for severe curvature is equivalent to 1 in 25. The Kalka–Simla line is one of only two 'hill' railways in India to have a 'straight' run without any aids to traction such as a rack, or a zig-zag as on the Darjeeling line. The other is the Matheran, near Bombay.

The rail-car mounted the hill steadily at about 15 m.p.h. By the nature of the country it was difficult to obtain any long vistas, and instead of the beautiful winter sunshine we had left behind in Delhi, clouds were low on these densely wooded hillsides, and it was inclined to rain. There are no fewer than 869 bridges on the Kalka–Simla railway; while the majority are relatively small culverts, the larger ones are of the arch gallery type, with successive tiers of arches built one upon each other up from the valley below. One of the largest and most picturesque comes at a point where the line is wriggling its way round the hillsides and the viaduct, looking for all the world like some Roman aqueduct, is seen almost broadside-on over on the opposite slope (see plate 9b). As can well be imagined there are numerous tunnels—102 of them. The longest, the 3752 ft.-long Barog Tunnel, leads immediately into Barog station where there is a refreshment room, and the morning 'up' train stops 15 minutes for breakfast. Thus fortified we continued uphill, into increasingly wild country; we came shortly after 11 o'clock to

Summer Hill station the nearest point to the one-time Vice-regal Lodge. From there after a long tunnel we came into the pleasant station of Simla itself, built like most of the line all the way up from Kalka, on the side of a precipitous mountain slope.

In the car sheds and small motive power depot beside the station I was able to see some of the latest rolling stock. There are now no steam locomotives in regular use, but a few of the 'K' class 2–6–2 tanks of 1905 are stored in sidings at Kalka awaiting disposal. The original 26 locomotives of this design, all built by the North British Locomotive Company between 1904 and 1910, worked the whole of the traffic until 1956, when the first diesels were introduced. The 'K' class had cylinders 14 in. diameter by 16 in. stroke, coupled wheels 2 ft. 6 in. diameter and carried a boiler pressure of 180 lb. per sq. in. They were massive little jobs with an all-up weight of 37½ tons, and a tractive effort of 15,990 lb. From 1907 the railway was worked by the North Western, and the 2–6–2 tank engines were painted black and carried the initials NWR. The engines I saw at Kalka recently were finished in the present standard style of the Indian Railways, with half the side tanks painted in the red-brown colour of the Northern Railway.

The first diesel-hydraulic locomotives were imported from Western Germany, but they have now been superseded in service on the Kalka–Simla line by the 'ZDM-3' class, of the B-B wheel arrangement and built at the Indian Railways' own locomotive works at Chittaranjan, to which more extensive reference is made in a subsequent chapter. These powerful locomotives, weighing 35 tons in working order have an engine horsepower of 700, and are used on all the ordinary services over the line. At Simla the turntable used for the steam 2–6–2 tank engines is still in commission, being needed now for turning the railcars which have their engine under a 'bonnet' at one end.

It was very cold up at Simla, and we had not been there long before it began to snow. During the night there was a considerable fall, but the storm had passed by morning. Unlike Darjeeling the great mountains of the Himalayas are some distance away from Simla, and one has to climb high above the station into the town itself to a lookout terrace to see the range of perpetual snow, some 50 miles away. But there was plenty of snow around Simla that morning, and on a short sightseeing tour we were occasionally up to our knees in it. We left on the railcar at 16.50, and from the front seat I was once again able to enjoy the scenic wonders of the line. The 60-mile run down to Kalka took 4½ hours, while the ordinary passenger train that followed is scheduled to make the run in 5½ hours. The uphill runs are made in about the same times, as it is the curves rather than the gradients that govern the speed on this fascinating line. It was raining hard when we got down to Kalka. There was a glimpse of one of the 2–6–2 tank engines, on shed, as we ran in; and then we made for the Kalka–Delhi–Howrah Mail, and the comfort of that officers' saloon.

CHAPTER SIX

The years of evolution

In 1898 Lord Curzon was appointed Viceroy of India, and with characteristic energy and far-sightedness he analysed the existing position of railway administration and management. The first supervisory authority set up by the Government of India had been the Central Public Works Department, and in this secretariat a Railway Branch had been formed in 1886. Control had necessarily to be decentralised to a considerable extent, for the field was too vast for the one Consulting Engineer of the Central Public Works Department to cope with in any detail. Consequently much was left to consulting engineers attached to the Provincial Governments, and much friction arose between them and the railway engineers. The latter felt that the Government officers did not possess the necessary professional competence, and were apt to be over zealous to the point of becoming officious. But the arrangements set up in 1866 remained in force for the rest of the nineteenth century, with some strengthening of the centralised control in 1871 and again in 1882.

So far as the actual railways themselves were concerned there had been three distinct phases in their inauguration and management set-up. The first lasted until 1869 by which time 11 railways had been incorporated in England, under the following broad terms from the Government of India:

1. A free grant of land.
2. A guaranteed rate of interest ranging from 4½ to 5 per cent.
3. Utilisation of half the surplus profits earned by the companies to repay to the government any sums which might previously have been spent to make good the guaranteed rate of interest.

4. Reservation of certain powers of supervision and control by the Government.
5. Option to the Government to purchase the lines after 25 or 50 years.

The six original companies, according with the Dalhousie plan of development and in contract with the East India Company, were the Great Indian Peninsula; the East Indian; the Madras; the Bombay, Baroda and Central India; the South Indian; and the Scinde, Punjab and Delhi—later to become the North Western. With these railways, and the five incorporated up to the year 1869 the working was left entirely to the companies, with some form of financial guarantee; but between 1870 and 1880 all new lines, including the metre gauge feeder systems recommended by Lord Mayo, were built under State supervision and management and with State funds. From then onwards, until the year 1907, new lines expected to be profitable were left to private enterprise with no Government assistance except a free land grant, while lines that were urgently needed for strategic or sociological reasons and were not expected to be viable, were built or directly assisted by the State. The following important lines were inaugurated, under company management, and no more than limited guarantees:

1881	Southern Mahratta
1882	Bengal and North Western
1885	Bengal Nagpur
1887	Indian Midland

All were regarded as State property from the outset. The Indian Midland was absorbed into the G.I.P.R. in 1900, while the Southern Mahratta was amalgamated with the Madras to form the M. & S.M. in 1903.

At the time of this latter merger the Madras was a purely broad gauge line, while the Southern Mahratta was entirely metre gauge. The amalgamation gave rise to a great deal of comment on Indian railway gauges, and the suggestion was strongly advanced that there ought to be unification. It was argued that India had not benefited from the adoption of the 5 ft. 6 in. gauge, and that the metre gauge lines had been built wider than necessary, so far as structural clearances were concerned, so why not alter the whole lot to 4 ft. 8½ in.! At the instigation of Lord Curzon, the Secretary of State for India appointed Sir Thomas Robertson to enquire into the administration and working of the railways, and the outcome was a recommendation that the Railway Branch of the Public Works Department should be replaced by a Railway Board—'a body of practical businessmen entrusted with full authority to manage the railways of India on commercial principles, free from all non-essential restrictions or inelastic rules'. The first Railway Board was appointed in 1905, by Lord Curzon's Government.

In view of the discussions that took place about that time over the gauges of Indian railways, it is interesting to study some of the locomotive designs for the metre gauge railways introduced around the turn of the century. On both the South Indian and on the Southern Mahratta engines of various wheel arrangements were built with outside frames, outside cylinders, and necessarily outside cranks. The Southern Mahratta had some quaint little 2–6–0s of this type which, with the dome placed on the forward ring of the boiler barrel just behind the chimney, had something of a Great Eastern look. There were some passenger 4–4–0s in the same style on the South Indian. All the engines working in the deep south burned wood, and their tenders were fitted with large open cages extending up to the full height of the cabs to carry a maximum number of logs. The use of such prominent outside frames suggested that the engines were designed for easy conversion to broad gauge, by merely lengthening the axles, and moving the wheels from the inside to the outside of the frames. Be that as it may, 4–4–0 tender engines with outside frames were built for the metre gauge sections of the South Indian Railway as recently as 1919; but in contrast to earlier examples of the same type, these later engines were superheated and had outside Walschaerts valve gear.

On the Madras and Southern Mahratta, after the amalgamation, the 4–6–0 type was introduced for the mail trains on the metre gauge and these engines, and the superheated variety that followed, formed a general standard for State-owned as well as private metre gauge lines. All had 4 ft. diameter coupled wheels. The saturated engines had cylinders 15 in. diameter by 22 in. stroke, and the superheated 16 in. diameter cylinders. The former worked at 180 lb. per sq. in. and the latter at 160. They were neat and compact little engines, but of very modest tractive power, only 14,000 lb. at 75 per cent. boiler pressure. So successful was this general type on metre gauge lines that additions were made down to the year 1939, when the Hunslet Engine Company built six for the Bombay, Baroda and Central India Railway.

The years between Lord Curzon's Viceroyalty and the outbreak of the First World War marked the zenith of British influence on the Indian railways, and the companies although under State ownership, displayed all the individual style and elegance of the British home railways prior to the Grouping of 1923. Locomotives and rolling stock were kept in immaculate condition, the coats of arms were carried with pride, but perhaps in no respect was the splendour of the Indian railways more grandly manifested than in the architecture of the principal stations. I have referred earlier to the massive construction of the smaller country stations, and in the great cities the railway stations displayed a trend in building that was continued into the period of transition, between the two World Wars. In earlier days the architecture of India and the consummate skill of her craftsmen has produced some of the glories and wonders of the world, and when railways began to pass from the primitive pioneer stages, it was no surprise that buildings of great beauty and architectural distinction were raised at the principal stations, and at the headquarter offices of the major companies. There was one large station, however, that for a time stood apart from Indian architectural style. The great English engineer, Isambard Kingdom Brunel was consulting engineer to the Eastern Bengal Railway, and he designed the first terminal station in Calcutta, Sealdah, which was opened in 1862. Here was no attempt to imitate Indian architectural style: it was just pure Brunel, with its low-pointed all-over roofs of which there were at one time many examples in the south-west of England.

One of the grandest of Indian stations is the terminus of the G.I.P.R. in Bombay, opened on the day of Queen Victoria's Golden Jubilee in 1887, and appropriately named Victoria Terminus. It is impressive enough from the street, and in those parts frequented by passengers; but while in Bombay I had the privilege of addressing a meeting of the Institute of Rail Transport in 'VT', as it is always affectionately called by Indian railwaymen, and I was able to see the remarkable interior. It was designed by F. W. Stevens—Gothic-Saracenic in style, with the look of a great cathedral, with a central dome set off by a number of smaller domes. It is deeply moving to stand beneath the central dome and look upwards, see the beautiful stained glass in the lancet windows, and admire the solid cut stone masonry. It is difficult to believe one is *not* in a cathedral, but merely in the centrepiece of a railway station!

There is, however, nothing of the cathedral-close calm of atmosphere in running the trains from 'VT', and in Bombay, as in Calcutta and Madras, the suburban traffic problem is one of the most severe items with which Indian railway operating men have to contend. At the time of which I am now writing, it was not greatly different from that currently facing the men of the Great Eastern, the Brighton, or the London and South Western in England. The suburban trains from Bombay were all steam worked, and wholly in the contemporary English style by powerful side tank engines. As in England, the 0–6–2 was a favourite type both on the G.I.P.R. and on the Bombay, Baroda and Central India. The passenger carriages were designed for bulk transport, since the Indian commuter did not look for comfort on his way to and from work. He was quite prepared to sit on the floor or hang on to the rails outside the carriage doors, and this tradition, so evident on the intense multiple-unit electric services of today, is as old as Indian railways themselves. It is important to realise that busy steam-hauled suburban services out of Bombay were being worked while Indian signalling was in its infancy, and that it was not until 1912 that the G.I.P.R. had completed their cabin interlocking on the main line between Bombay and Delhi. Little had been done before 1905.

* * * * * *

It is a far cry from the teeming suburban traffic areas of 'VT', and the B.B. & C.I.R. lines around Bombay, to the North West Frontier; and the story of how the line was carried through the wild and inhospitable mountain ranges of Baluchistan, through Quetta to

Chaman, with the buffer stops only a few hundred yards short of the Afghan frontier recalls one of the most remarkable feats of construction anywhere on the world's railways. That unlikely terminus was reached in 1893, and a large depot was set up there containing materials for continuing the line to Kandahar, if necessary, 67 miles farther on. But the interesting feature of this extraordinary railway—or group of railways to the North West Frontier, was that there were two alternative routes from Sibi. One went through the Bolan Pass, and the other took the well-nigh incredible track through the Chappar Rift. They joined at Bostan, 21 miles north of Quetta. Sibi lies no more than 433 ft. above sea level. It was the railhead when construction started, and no more terrible base of operations could be imagined. Shut in by the mountain ranges to the north and a vast waterless desert to the south, it is one of the hottest places in all the Indian sub-continent. The geology of the mountains beyond veritably defies description. I can only commend pictures taken in the Chappar Rift (plate 5b), and in the Bolan Pass and hope that the reader will be able to gain some idea of what the engineers were up against!

Troubles did not cease when the line was built and the trains began to run. There had been fearful conditions—visitations of cholera epidemic, attacks by tribesmen and plain marauders, torrential rainfall, and such terrific heat that in one summer work had to be suspended for a time because of disease. One also might have expected interference from natural causes in such a gigantic freak of nature as the Chappar Rift, where the whole mountain range has been split open with a great crack cutting completely athwart its natural contours. And through this great crack, blasting the track and its tunnels out of the solid rock, was taken the line to Bostan. As it turned out however it was the next section, through the aptly named Mudgorge that the greatest troubles subsequently occurred. Here, nearly 5900 ft. above sea level, the line was taken through a deep glen three miles long filled with dried mud 1700 ft. deep—*one thousand seven hundred feet!*—the accumulation of centuries. In dry weather the mud was almost rock hard, but in the rains, it is just one vast unstable bog. The railway was taken through Mudgorge in a tunnel made by cut and cover methods, excavated in the dry season, and built so massively—or so it was hoped—to withstand all the unstable conditions of the rains. Slips and washaways were frequent; damage to the track led to derailments and one incident, laconically reported as 'Obliteration of Line', took 19 days to clear. But there was never any thought of giving up; the trains continued to go through!

On the Chappar Rift–Mudgorge route, and in the Bolan Pass the steepest gradient was 1 in 25. Small-wheeled 4–6–0s of the 'L' class were used in the early days, but the real heroes of train operation on the North West Frontier were the 'HG' and 'HG/S' 2–8–0s. They were a standard N.W.R. heavy freight engine, introduced in 1906, and a type that with local variations such as the style of cab and tender was adopted as an Indian standard, and used also on the East Indian, the G.I.P.R. and the B.B. & C.I. Railways. The 'HG' class were non-superheated and had inside Stephenson link motion. The 21 in. by 26 in. cylinders drove on to the second pair of coupled wheels. The 'HG/S' superheated variety had outside Walschaerts gear, and drove on to the third pair of coupled axles. Although designed as a general purpose heavy freight locomotive they proved ideal on the mountain sections, slogging hard up the 1 in 25 gradients and running freely at about the maximum speed permitted on the easier stretches—45 m.p.h. With a little hindsight one wonders how much better still they might have been on the 1 in 25 gradients with long-travel Stephenson link motion *outside*, as on the classic LMS 'Black Five' 4–6–0 No. 4767, in England.

Beside the natural hazards, warlike excitements and disasters of the North West Frontier, the railways on the present North East Frontier of India have not had the same attention from writers and visitors. There is a natural tendency to make for Darjeeling, and to leave it at that. The original main line of the Eastern Bengal Railway, planned in part by Brunel and now mostly in Bangladesh, ran almost due north from Calcutta to Haldibari. The connection northward to Siliguri was made in 1878–9. There is now a direct route west of the international frontier from Calcutta to Siliguri. The other component of what is now the North-East Frontier Railway in the nationalised Indian railway system, was the Assam Bengal, a metre gauge railway originally laid out as a channel of outlet for the tea growing areas of upper Assam. Just as the Ganga formed the guide line for develop-

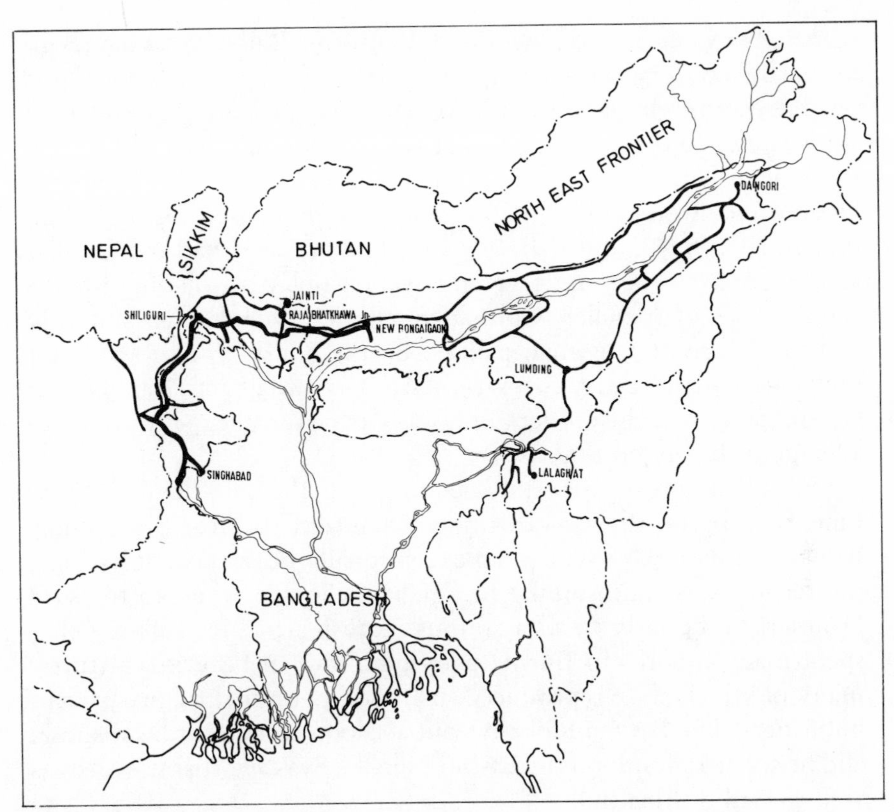

8. Railways on the North East Frontier

ment of the East Indian Railway so the Brahmaputra River was the trading route of the Assam Bengal, the traffic from which was concentrated at the junction of Lumding, and continued south to Chittagong. There were connections across the Jamuna River to the broad gauge Eastern Bengal Railway, but most of the traffic remained on the metre gauge Assam Bengal Railway. The profound changes in this area since Independence are described in a later chapter of this book.

Moving still further eastwards there was the Burma Railway, another significant metre gauge system. Construction began in 1887 and the line was carried for 386 miles up country to Mandalay. This section runs through fairly level country, but at Mandalay, which is in many ways the grand junction of the Burma Railways two lines go forward into very difficult regions. Until 1937, when Burma was separated from India, the railway was operated and managed on similar lines to those of India itself, and the locomotives and rolling stock were for the most part of standard types. The passenger locomotives were 4–6–0s of the same design as used on the South Indian, M. & S.M., and B.B. & C.I.R. The carriages had the familiar sunshades over the windows and were painted to distinguish the three classes of traveller. Compartments reserved for women only had the figure of a woman painted on the doors. Speeds were not high, and in the early 1900s the Mandalay Mail left Rangoon at 6 p.m. and took just over 20 hours to cover the 386 miles—an average of barely 20 m.p.h.

One of the most interesting sections was the very severe Lashio Line, running north-eastwards from Mandalay towards the Chinese frontier. Although providing an exceptionally heavy task of haulage, the terrain was quite unlike the great inclines of the North West Frontier. In the early 1900s a famous English artist, R. Talbot Kelly, spent many months in Burma painting a host of beautiful pictures, many of which were reproduced in a book published by my present publishers. The Burma Railways put a saloon carriage at his disposal and he spent a month on the Lashio Line. He was an artist in words as well as with his brush:

> By a series of reversing stations, up gradients of 1 in 25, we slowly zigzagged up the face of the mountain, while below the broad plain of Ava rose slowly into the sky, a sea of paddy land and jungle which disappeared into blue distance, and at our feet, far below, lay the little station we had left. Along the foot hills wound a sluggish stream, and through the distant haze peeped the pink tops of the Sagaing hills. Mounting still higher, Mandalay hill appeared above an intervening spur of the mountain whose broad shadow stretched half a mile across the plain, while like a silver ribbon the Irrawaddy gleamed through the mist which still obscured the horizon.
>
> Reaching the crest, the line wound along a ridge bordered by deep valleys filled with trees, glorious in autumn tints which ranged from the crimson and scarlet of the dhak and cotton-tree to the pale yellow of the bamboo.

Despite the ever increasing altitude it is jungle, jungle all the way, and Kelly wrote:

From Goekteik to Hsipaw, my next headquarters, the journey was much as I have already described, and as we mounted higher into the heart of the Shan hills the country seemed to expand itself into an immense sea of tree-clad undulations. The exuberance of the vegetation is extraordinary; every inch of ground supports some form of growth, each elbowing the other for space in which to reach the light and air. Should a tree die, a dozen creepers fight for its possession, while its topmost branches are crowned with orchids. In many places are clearings, where, in made terraces flooded with irrigation water, Shans and Shan-tiloks are planting paddy, their little hamlets being almost lost to sight amidst the vegetation, from which at times rises a long bamboo flagstaff erected as a "tagundaing" to mark a holy place. Cart roads and gharries are almost unknown in this district, but in their place large herds of pack ponies browse upon the hill-sides, or, heavily laden, wind their devious way through the forest.

To cope with 1 in 25 inclines on this extraordinary line the Burma Railways introduced some powerful Mallet 4-cylinder compound articulated locomotives of the 0–6–6–0 type. In haulage power they were the equivalent of two ordinary 0–6–0 goods engines, and because of the articulation they were able to negotiate the many sharp curves of the Lashio Line, despite their unusual length. The high pressure cylinders drove on to the rear group of wheels, carried on the locomotive frame, while the large low pressure cylinders out in front of the smokebox, drove on to the leading group of wheels, carried on the articulated truck. One of the most spectacular parts of the Lashio Line is the Goekteik Viaduct, a steel trestle 2100 ft. long with a maximum height of 320 ft. Although designed by Sir Alexander Rendel the steelwork was supplied and erected by an American firm.

The Mallet locomotives were introduced in 1911, the year that probably marked the zenith of British influence on the railways of the Indian sub-continent. In December of that year King George V, with Queen Mary, paid his great ceremonial visit, the only one of the five British monarchs to bear the title 'Emperor' to visit India in full Imperial State. The Coronation Durbar required the running of many Royal trains, and special trains for the native princes, most of whom had their own private trains. The Royal Train used by the King and Queen was one built by the East Indian Railway in 1904–5 for the earlier visit of King George and Queen Mary, when Prince and Princess of Wales. For the Durbar a supplemental Royal Train was built by the G.I.P.R. The latter company adopted a special painting style for all locomotives working the Royal Train—dark blue with chocolate framing, gold lines, brass tops to the chimneys, and polished brass domes. Four 4–4–0s, two 4–6–0s and five 'Atlantics' were so treated, and all were given names of members of the Royal Family. In addition, even the Ghat bank engines of the 2–8–4 type were painted blue, though these two engines were not named. Locomotives of the East Indian, Bengal Nagpur, and B.B. & C.I. Railways, although given a superlative finish and appropriate decoration on the buffer beams, retained their standard colours. The Bengal Nagpur used their de Glehn compound 'Atlantics' exclusively for the Royal Train.

An event of great significance at the time of the Durbar celebrations was the announcement that the Government of India would be transferred from Calcutta to the traditional capital, Delhi, and that a great new city would arise there. On December 15, 1911, King George V laid its foundation stones. This was a move that in due course would change the pattern of Indian train services, although of course the commercial pre-eminence of Calcutta would remain. Until this time Delhi had lain a little to one side of one of the principal arteries of railway traffic. Although Delhi had been the goal of the East Indian, the building of the Oudh and Rohilkund Railway with its trans-Ganga connection between Varanasi and Mughal Sarai, had made the new route via Lucknow the most direct from Calcutta to the cities of the Punjab, and thence to the North West Frontier. This route completely by-passed Delhi. The situation of the new seat of Government in the very heart of India, instead of in the eastern corner, made some replanning necessary; and like all fundamental changes it was at first not to the liking of everybody.

PLATE I

James Andrew Broun Ramsay, tenth Earl and first Marquis of Dalhousie: Governor General of India 1848–1856: architect of the original railway network in India, and of the introduction of the electric telegraph

PLATE 2 Railway coats of arms

(*a*) North Western

(*b*) Oudh and Rohilkund

(*c*) Bombay, Baroda and Central India

(*d*) Great Indian Peninsula, from a 'relief' on a wall at Victoria Terminus, Bombay

(*a*) Metre gauge 4–4–0 passenger locomotive, South Indian Railway: a later example built 1920 at the Atlas Works of North British Loco. Co. Ltd.

PLATE 3

(*b*) The standard metre gauge 4–6–0 locomotive: an example built for the South Indian Railway in 1905 at Hyde Park Works, N.B.L. Co. Ltd.

(*c*) The most beautiful of all Indian passenger locomotives: the 'C/5' class 4–4–0 of the G.I.P.R.

(*d*) The B.E.S.A. standard 4–4–0 passenger locomotive for broad gauge line: an example built 1908 at the Atlas Works, N.B.L. Co. Ltd.

PLATE 4 Notable Indian stations

(*a*) Lucknow: formerly East Indian, and now Northern Railway

(*b*) Madras Egmore

(*c*) Not a cathedral, but part of Victoria Terminus, Bombay: the initials G.I.P.R. over one of the entrances

(*a*) The Lansdowne Bridge

LATE 5 Towards the orth-West Frontier—in pre-war days

(*b*) In the Chappar Rift: Iron Gate Tunnel with an 'XA' 'Pacific' working a down mixed train

(*c*) The famous road and railway bridge across the Indus, at Attock, with a 'WL' 'Pacific' crossing with a Peshawar–Bombay express

PLATE 6 Locomotives on the narrow gauge

(*a*) South Central Railway: 'Barsi Light' section 'G' class 4–6–4 No. 730 at Miraj (March 1973)

(*b*) Western Railway: 'W' class 0–6–2 No. 569 at Nadiad (February 1973)

(*c*) A 'ZB' class 2–6–2 No. 91 at Dabhoi (February 1973)

(*d*) Southern Railway: A Kerr Stuart-built 4–6–2 of class 'ES', working on the Bangalore–Bangarapet section, on shed at Yelahanka (March 1973)

(*a*) Train from New Jalpaiguri to Darjeeling leaving Paglajora, on the way up. Note the men riding on the front to apply sand to the rails if necessary

PLATE 7 Darjeeling Himalayan Railway

(*b*) The spectacular Ghoom Loop: see the lower alignment at the extreme left and right of the picture

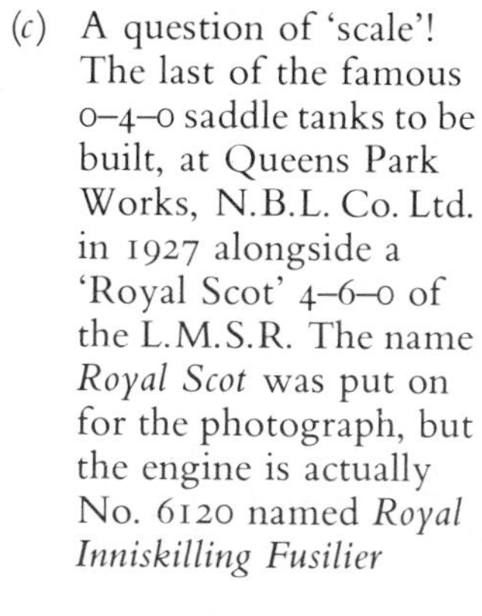

(*c*) A question of 'scale'! The last of the famous 0–4–0 saddle tanks to be built, at Queens Park Works, N.B.L. Co. Ltd. in 1927 alongside a 'Royal Scot' 4–6–0 of the L.M.S.R. The name *Royal Scot* was put on for the photograph, but the engine is actually No. 6120 named *Royal Inniskilling Fusilier*

(*a*) Bengal Nagpur de Glehn 4-cylinder compound 'Atlantic', built at the Hyde Park Works, N.B.L. Co. Ltd. in 1910

PLATE 8 Broad gauge locomotives of the Imperial days

(*b*) 4–6–0 express locomotive No. 1151, built at the Atlas Works in 1904 for the East Indian Railway, but afterwards transferred to the Oudh and Rohilkund Railway

(*c*) Bengal Nagpur Railway: a handsome variant of the popular 2–8–0 heavy freight design used on many of the broad gauge lines: built at the Queens Park Works, N.B.L. Co. Ltd. in 1909

(*d*) One of the monster 4-cylinder 2–10–0 heavy freight engines of the G.I.P.R. of which 30 were built in Glasgow in 1919

PLATE 9 The Kalka–Simla line

(*a*) The passenger terminus at Simla. The line to the goods terminal can be seen curving round to the left beyond the station buildings

(*b*) The most spectacular of the arched viaducts on the line

(*a*) North Western Railway—Kalka–Simla section: 2–6–2 tank engine No. 75, as originally built

(*b*) Oudh and Rohilkund Railway: one of the original 0–6–0 engines, No. 26, as preserved in Lucknow locomotive works

(*c*) Western Railway, metre gauge 'HPS' class 4–6–0 No. 31080 at Dhola Junction, in November 1970

(*a*) Heavy train hauled by a standard 'WG' 2–8–2 engine crossing the Auranga bridge, Bombay–Surat section of Western Railway, showing construction of new piers between the old ones of the bridge

PLATE 11 Modern freight traffic

(*b*) At Lonavla, summit of Ghats on Bombay–Pune (Poona) line, showing vacuum brake cylinders held in readiness for substitution of any found below standard on trains about to descend the Ghats

(*c*) Mughal Sarai marshalling yard: one of the electro-pneumatic wagon retarders. Control Tower in the background

PLATE 12 In the Chappar Rift

(*a*) (above) a mixed train, Sibi to Quetta crossing the Louise Margaret bridge, hauled by an 'XA' 'Pacific'

(*b*) (above right) Looking up Tunnel No. 9, leading into the Chappar Rift

(*c*) A dramatic view of the Louise Margaret bridge 230 ft. above the bed of the stream below

PLATE 13

(*a*) Electric train for Bombay (Churchgate) entering Grant Road station

(*b*) Crowded carriages on Western Railway train in Bombay suburban area

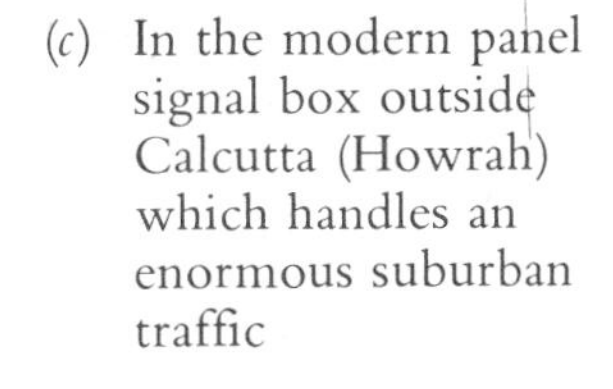

(*c*) In the modern panel signal box outside Calcutta (Howrah) which handles an enormous suburban traffic

TE 14 Work on the line

Rolling in new girders for bridge reconstruction, Cochin–Trivandrum gauge conversion scheme, Southern Railway

Machine for mechanised laying of pre-fabricated track using concrete 'pot' sleepers

What sometimes happens in floods: spill of the Tapi River, 1970, on Utran–Sayan section, Western Railway, showing track formation with cast iron sleepers

PLATE 15

(*a*) South Central Railway—Miraj to Poona: train leaving Miraj hauled by standard 'WG' class 2–8–2 No. 10091

(*b*) Southern Railway, metre gauge section: express from Bangalore arriving at Mysore hauled by standard 'YP' class 4–6–2 No. 2733

(*c*) Western Railway, northbound express from Bombay hauled by standard 'WP' class semi-streamlined 4–6–2

(*a*) One of the original electric freight locomotives of the G.I.P.R.—'EF/1' class for the Ghat electrification

(*b*) Metre gauge electric locomotive, class 'YAMI' at Madras Egmore

PLATE 16 Electric and diesel locomotives

(*c*) Modern electric passenger locomotive, class 'WCM4' on the 'Deccan Express' at Lonavla, Central Railway

(*d*) The standard broad and metre gauge main line diesel locomotives, classes 'WDM' and 'YDM' alongside at Varanasi locomotive works

CHAPTER SEVEN

'The years between'

I have 'lifted' the title of this chapter from Rudyard Kipling, who knew and loved India so well, and in his regard for railways too did not forget the humble commuter train; for it was he who reminded us that 'romance brought up the nine fifteen'. In this book of mine 'the years between' is an apt title for the time between the pinnacle of the British Raj, as epitomised in the Coronation Durbar of 1911, and the granting of Independence. They were restless years, on the railways as in India herself; but nevertheless years of great technical achievement, and in every way stepping stones to the new era that began on August 15, 1947. In this book I am concerned primarily with the engineering and operation of railways, but I cannot pass on to purely material things without mentioning the important moves towards direct State management of the entire Indian railway network. During the First World War the Imperial Legislative Council had repeatedly urged the appointment of a committee to examine the general situation, and in 1920 the East India Railway Committee was set up:

> to recommend suitable methods of management, to examine the functions, status and constitution of the Railway Board and the system of Government control over the Railway administration, to consider arrangements for the financing of railways in India, and to make such other recommendations that may seem germane to the enquiry.

The chairman of the Committee was Sir William Acworth, who was not only an English railway director of wide experience, but a thorough-going railway enthusiast. He was also the author of several important books on railway operation. His chairmanship of the East

India Railway Committee was an assurance that the whole question would be most sympathetically reviewed. Without going into fine detail the two principal changes arising from the recommendations of the Committee were that the Government gradually took over the management of the railways, and that railway finance was separated from the general finance of the Government of India. In 1925 the management of both the G.I.P.R. and the East Indian was taken over, and an important side effect of the latter was that the Oudh and Rohilkund, which had been State-managed for practically its entire existence, was incorporated into the East Indian, with the enlarged organisation keeping the latter name. The loss of individual identity by the O. & R. was of course much regretted by all those who had served that company, and had contributed to its individuality and prowess. But it was the way of all amalgamations. Nevertheless I found the memory of the old company still very much alive when I visited the locomotive shops at Lucknow 50 years later. Another change at that time was the transfer of the Allahabad–Jabalpur section of the East Indian to the G.I.P.R.

The North Western had been State-managed since 1886, and immediately after the First World War it was faced with a tremendous problem on the North West Frontier. Whatever may have been done on the route to Kandahar the Khyber Pass remained the most important strategic point in the defence of India from the North West. About the turn of the century a famous Commander-in-Chief had said:

> It's impregnable. I'm no believer in sitting still in a defensive position. But this—it's different. Give me two Army Corps and a railway behind me and I'll defy the whole of Asia, and Europe too. But, of course, it's too good to be true.

The difficulties were not only those of terrain and engineering. Between the frontier of British India and Afghanistan lay a belt of Tribal Territory, a kind of no man's land where there was no law and order save for tribal custom; and in the early 1900s, the tribes just forbade the construction of a railway. In 1919 however came the third Afghan War, and afterwards a brigade of troops was quartered in the Khyber. The Government decided it was time to build the 'impossible' railway through this no man's land to the frontier of Afghanistan. Victor Bayley, the Resident Engineer, has told the amazing story of its construction in a splendid book, *Permanent Way through the Khyber*, in which his own fortitude, professional skill and incredible diplomacy is thinly veiled behind the modesty of his flowing English, and a rare sense of humour that no doubt sustained him in the more difficult moments. This was no game of 'cowboys and Indians' out on the prairies of North America, but the 1920s, when he had to recruit his labour from the warlike tribesmen; arrange the allocation of duties to keep potentially hostile groups apart; and prevent, as far as possible, the stealing of the dynamite needed for blasting the rocks for use in bloody affrays. All this was a constant background to the progress of the work, as if the rugged terrain, the difficulty of bringing up supplies from Peshawar and the almost unbelievable heat of the summer months were not enough.

The Political Agent for 'no man's land' was a staunch ally. He had no jurisdiction over the British troops and made it clear to Bayley from the start that he could expect no military escorts for working parties. 'That would simply mean a Frontier war', he explained. But he did a mammoth job in adjusting matters between the Tribes. Bayley would ask him to nominate a contractor for a particular job, and then, in his own words: '. . . after a few days an unspeakable ruffian with two attendant murderers, all three armed to the teeth, would turn up with a letter from the Political Agent and announce himself as contractor for the work'!

On purely engineering matters the problems were peculiar. One might have thought that in such a stark, treeless mountain country there would have been ample good stone for building; but much of the rock was shale, and the limestone was so fissured that it disintegrated immediately one tried to dress or shape it. But there was a large deposit of brick clay near Landi Kotal, the summit of the pass, and where the British troops were quartered; and the intrepid engineer set up a brick kiln, and with coal brought up by road from the railroad near Peshawar, he organised the expert job of brick manufacture in the Khyber Pass. He burned the friable limestone to make lime, and mixed it with brick dust to make excellent mortar. Against such a fantastic background statistics are mere figures, but must be quoted for the record. From the entrance to the pass to Landi Kotal, there was a rise of 2,000 ft. in 21 miles, four reversing stations, six ordinary stations, 34 tunnels, 92 bridges, and four locomotive watering stations. From Landi Kotal down to the Afghan frontier the line descends 872 ft. in 4½ miles. The stations were built like forts, and were actually so. On the drawings one finds instructions such as 'Combined Booking Office Window and Machine Gun Loophole'. The line was laid out for standard broad gauge operation and, as in the Bolan Pass and the Chappar Rift, the standard engines used were the incomparable 'HG/S' 2–8–0s of the North Western Railway.

During four years of unremitting toil there were many distinguished visitors, including ladies. Bayley was a psychologist in addition to all his other sterling qualities. He wrote:

> We had a real job of work to tackle, and there would be steady collar-work required over a period of years. Much better to build the railway to the accompaniment of a ripple of laughter than to pull a long face, proclaim ourselves miserable sinners and suffer from overwork and repression. So when vexations gathered about us and things looked black, when tempers grew short and difficulties loomed, I would give my young men a car and my blessing and tell them to go and bring the prettiest girls from Peshawar to lunch. Perhaps I even went and fetched them myself.
>
> My wife and daughter came up several times. The latter was five years old the first time she made the journey and ten the last time, when she drove the last spike, and then, triumphantly, albeit a bit scared, piloted the first train, whistling madly, into Landi Kotal Station.

There were American tourists, diplomatic high-ups and at last the Prince of Wales, later Duke of Windsor. The authorities held their breaths, but the tribesmen loved it. To quote Bayley again:

> The dear old savages! Their feelings were of intense reverence and genuine love for the Crown, and they would have delighted in indulging in an orgy of bloodshed in order to demonstrate their feelings.
>
> I have often wondered if our distinguished visitors ever realised what great pleasure they gave to us all. In the remote Khyber, outside the boundaries of the Empire, we sometimes felt ourselves forgotten. But not by every one. Although we lived outside the British Empire, the Income Tax collector never failed to deduct Income Tax at the source. He did not, however, visit the Khyber. . . .

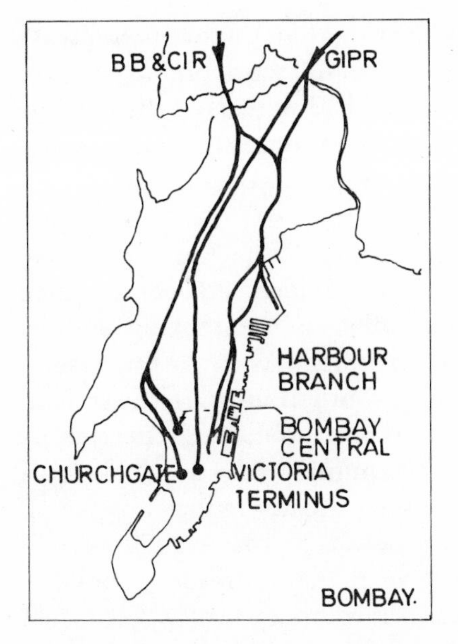

9. Bombay: the electrified local lines

The Khyber Railway was opened on November 2, 1925, by which time the almost unbelievable contrasts in Indian railway engineering and operation were about to be further manifested in the electrification of the Bombay suburban area of the G.I.P.R. The population of that great city was just exploding. People were living further out, beyond the creeks, and the two railways were called upon to carry vastly more people. How they both applied electrification can be seen from the accompanying map. The G.I.P.R. built what was virtually a new line, the Harbour Branch serving a densely populated area, and completely remodelled the train accommodation at Victoria Terminus. Hirtherto that station had seven platforms and two stabling tracks under the roof; as reconstructed it had nine platforms for suburban and six for main line trains, with a sextuple-tracked approach. At first only the suburban lines were electrified, but in a very few years both the South East and the North East main lines were electrified, over the Thul and Bhor Ghats to Igatpuri and Poona respectively. The system of electrification was 1500 volts direct current, following the precedent of the Newport–Shildon line on the North Eastern Railway in England, and in line with that currently being installed on the Victorian Railways around Melbourne, Australia. Early in 1925 the work on the Harbour Branch was finished, and just as Bombay had witnessed the running of the very first train in India in 1853, so, on February 7, 1925 the city saw the despatch, from the same starting point, of the first electric train in India.

With the remodelling of the layout at 'VT' came complete resignalling. It was fitting that the G.I.P.R., which had been so much to the fore in earlier days in putting in full cabin interlocking, and the development of signalling generally, should have been the first to install colour light signalling on the Harbour Branch. Then at 'VT' there came a splendid new power interlocking, with the points electro-pneumatically operated, and the number of individual signal heads on the approach and departure lines greatly reduced by route, and platform number indicators of a new type that was just being introduced on the Southern Railway, in England. Inside, a multiple sector plate carried a series of optical projectors each of which when illuminated threw a letter or figure on to a ground glass screen. As many as thirteen different indications as required, could be displayed. In the smoky atmosphere around London the front glasses of these indicators soon got dirty, and efforts to wipe them clean destroyed the ground glass surface. They were soon superseded by a later design. But in the clear atmosphere of Bombay they are still in service, after fifty years! The cabin equipment has been partially modernised, but of the original miniature-lever interlocking frame there is a story to be told.

The standard casings for these beautiful control machines were of teak, usually polished most lovingly by the staff. But the engineers of the G.I.P.R. felt they could not risk the use of teak, due to the risk of depredation by white ants. As a young draughtsman I had the job of designing a steel casing for the big interlocking machine for 'VT', and it was not a very easy task. An amusing sequel came only a short time later. As will be seen from the map on page 65 the B.B. & C.I.R. had two terminal stations in Bombay: Churchgate which dealt with the heavy suburban traffic, and Bombay Central from which the steam-hauled long distance trains departed. Before the work at 'VT' was finished we were awarded a contract for resignalling at Bombay

Central, and then it appeared that the white ants were quite selective in their predatory activities, for the B.B. & C.I.R. were quite content to accept an interlocking machine with our standard teak casing! Although the railways of India were all State-owned, if not then all of them State-managed, there was considerable rivalry between them, and I have been told that at one time the G.I.P.R. and the B.B. & C.I.R. were on cat and dog terms.

The main line electrification of the G.I.P.R. to Igatpuri and Poona transformed train operation on the Ghat inclines. To operate these services, both of which had been completed by June 1930, 24 locomotives for passengers and 41 for freight were introduced. The former had a 4-wheeled bogie at one end, a pony truck at the other, and three driving axles with individual drive, and a total capacity of 2160 horsepower. The freight locomotives were carried on two articulated 3-axle bogies. The wheels were coupled, and driven from jack shafts. These locomotives, some of which are still in service today after nearly fifty years, are of 2600 horsepower. All the 65 original electric locomotives of the G.I.P.R. were British built. On the Ghat inclines all trains had a freight locomotive banking in rear. On passenger runs the train engine worked through from Bombay to Igatpuri, or Poona. The ascending speed with passenger trains was 30 m.p.h. Descending the Ghats all freight trains and most passenger trains had a freight engine coupled in front of the train engine, and with a freight engine in front, trains came down with the regenerative brake of the leading engine in action, and the train brakes released.

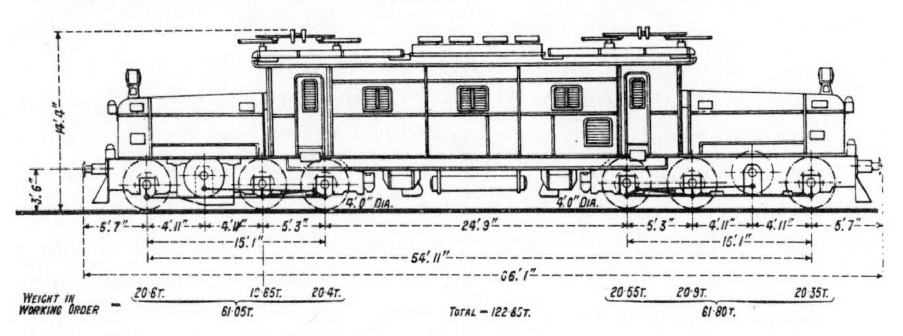

10. G.I.P.R. electric freight locomotive

In readiness for the improved service that the G.I.P.R. intended to put on after electrification, the tremendous task of realignment on the Bhor Ghat incline was commenced in December 1926. To avoid the time-consuming inconvenience of reversing on the zig-zag it was necessary to cut three tunnels below Khandala station, one of which was 3100 ft. long. At one time nearly 4500 men were engaged on this work, and it was completed in December 1928. It was in the latter year that the celebrated Imperial Indian Mail trains were introduced, jointly by the G.I.P.R. and the East Indian Railways, to provide a luxury service between Bombay and Calcutta, in connection with the sailings from England of the P. & O. mail steamers. The trains, one built by each railway, consisted of seven vehicles. The changeover point in haulage was at the new 'frontier' station of Allahabad instead of at Jabalpur. The 'joint' nature of the service was emphasised by the coats of arms of both railways and of the P. & O. being carried on the body panels of each vehicle, while accommodation on the trains could be reserved at the offices of the P. & O. in London. The trains were normally hauled by the standard superheater 4–6–0s of the two railways. Apart from colour the principal detail differences between the locomotives of the two companies were to be seen in the cabs—louvred side windows on the E.I.R., and a large open window on the G.I.P.R.—and in the chimneys. The East Indian had a shapely cast iron type, while the G.I.P.R. continued to favour the stove-pipe. One of the latter was designated as a War Memorial engine, named 'Hero', and carried the inscription: 'In memory of G.I.P. Railway employees who gave their lives in the Great War 1914–1918'.

In 'the years between' an interesting range of new high power locomotives of standard design was introduced for passenger and heavy freight working on the broad gauge lines. These were of the 'Pacific' type for passenger and 2–8–2 for freight. The size and power of the passenger engines were governed by the weight restrictions on the classes of lines concerned. The basic parameters and dimensions are shown in the following table. These designs were the first products of the Indian Locomotive Standards Committee set up in 1924, and large orders were placed with British manufacturers soon afterwards. Although there were teething troubles, and at least one serious accident—attributable as much to the track however as to

11. Standard steam locomotives:

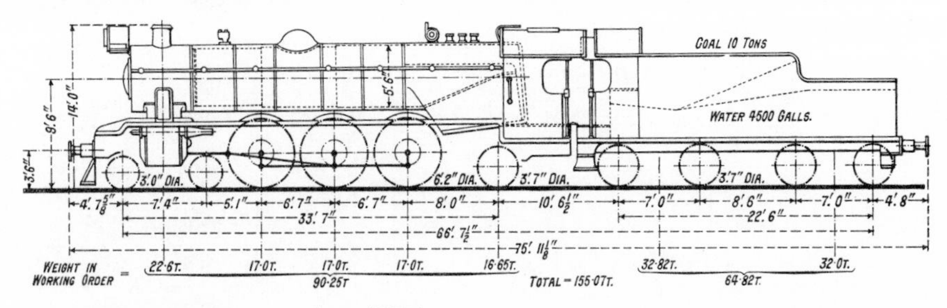

(*a*) Express passenger class 'XB'

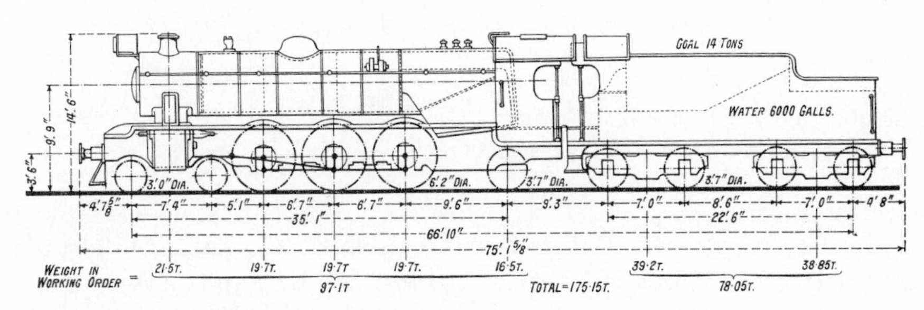

(*b*) Express passenger class 'XC'

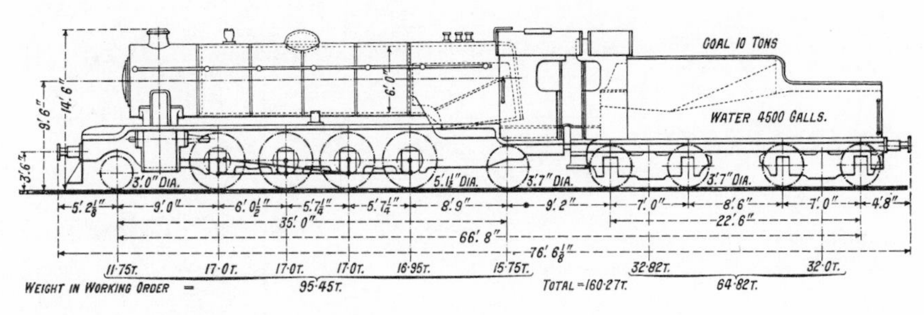

(*c*) Heavy freight class 'XD'

locomotive design—the 'XA', 'XB' and 'XC' engines have rendered good service, and I saw a number of them still at work when I was in India in 1975.

Indian standard 'Pacific' locomotives

Class	'XA'	'XB'	'XC'
Duty	Branch Lines	Light Main Lines	Heavy Main Lines
Maximum permitted axle load, tons	13·1	17	19·8
Cylinders			
dia. in.	18	21½	23
stroke in.	26	28	28
Coupled wheels dia. ft. in.	5–1½	6–2	6–2
Combined total heating surface sq. ft.	1747	2303	3065
Grate area sq. ft.	32	45	51
Boiler pressure per sq. in.	180	180	180
Total engine weight, tons	66·5	90·25	97
Nominal tractive effort (85% boiler pressure) lb.	20,960	26,760	30,625

I always thought the 'XC' was a very handsome design, but as it became 'watered down' as it were, into the 'XB' and 'XA' classes something of its balanced style and symmetry was lost. The freight engines of the 'XD' and 'XE' classes were grand looking machines. Their basic dimensions were:

Indian standard 2–8–2 locomotives

Class	'XD'	'XE'
Cylinders		
dia. in.	22½	23½
stroke in.	28	30
Coupled wheels dia. ft. in.	5–1½	5–1½
Combined total heating surface sq. ft.	2316	3777
Grate area sq. ft.	45	60
Boiler pressure per sq. in.	180	210
Nominal tractive effort (85% boiler pressure) lb.	35,260	48,086

The 'XDs' in particular were very long-lived engines, and I saw many of them in my Indian travels in 1975. The standard locomotives were allocated to the majority of the broad gauge lines, though I believe the 'XE' 2–8–2s were confined to the East Indian. Mention must also be made of the very popular 'HPS' standard 4–6–0 passenger engine of 1924. This had 20½ in. by 26 in. cylinders, 6 ft. 2 in. coupled wheels, and a boiler pressure of 180 lb. per sq. in. Despite the marked trend towards larger locomotives, the 'HPS' has remained a standard in India, and further large repeat orders were placed with the Vulcan Foundry of Newton-le-Willows, Lancashire, as recently as 1947. Although the basic standard 'Pacifics' were widely introduced after 1925, no restrictions were placed upon the development of individual variations. The G.I.P.R. obtained an experimental variation of the 'XB' class, with higher boiler pressure and Caprotti valve gear, while the North Western had a 4-cylinder variation of the 'XC'.

In the years between, however, it was the Bengal Nagpur that displayed the greatest distinction from current Indian standard practice. This line did not become State-managed until almost the very end of British rule in India, and its locomotive designs lay for the most part quite apart from the rest. After many years of successful experience with the de Glehn compound 'Atlantics', the company took delivery in 1929 of the first of an order for 18 enormous 4-cylinder compound 'Pacifics'. They conformed to Indian standards so far as the wheelbase, frame details, springing and tender were concerned, but as to the boiler, firebox and machinery they were quite distinct. It is interesting to compare their proportions to those of the contemporary de Glehn compound 'Pacifics' on the Northern Railway of France, introduced by Monsieur Collin.

Apart from the grate areas there is remarkable similarity, though the French engine despite its smaller grate had a larger firebox heating surface.

Another important feature of Bengal Nagpur locomotive practice was its use of the Beyer–Garratt type of articulated locomotive. The railway served no fewer than five coalfields and areas of extensive mineral deposits of iron ore, manganese and limestone, all of which produced bulk traffics of constantly increasing tonnage. Trains of

4-cylinder de Glehn compound 4–6–2s

Railway	Bengal Nagpur	Northern of France
Gauge ft. in.	5–6	4–8½
Cylinders		
h.p. dia. in.	16½	17·3
stroke in.	26	26
l.p. dia. in.	25	24·4
stroke in.	26	27·2
Coupled wheel dia. ft. in.	6–2	6–2·8
Heating surfaces sq. ft.		
Tubes	2228	2099
Firebox	211	248
Total evaporative	2439	2347
Superheater	637	616
Combined total	3076	2963
Grate area sq. ft.	51	37·7
Boiler pressure p.s.i.	250	245
Total engine weight tons	105	100·5

1650 tons had to be operated, and a pair of 2–8–0 tender engines were needed. Following tests in 1926 a batch of 16 Beyer-Garratt locomotives of the 4–8–0 + 0–8–4 type was obtained and these enormous units, with a tractive effort of 70,000 lb., were able to handle 2000 ton trains at practically double the speeds made with the previous 1650 ton trains, double-headed with two 2–8–0s. By the outbreak of war in 1939 the Bengal Nagpur Railway had 26 Garratts of the 4–8–0 + 0–8–4 type at work, in addition to the two experimental 2–8–0 + 0–8–2 units of 1926, and in 1940 delivery was taken of four additional engines of the 4–8–2 + 2–8–4 type specially for the Anuppur–Chirmiri section, where the 4–8–0 + 0–8–4 type with their 20¼ ton axle load could not be used.

In 'the years between' some interesting developments in signalling practice, away from the great cities, took place in India. As in Great Britain the experience of accidents pointed to the need for safeguards beyond the ordinary routine of the blockworking regulations, as well as some form of interlocking between the block instruments and the actual signals. On the Madras and Southern Mahratta for example, space had to be found within the crowded interiors of the Neale's single-line instruments for additional electrical contacts to be made when the operating handle was in the TRAIN GOING TO position. Only when a circuit was made through these contacts could an electric lock on the starting signal lever be released. In other words it was electrically impossible to signal a train away into a single line section unless the correct co-operative action between the signalmen at both ends had taken place with their respective Neale's instruments. Splendid in theory—but what a job we had getting those extra contacts into an already crowded box of tricks!

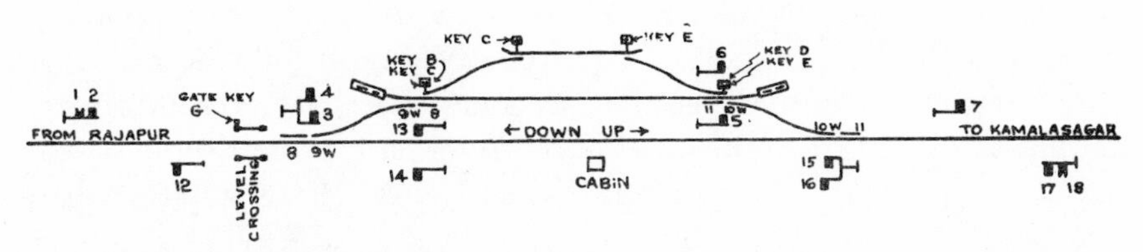

12. Assam Bengal Railway: layout of station with double-wire working of signals and points

Another interesting signalling development took place on the metre gauge Assam Bengal Railway. There, the signal engineer sought to obtain fully interlocked operation of passing stations on a single line railway without going to the expense of separate cabin interlockings at each end of a loop, as on the G.I.P.R. The double wire system of point operation, widely used on the continent of Europe, had been adapted for use in British overseas territories and installed in Nigeria, the Gold Coast and elsewhere. With the ready co-operation of Saxby and Farmer (India) Ltd. in Calcutta, the apparatus was made available to the Assam Bengal Railway. The advantage was that the points and signals at both ends of a loop could be operated from a central cabin, under the immediate jurisdiction of the station master. As might be imagined there were numerous teething troubles in the introduction of apparatus so novel to Indian practice; but these were successfully overcome. The above diagram shows the layout of a typical station.

CHAPTER EIGHT

Independence—locomotive building

The period of the Second World War threw immense strain upon the railways of India, particularly after the opening up of a large area of direct naval and military conflict in South East Asia. The strategic emphasis shifted from the historic North West Frontier to the North East, and it was the metre gauge Assam Bengal Railway rather than the North Western routes into Baluchistan and the Khyber Pass, that became a major military supply line. It so happened that the attack on Pearl Harbour in December 1941, and the swift moves that followed, coincided almost exactly with the amalgamation of the metre gauge Assam Bengal Railway with the broad gauge Eastern Bengal, to become the Bengal and Assam, so that the administrative upheavals of railway amalgamation were added to the wartime work-load. The merging of an all-broad gauge line, with an all-metre gauge had already had its precedent in India, with the formation of the Madras and Southern Mahratta in 1908, but in considerably less exacting conditions.

In 1942 however it was the metre gauge section of the new railway that led to what was rapidly becoming a potentially hostile frontier. New locomotives were needed to haul greatly enhanced loads and yet not exceed the relatively light axle load restrictions of the line, and, in conjunction with the British Ministry of War Transport, Messrs. Beyer, Peacock & Co. of Manchester urgently worked out a design of Beyer-Garratt articulated locomotive that could be used in a number of overseas territories that were in need of increased and additional motive power. By having a standard design, applicable to a number of railways, the advantages of quantity-production could be realised. Before that, however, 22 Garratts ordered by the Burma

Railways were temporarily diverted to the Bengal and Assam, which with the War Standard Light type, of which nine were allocated to the B. & A. proved an absolute godsend during the build-up and progress of the campaign for the liberation of Burma.

North-East Frontier Garratts: B. & A.R.

Affiliation	Type	Maximum axle load tons	Nominal tractive effort	Total weight tons	Number in service
Burma	2–8–0 + 0–8–2	10·5	41,890	103·4	10
Burma	2–8–2 + 2–8–2	10·5	41,890	117·9	12
War Standard Light	4–8–2 + 2–8–4	10	43,520	136·8	9

Of the larger Burma class, which was used in Assam during the war, there should have been 14 but two were on a ship that was lost at sea. Of the War Standard Light type, a further nine were sent to Burma after the liberation of that country, and the remaining two were allocated to the Kenya and Uganda Railway.

On the Indian broad gauge lines there were some interesting developments. In pre-electrification days the G.I.P.R. had introduced a class of very powerful 2–10–0 freight engines, known as class 'N/1'. They were 4-cylinder simples, with a tractive effort, at 85 per cent. boiler pressure, of 50,000 lb. There were 26 of these monsters, built in 1919 by the North British Locomotive Company, but after electrification of the Ghat sections they were not required and were transferred to the North Western for service on the heavily graded frontier lines. They were oil-fired, but when war came and there was a need to minimise oil imports the North Western converted them to coal burners. Because of the high firing rate involved when these engines were working at high capacity they were equipped with mechanical stokers.

For general freight service in India the 2–8–2 type has remained standard until the present day. While the 'XE' was the most powerful of the standard designs introduced between the two World Wars the 'XD', so far as tractive capacity was concerned, was chosen as the future national standard. Large additions to the type were made before the new Indian standard 'WG' design was evolved. Because of the heavy pre-occupation of British industry with wartime production in 1943–4, orders were placed in Canada for a total of 145 broad gauge 2–8–2s, shared almost equally between the Canadian Locomotive Company of Kingston, Ontario, and the Montreal Locomotive Works. Although the basic proportions corresponded generally to those of the 'XD' class, the design of the new locomotives was essentially North American in detail, with cast-steel bar type frames, the smokebox saddle being cast in two halves, each having the outside cylinder and steam chest cast integral with it. As distinct from the British built 'XD' the new engines were classed 'X-Dominion' and a total of 400 was eventually shipped from Canada. The comparative dimensions of the two varieties of 2–8–2 are:

Class	'XD'	'X-Dominion'
Cylinders		
dia. in.	22½	21
stroke in.	28	28
Coupled wheel dia. ft. in.	5–1½	5–0
Heating surfaces sq. ft.		
Total evaporative	2145	2164
Superheater	540	623
Combined total	2685	2787
Grate area sq. ft.	45	47
Boiler pressure p.s.i.	180	200
Total weight in working order tons		
Engine	98·35	88·35
Tender	66·5	55·2
Tractive effort at 85% boiler pressure lb.	35,250	35,200

While the Canadian builders were supplying large numbers of the 'X-Dominion' series, the North British Locomotive Company built a further 110 of the 'XD' class, generally similar to the original Indian standard design of the 1920s, but with slightly larger heating surfaces. As previously these engines had plate frames, but one of the most distinctive changes was the use of a hind pony truck of the radial arm type, instead of the radial axle box with Cartazzi slides used on the earlier engines, and also on the 'XA', 'XB' and 'XC' standard 'Pacifics'.

In the meantime, following extensive experience on the broad gauge lines with the three 'X' series of standard 'Pacifics', a new general purpose 'Pacific' design had been worked out in India, known as the 'WP', and the first orders for these were placed with the Baldwin Locomotive Works of Philadelphia, U.S.A., and completed in 1942. In external appearance they marked a striking departure from previous Indian practice. With a bullet nosed front and deeply styled valences they had something of the look of a Norfolk and Western streamlined 4–8–4, while Box-pok cast driving wheel centres and typical American outside running gear, gave them very much of a new look. First deliveries were made in the middle of the war, and the engines were finished plain black, but more recently some highly decorative adornments have been added to them, as will be told later. The nominal tractive effort of 30,600 lb. was approximately the same as the previous standard 'XC' class, but on the new engines the coupled wheel diameter is 5 ft. 7 in., against 6 ft. 2 in. and the cylinder 20¼ in. by 28 in. against 23 in. by 28 in. The grate area was reduced from 51 to 46 sq. ft., but with boiler pressure raised from 180 to 210 lb. per sq. in. The first engines gave successful results and the design was adopted as the Indian standard for passenger traffic on the broad gauge lines.

On August 15, 1947, India was granted Independence and became a self-governing Dominion, within the British Commonwealth. The partitioning off of predominantly Muslim areas into the second new Dominion of Pakistan, brought great problems to certain parts of the railway system apart from the disturbances and movement of population that took place around the time of Independence. The railways directly affected were the North Western, with the 1947 partition line crossing one of its principal main routes mid-way between Lahore and Amritsar, and the Bengal and Assam. While in the former case it meant that Amritsar, instead of Lahore, Rawalpindi, or even Peshawar became the Indian terminus of the long distance expresses from Bombay or Calcutta, the whole operating set-up of the Bengal and Assam—or its constituent parts—was changed. The main outlet of the original system, namely to Calcutta, was completely severed, and the broad gauge lines in East Pakistan rendered of little value. Chittagong was the only port in the country, and the 208½ mile single-tracked metre gauge length northward to Narayanganj became the principal main line of the new country.

Quite apart from the new geographical situation, and the immediate railway problems arising from it, there was the vital question of economics. India was indeed independent. She was equally on her own, and self-reliance became one of the greatest aims of national policy. How this has developed on the railways is one of the phenomena of world transport history. It has taken place in two distinct, yet closely connected ways—administratively, and technically. Up to the outbreak of the First World War, as I have indicated in earlier chapters of this book, the management of the railways was almost entirely British; and then, in the years between, there was a gradual devolution. Indians began to enter positions in middle-management, technical and otherwise; and the age-old traditions and skills in civil engineering and mechanics, amply manifested in the exquisite architectural heritage of the country, and the craftsmanship of countless individual workers, were developed and trained towards the assumption of full control, which the more far-sighted executives of British nationality saw to be the eventual outcome of the period of the British Raj. When Independence did come the actual transition, with the Indian 'seconds-in-command' stepping up into the shoes of their mentors, was swift, smooth and cordial. Rarely can such a momentous changeover have taken place with so little dislocation at top level, particularly in view of the many incidental setbacks and disturbances from causes entirely outside the railway service.

The setting up of the new international frontiers, and the severing of railway connections some of which were upwards of a hundred years old, posed some immediate problems, while the bringing of the entire Indian railway network under direct State control revived again the suggestions that had been made at several times during their history for the grouping of the railways. The truncated sections of the North Western and the Bengal and Assam remaining in Indian territory were obviously anachronisms, while even more serious than any questions of mere size was that, under the new political divisions, Assam had no direct rail link with the rest of India. Grouping procedures in Great Britain and France were studied, and as in Great Britain the first zones set-up in India, in April 1951, did

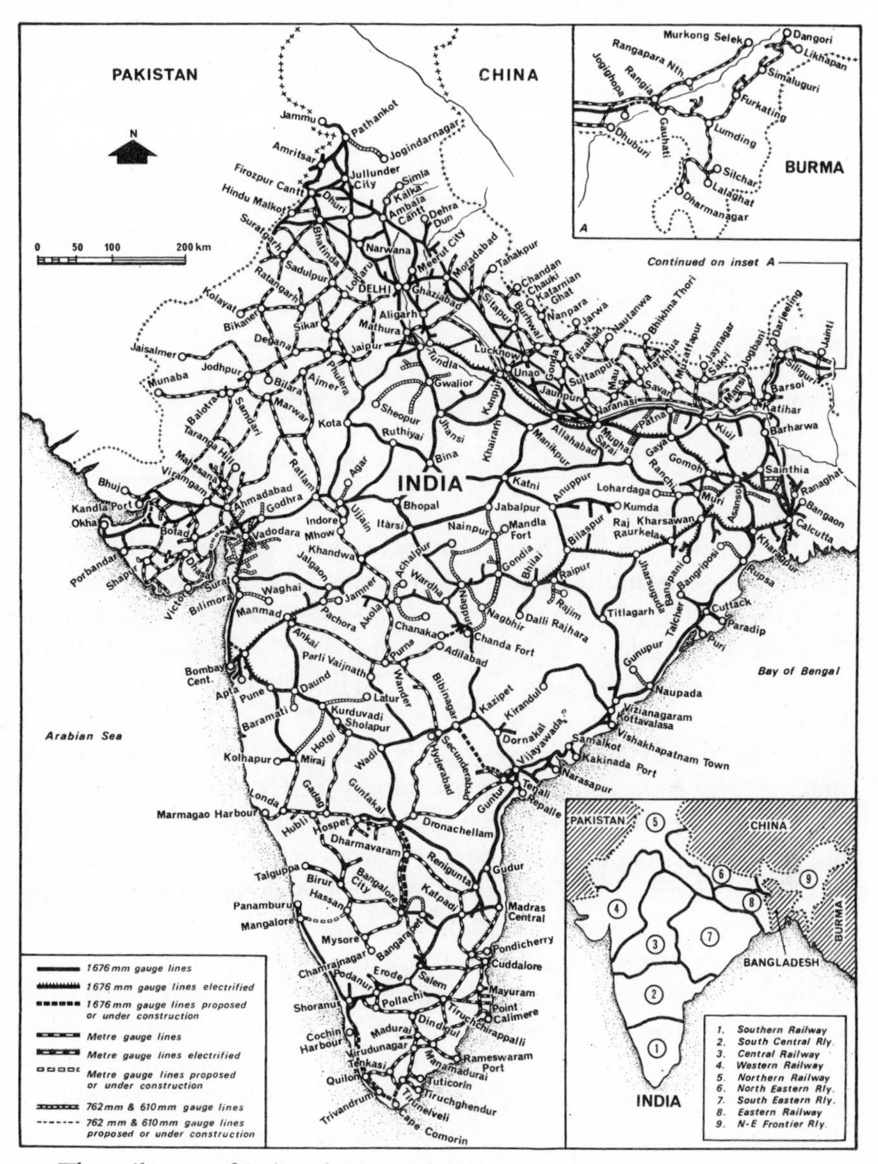

13. The railways of India, showing the present zones

not prove to be the final one. A second phase came a year later, but I can pass over the intermediate stages and proceed to the present set-up, which consists of nine zones, with their headquarters as under:

Railway Zone	Headquarters
Central	Victoria Terminus, Bombay
Eastern	Howrah, Calcutta
North Eastern	Gorakhpur
Northeast Frontier	Maligaon
Northern	New Delhi
South Central	Secunderabad
South Eastern	Garden Reach, Calcutta
Southern	Madras
Western	Churchgate, Bombay

A study of the map on page 79 shows there is something Beeching-like in the geographical distribution of the railway network between the zones and at the same time it will be appreciated that the Central is based on the old G.I.P.R.; the Western on the B.B. & C.I.R.; the South Eastern on the Bengal Nagpur. The others are not so clearly recognisable.

One of the first steps towards the policy of self-reliance was in making provision for the further supply of locomotives. While in 1947 the general trends on railways all over the world were towards the elimination of steam traction, the economic situation in India, as in Great Britain also at that time, made it essential to rely as far as possible on indigenous fuel. India has large deposits of coal suitable for locomotive purposes, and so it became a point of major policy to continue with steam as the principal source of motive power. Locomotives had been built in India since 1885, but on no more than a small scale. In that year the East Indian Railway built its first new one in the shops at Jamalpur, and in 1896 the B.B. & C.I.R. built its first locomotive for the metre gauge in its shops at Ajmer; but an overwhelming proportion of new power had always to be imported.

The decision to set up a new works for large scale production of broad gauge steam locomotives was a sociological as much as an engineering project. It had been discussed and broad principles agreed even before the Second World War, and the conception of an entirely new site away from existing industrial complexes generally accepted. But war conditions, and the subsequent uncertainties over the political situation and the impending partition of India caused further postponement. It was not until after partition in 1947 that a site was chosen. This was in open country beside the first Chord Line of the East Indian Railway, that runs from Asansol northwestwards to join the original river valley route near Patna. The main considerations determining the choice of the site were an expansive area of cheap waste land available for building purposes, a natural undulating landscape suitable for town planning, good water supplies and proximity to coal and steel producing areas. It was not only the works that was to be new; everything was to be new. It was like building another Crewe, on the borders of Bihar and West Bengal. The new city was named Chittaranjan, after the great Indian patriot Deshabandhu Chittaranjan Das. It is about 16 miles from the major junction of Asansol.

When the site was chosen it was infested with the worst kind of malarial mosquitoes. But the activities of the Public Health Department were as vigorous and successful as those of the men who planned the quantity-production of locomotives, and with a good climate Chittaranjan has become a very pleasant place to live. The town is built on a series of hills. The houses rise tier upon tier in terraces, and at night when all the lights are on the scene is beautiful. With close attention given to every facet of the social services, health and education, it is a remarkable example of modern town planning. Every worker in the factory, and his family, had in the first place to be brought from distant parts of India. Work was commenced on the site in 1948, and the first locomotive was steamed off the assembly lines in November 1950.

Taken all round Chittaranjan was a mighty project. It became the largest locomotive building plant in Asia, and its equipment was the most modern in the world. Never before was a works planned for such a purpose on such a scale, and British engineers may in all modesty add that never before did the sponsors of such a scheme have a comparable wealth of experience and assistance to draw upon, as that given by the Locomotive Manufacturers' Association of Great Britain. The original aim was to produce 120 steam locomotives and

60 spare boilers a year. By the time Chittaranjan finished building steam in 1972, the record stood at 2344 locomotives and 2305 boilers, in a span of 21 years. Allowing for the building up period at the start these averages of 112 locomotives, and 109 spare boilers constitute a magnificent record of achievement, and fully justify all the careful planning put into the works and its environment.

At first production was concentrated on the 'WG' heavy freight 2–8–2, a design developed by the Central Standard Office of the Ministry of Railways, New Delhi, in collaboration with the English firm who had been consulting engineers to the Indian Government for about fifty years. The 'WG' was in some ways a synthesis of the best features of the British-built 'XD' and the Canadian 'X-Dominion', and had bar frames and many features interchangeable with the well-tried 'WP' 'Pacifics'. While Chittaranjan Works was getting into its stride an order for 100 'WG' class 2–8–2s was given to the North British Locomotive Company, and the first engines of this now very numerous class actually came from Glasgow. However it later became very much the 'Chittaranjan Engine', and the great new works certainly 'cut its teeth' on this successful design.

Details of the latest British and American practice were closely studied to give trouble free service and, if possible, mileages of around 200,000 between successive visits to plant for general overhaul. A thermic siphon was included in the firebox to improve circulation of water in the boiler, and a rocking grate was used to facilitate cleaning of fires on a long run. The use of bar frames was adopted to provide increased accessibility, though of course all the motion was outside. Bar frames naturally induce a degree of longitudinal stiffness not inherent in plate frames of the traditional British type and, to counteract this, frame deflection plates were located between the coupled wheels to reduce bending stresses in the frames. The basic dimensions were cylinders $21\frac{7}{8}$ in. diameter by 28 in. stroke; coupled wheels 5 ft. $1\frac{1}{2}$ in. diameter; boiler pressure 210 lb. per sq. in. and nominal tractive effort 38,890 lb. As the locomotives are used on mixed traffic duties they have the vacuum automatic brake for operating passenger trains, as required.

The last order for steam at Chittaranjan was completed in

1972—50 metre gauge 'Pacifics' of the 'YP' class. Since then all new work has been with electric locomotives. As with the broad gauge, the metre gauge standard types are of the 4–6–2 and 2–8–2 wheel arrangements, with a maximum number of parts interchangeable between the two. Not all of these smart little engines were built at Chittaranjan; some came from Great Britain and others from Germany. The design followed the same principles as those of the broad gauge, with bar frames, thermic syphon and two arch tubes in the firebox. They were built down to severely restricted axle-loading, and the adhesion weight of the 'Pacifics', for example, is only $31\frac{3}{4}$ tons. The cylinders are $15\frac{1}{4}$ in. diameter by 24 in. stroke; coupled wheels 4 ft. 6 in. diameter, and boiler pressure 210 lb. per sq. in. At 85 per cent. boiler pressure the tractive effort is 18,450 lb. Since the formation of the new zones, as enumerated on page 80 a touch of gaiety has been added to all the standard locomotives by applying zonal colours to the tenders and smoke deflecting plates, such as orange for the Southern Railway, leaf green for the Central, blue-green for the Eastern and so on.

CHAPTER NINE

Modernising—1 a.c. electrification

While the first major movement towards self-reliance on the railways of India was for bulk replacement of obsolete motive power, and of making up the arrears that had accumulated during the years of the Second World War, it was realised that steam traction would not provide the answer indefinitely—even in a country with such ample supplies of coal as India. In all the advanced countries of the world there was a definite trend to phase out steam, though not everywhere with the breathless haste evident in the U.S.A.; and in India, while finance was not yet available for their implementation, plans were initiated for a general modernisation of the railways, in much the same way as studies were inaugurated in Great Britain. The situations in the two countries were remarkably alike in their difficulties. Unlike those of certain European countries like France and Holland, whose railways had been wrecked on a devastating scale in the military campaigns fought along them, and in the strategic bombing of railway targets as a preliminary, the Indian railways, like the British, had been worked to the limit of their capacity, with nothing in the way of normal replacement, and with considerably less than normal maintenance. In this chapter, and the next which deals with the modernisation that has been gathering momentum strongly since 1960, I have taken the diverse engineering and operational disciplines in groups rather than treating the period in true historical sequence, and so begin with the development of electric traction, and its associated problems.

I have told in chapter 7 how suburban electrification, with the 1500 volt d.c. traction system, was inaugurated on both the G.I.P.R. and the B.B. & C.I.R. in Bombay, and of the extension of the

G.I.P.R. system over the Ghat inclines to Igatpuri and to Poona. The system chosen followed contemporary trends in both Great Britain and France. At the end of the Second World War electrification policy in Great Britain and France remained the same, and some notable installations were made in both countries of the 1500 volt d.c. system, with overhead wire current collection. At the same time Italy abandoned her previous use of the 3-phase a.c. traction system in favour of 3000 volts d.c., and Belgium adopted the same system, while Germany, Austria and Switzerland had standardised the single-phase a.c. system at 15,000 volts, 16⅔ cycles. The engineers of Indian Railways, studying world trends, were thus faced with a somewhat confusing divergency of preferences on railways with long experience of heavy passenger and freight traffic.

In the meantime the situation in the suburban areas of Calcutta was becoming extremely urgent, and in 1957 the first 20 miles of the original East Indian line out of the Howrah terminus, as far as Bandel, was equipped on the 3000 volt d.c. system. Bandel is the point of bifurcation of the loop line following the valley of the Ganga and the old East Indian main line through Burdwan, Asansol, and then northwestwards to join the loop line near Patna. At the same time the rapid development in Europe of national power networks at a frequency of 50 cycles per second, and successful experience with an experimental installation, had led the French National Railways to adopt 25,000 volts single phase a.c. at 50 cycles per second as the future standard for traction; and electrification by British Railways had quickly followed on the very busy main lines of the former London and North Western Railway, between Liverpool, Manchester, Birmingham and London (Euston). The British decision came in 1955, and with the accumulating experience in France on the heavily used freight lines between Thionville and Valenciennes, the Indian Railways decided to do the same. In 1958 work began between the steel centre of Durgapur (near Asansol) through the Bengal coalfields and northwestwards along the Grand Chord Line to Gomoh.

Before describing this work in any detail a word of explanation is needed concerning the historic build-up of the East Indian Railway main line network. As can be seen from the accompanying map, the

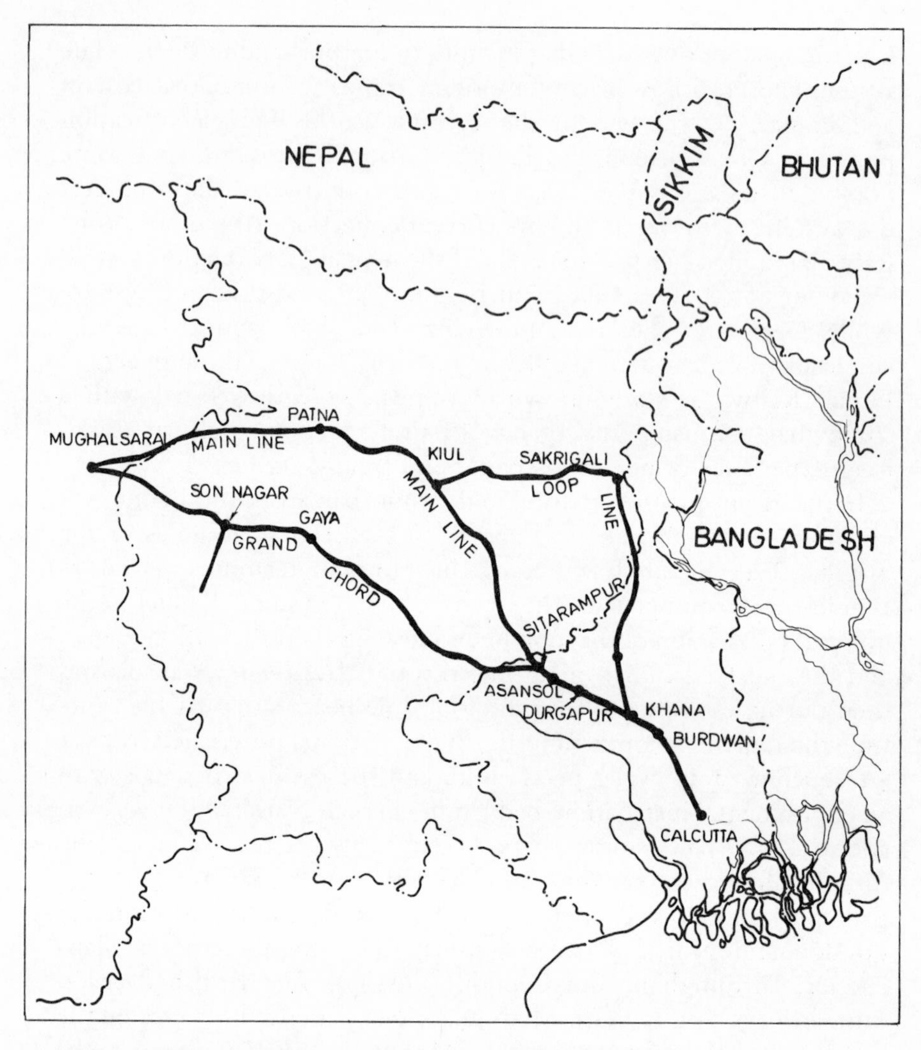

14. East Indian Railway: the Main, Loop and Grand Chord Lines

so-called Loop Line ran roughly due north from the bifurcation at Bandel, until at Sakrigali it turned through a right angle to continue west, and near to the right bank of the Ganga. What is known as the Old Main Line ran through Burdwan, past Durgapur and Asansol and then ran northwest to join the Loop Line at Kiul, after which it continued in general proximity to the Ganga through Patna to Mughal Sarāi. Then, in 1906, the Grand Chord Line from Sitarampur was opened, providing a much shorter route for heavy freight and mineral traffic from the Bengal coalfields area to Delhi and the North

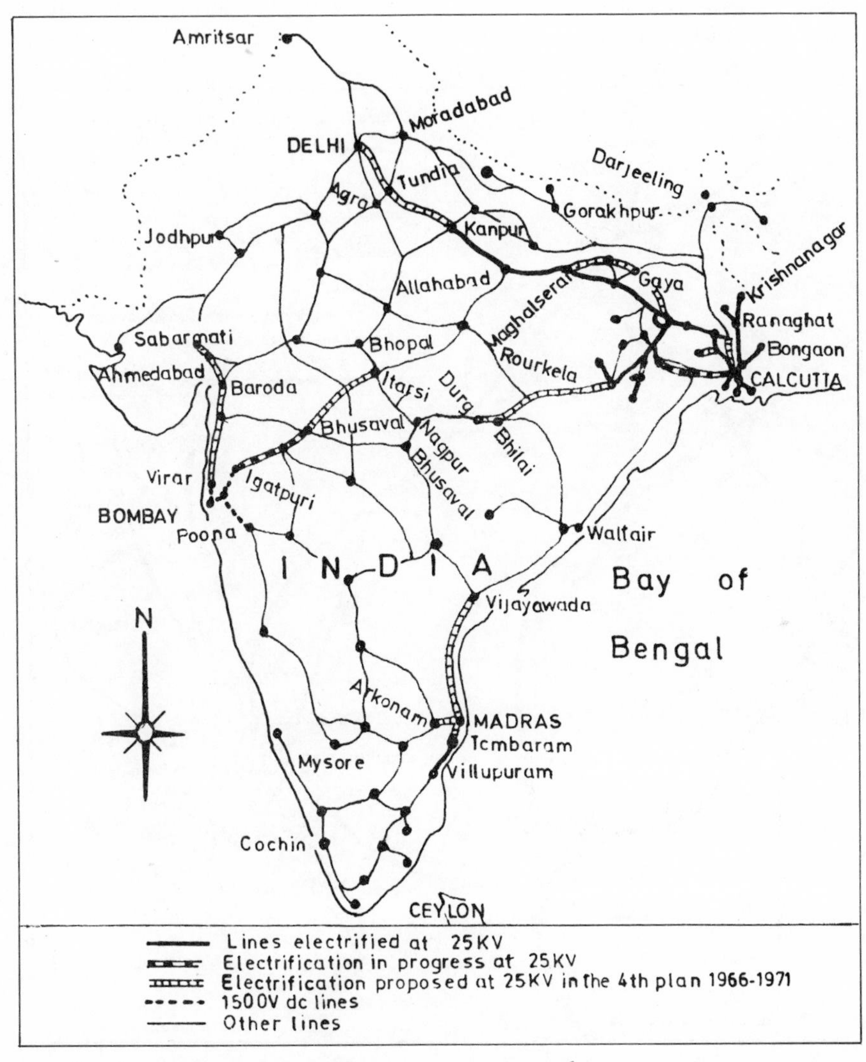

15. The first stages of electrification at 25,000 volts

West. The first stage of 25,000 volt a.c. electrification was brought into service in July 1961 to the extent indicated on the second map. The area was mostly that of the former Bengal Nagpur Railway, though the position of the East India Grand Chord Line will also be apparent. The districts in which the Beyer-Garratt locomotives of the Bengal Nagpur Railway operated, referred to in chapter 7, can also be traced on this map.

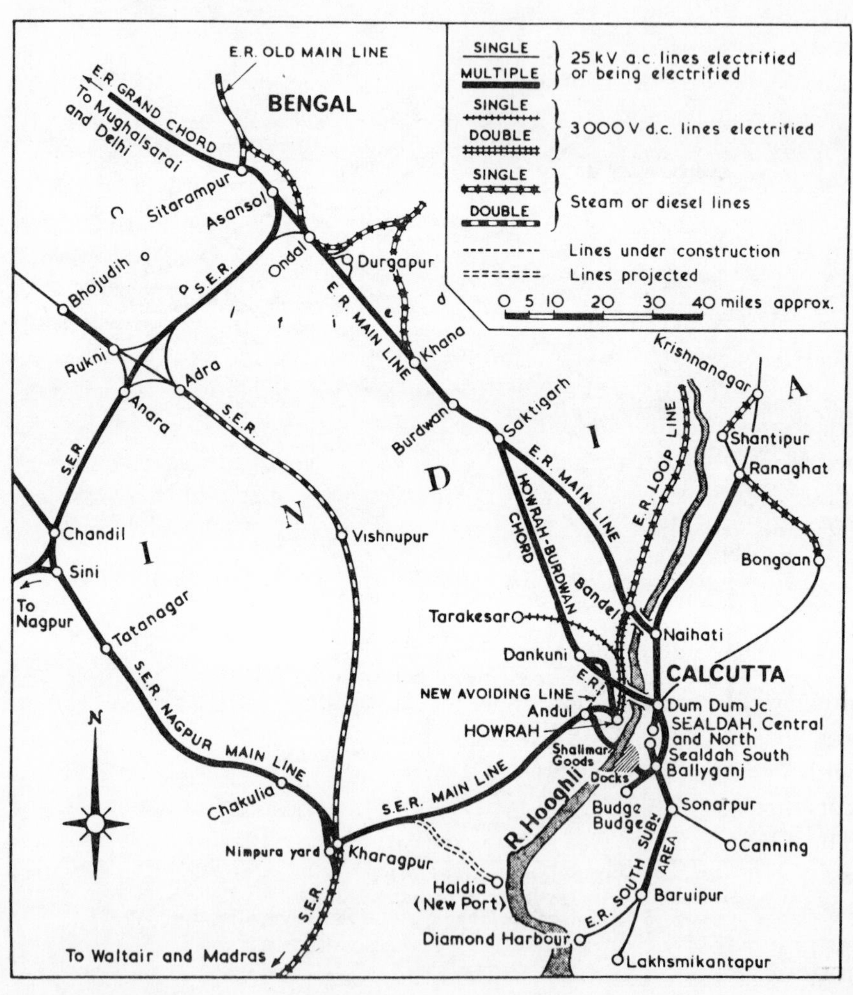

16. Electrification around Calcutta

The next area to be considered was in Calcutta itself. By parallel connections across the Hooghly River, from Bandel to Naihati, and from Dankuni to Dum Dum Junction, there are direct lines from the former East Indian system to the Calcutta docks, which were heavily utilised for export coal traffic. It seemed a logical development to electrify these lines, so that traffic from the colliery area west of Ondal could be expedited. This would bring a.c. electrification to the suburban lines of the former Eastern Bengal Railway from Sealdah station, although there was some hesitation in doing this, due to some extent to the amount of trespassing on the line, to a degree scarcely conceivable in European countries and in North America. But the decision was taken to carry the 25 KV a.c. line into Calcutta, and as a further map, of 1966, shows the original passenger electrification on 3000 volts d.c. from Howrah was encompassed on all sides. It has since been converted. The density of the rush hour traffic converging upon Howrah can be appreciated from there being six running lines, and it is no unusual thing for three multiple-unit electric trains to come in simultaneously, as I have seen myself, and discharge about 8000 passengers—*eight thousand!*—into the station concourse within a matter of seconds. There is however no segregation of the different forms of motive power in India. Steam and diesel locomotives work many of the longer distance trains out of Howrah, together with new 25 KV electrics, all 'under the wires' as the saying goes.

Chittaranjan Works are now building the main line electric locomotives, though when the programme was first launched their capacity was absorbed in building steam, and the majority of the new power had to be imported from Great Britain, and to an even greater extent from Japan. Typical freight locomotives were of the B-B type, with a continuous horsepower rating of 3200. The Grand Chord Line cuts through hilly country, with lengthy sections of 1 in 100 gradient. The 'WAG2' class was designed to operate trains of 1830 tons at 20 m.p.h. on such gradients. The passenger locomotives of Class 'WAM2' are also of the B-B type, with a rated maximum speed of 70 m.p.h. and a continuous horsepower rating of 2800. The line via Patna is still known as the main line, but with the mail trains there is a saving in time of about two hours by those trains that use the Grand

Chord. Two examples taken from the 1975 timetable may be quoted, as between Asansol and Mughal Sarai: the Amritsar Mail which takes the main line leaves at 23.16 and arrives at Mughal Sarai at 09.07, while for the Delhi–Kalka Mail, taking the Grand Chord, the corresponding times are 23.38 and 06.55.

Mughal Sarai is the grand junction of the Ganga plain. Into it feed five main routes. It is the point of convergence of the main and Grand Chord lines of the East Indian, while two routes of the former Oudh and Rohilkund from the north west converge at Varanasi, and the flow from these crosses the great bridge over the Ganga to join the main line from Allahabad just to the west of Mughal Sarai station. That is not all. Seventy-five miles to the east, at Son Nagar, the Grand Chord Line is joined by a line from Garhwa Road that carries an immense coal traffic, and the section of the Grand Chord between Son Nagar and Mughal Sarai is reputedly the busiest in the whole of India, apart of course from the intensely worked suburban routes around Bombay, Calcutta and Madras.

Traffic on the Grand Chord Line as far east as Gaya is regulated from Mughal Sarai, and I was privileged to spend some time in the control office. To watch and hear a controller at work is to me one of the most fascinating experiences one can have on a modern railway, and Mughal Sarai was no exception. By the courtesy of the Eastern Railway I was given one of the charts that had been compiled in that office, covering a whole day's working, and from one of its busiest portions the accompanying reproduction has been made. On the original diagrams the paths of passenger trains are shown in red crayon, electrically hauled freights are in blue, and diesel-hauled freights in green. Appropriate distinguishing codes have been chosen for the reproduction of the diagram, which shows the section of line between Mughal Sarai and Son Nagar between 1.00 and 9.00 a.m. It will be seen that the freights were leaving for the east thick and fast, each in turn having to be side-tracked further down the line to clear the way for the two express passenger trains. On the westbound road no fewer than 13 fast freights arrived at Mughal Sarai between 2.30 and 7.30 a.m. the last five of which had completely clear runs from Son Nagar. Of those 13 trains all except three were electrically hauled, and most had entered the Grand Chord Line at Son Nagar.

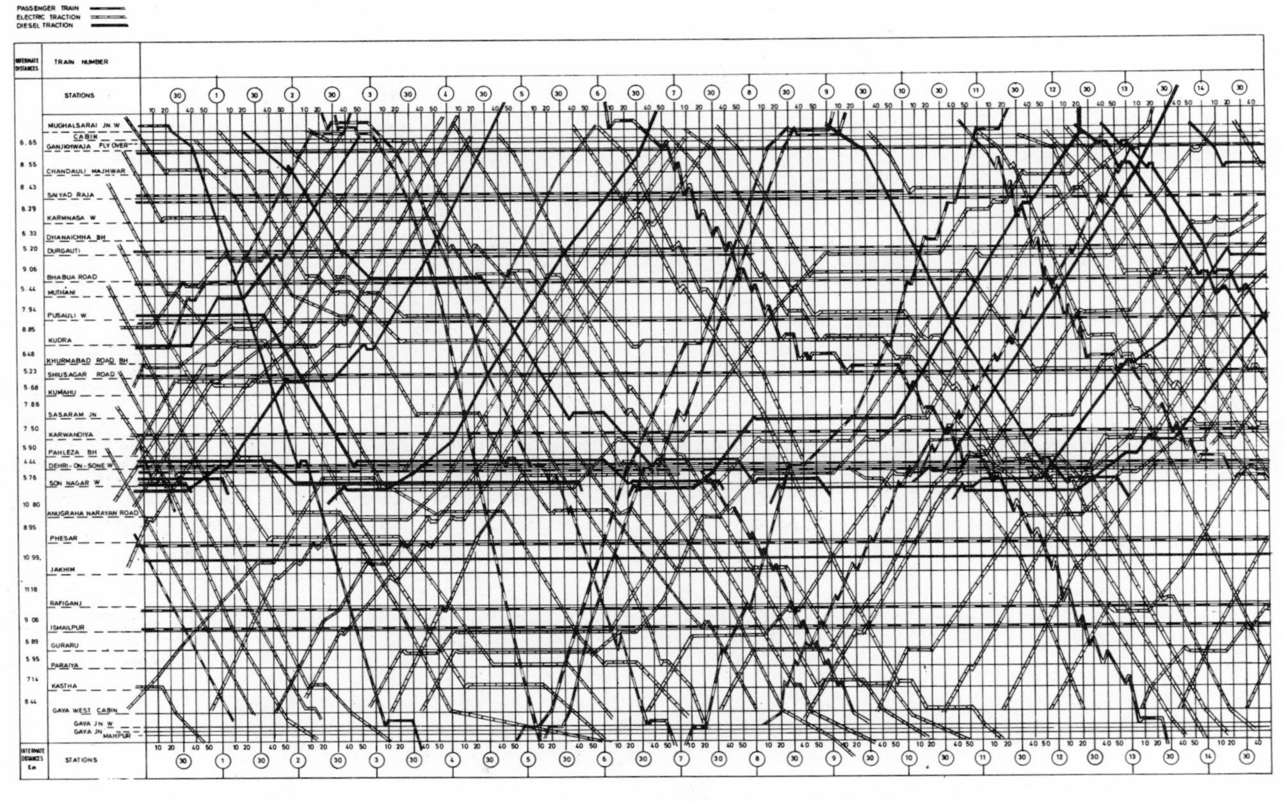

17. Timetable diagram showing operation on line between Mughal Sarai and Son Nagar

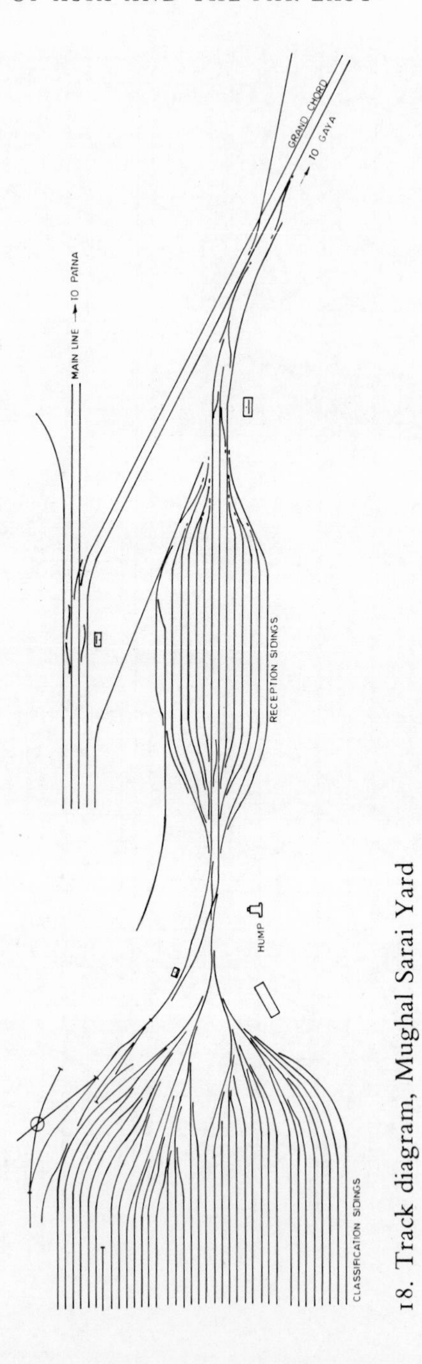

18. Track diagram, Mughal Sarai Yard

The network of the Northern Railway beyond the left bank of the Ganga extending to the frontier of Pakistan is in itself one of the most extensive group of lines in all India, while the electrified main line on the right bank not only reaches towards Delhi but makes important trunk line connection with the Central Railway at Allahabad and Kanpur. It is not surprising therefore that Mughal Sarai, poised in a position so 'strategic' for railway movements, should have become the site of the largest freight marshalling yard in India. The area dealing with 'up' traffic, that is from the direction of Calcutta, is located near the junction of the main and the Chord lines, and the track layout has been remodelled to facilitate the movement of trains from either line into the nest of 12 reception lines. As the accompanying diagram shows, departing traffic for the east from the 'down' yard is carried across what would be conflicting routes by 'flyover' crossings. In the fully mechanised 'up' yard trains from the reception sidings are propelled over the hump, and thence routed to the 22 classification lines, according to their content and destination west of Mughal Sarai. The yard was equipped in accordance with the current British practice in vogue at the time of its construction in 1962, with electro-pneumatic wagon retarders, and route setting with push button control from the tower. The operations were familiar to me from my professional association with many yards in Great Britain, but what was surprising in India was that the fine weather I had enjoyed in Madras and Calcutta had turned to unseasonably cold and drizzling rain—traditional enough in marshalling yards on Tees-side, or at Carlisle, but unexpected at Mughal Sarai!

It had been hoped to extend the 25 KV electrification by the end of the year 1971 to cover the following additional main lines:

Western Railway:	Bombay (Virar) to Baroda
Central Railway:	Bhusaval to Harsi
Northern Railway:	main line from the east into Delhi
Eastern Railway:	main line from Asansol to Mughal Sarai, via Patna
Southern and South Central Railways:	Madras northwards to Vijaywada

But these have not so far proved possible, and there have been just three major extensions; on the Northern from Kanpur to Tundla (near Agra); on the South Eastern, from Raurkela to Durg—former Bengal Nagpur main line from Calcutta towards Bombay—and the Central Railway extension from the previous 1500 volt d.c. railhead at Igatpuri to Bhusawal. This leaves only about 400 miles of the Bombay–Calcutta route (via Nagpur) that is not now electrified. The longest continuous electrification, all at 25 KV a.c. 50 cycles, is that from Calcutta via the Grand Chord to Mughal Sarai, Kanpur and Tundla, about 800 miles.

The density of traffic on the electrified main lines is not yet such as to demand continuous colour light signalling, but it is another matter in the approaches to the major city stations. Even before electrification, the situation outside Howrah had led to the installation of colour light signals and electrically operated points. This plant, which was commissioned in 1937 was actually the second generation of power signalling on the East Indian Railway. As early as 1906 increasing traffic on both the East Indian and Bengal Nagpur lines approaching the station led to the introduction of the earliest form of electro-pneumatic signalling with miniature lever frames in the station signal box (71 levers) and at the Bengal Nagpur junction (34 levers). The signals were electro-pneumatically operated semaphores, with a great proliferation of arms. It was only for shunting movements that any form of route indicating was used, and the array of semaphores on a great gantry spanning all the tracks at the entrance to the station was reminiscent of some of the most spectacular British layouts. At Howrah on the one gantry there were 24 arms for ingoing traffic alone.

The 1937 remodelling brought the entire area under the control of one signal box, substituting colour light signals of the searchlight type for the previous semaphores. Although no form of route indicating was included the number of individual signals was much reduced by having a single unit in each of the platform 'home' locations. If such a signal were in the clear position it could read into any one of the platforms ahead, usually not more than three, and the driver of an ingoing train would be prepared to act accordingly. The new interlocking frame of 82 levers was of the so-called 'pistol-grip' type, which was commonly used in North America at that time, and had been installed by the English manufacturers of the Howrah equipment on certain large interlockings on the Great Western Railway of England, notably at Paddington and Bristol.

Like its predecessor of 1906 the power interlocking of 1937 lasted for about 30 years, and then an increase in traffic of some 30 per cent. was planned. Had such traffic, amounting to about 650 train movements daily, been evenly spread over the 24 hours the older plant could have coped; but at Howrah, as at every other station dealing with a heavy suburban traffic, there is intense pressure for relatively short periods at the beginning and end of the working day, and my earlier reference to the discharging of 8000 passengers from the simultaneous arrival of three multiple-unit electric trains, was not of an exceptional occurrence. The new plant of 1968, which I had the pleasure of seeing in action during the morning rush hour, was designed to deal with more than 800 train movements daily. In 1975 at the time of my own visit there were in addition to the multiple-unit electrics many locomotive-hauled trains, powered variously by steam, diesel and electric units.

In signalling practice the Indian railways have always made careful studies of current developments in Great Britain, adapting established techniques to the local conditions. But as the traffic situations around the great city terminal stations have developed to correspond closely with British circumstances—at any rate so far as the actual running of trains is concerned—so the more advanced examples of Indian signalling are coming to correspond more closely with contemporary British practice. Until fairly recently the control instruments and most of the individual items of equipment were imported; but now, as with locomotives and other railway supplies, signalling products are being manufactured in the new Signal and Telecommunications shops at Podanur, beside the broad gauge main line of the Southern Railway, which runs southwest from Madras through Salem and Erode to reach Cochin Harbour terminus, in the State of Kerala. Podanur itself is almost at the border of the latter State, and is the junction for an important metre gauge network of the former South Indian Railway. Although they were not concerned with any electrification projects, the junctions of Salem and Erode were equipped with the later British type of miniature lever interlocking frames with electric, rather than mechanical, lever interlocking.

Although the national policy of self-reliance has established an important centre of signalling manufacture in the far south of the country, it has also led me far away from my immediate subject—the third generation of power signalling at Howrah. In this recent modernisation, the opportunity was taken to utilise the technique of route setting, rather than that of individual signal and point control, in order to minimise the number of operations to be made by the signalmen. The entrance-exit system of route switching was adopted, requiring a thumb switch to be operated at the entry to a route, and then selection to be made of the appropriate push-button at the exit point of the route. Providing the route is clear, and it is safe for such a route to be set up, all the intermediate switches on the track line up as initiated by the operations made on the panel by the signalman, and when the route is fully set the colour light signal at its entrance clears.

In view of the complexity of the track layout in the approach to Howrah terminus the panel equipment is extremely compact. As in many modern British signal boxes it has been arranged in two sections. The switches and push buttons for the route setting are accommodated on a sloping-top desk, of such proportions that a single operator can reach any function from a seated position. Ahead of the desk, displayed vertically is an enlarged representation of the track layout, with the usual illuminated indications of the movements of trains. In some earlier applications of the entrance-exit system of route-setting, the operating switches and push buttons were located on the actual illuminated diagram; but on a large installation such as Howrah this meant that the signalmen were standing for much of the time, and being in close proximity to the track diagram they did not have such a good overall picture of train movements as with the dual arrangements.

From the verandah of the signal box there is an excellent view of the trains constantly coming and going on the tracks below, though of course the signalman himself does not *see* any trains at all. He works entirely by the illuminated diagram, and in the air-conditioned cabin, with the sun-blinds lowered to keep out the strong light, there is a feeling of seclusion. There is certainly no feeling of seclusion outside, as the commuter trains come, one after another, with all the sliding doors open, and clusters of passengers hanging on around every one of these entrances. The electrified railways are certainly moving the people into and out of the great Indian cities. Outside Howrah the throng is indescribable in the peak periods, for nearly all the passengers arriving have, by some means, to make their way across the great Hooghly road bridge into Calcutta itself. When every train is bringing in at least 2500 people there can be quite a crowd in the roadway, and subway outside.

CHAPTER TEN

Modernising—2 the broadening field

Building carriages was one of the first ways in which the railways of India began to move towards self-reliance. The principal railways began in quite early days, and I have already referred to some of the magnificent special trains built by the East Indian, the G.I.P.R., and the Bengal Nagpur Railways. But after Independence, and the centralising of design and research activities, there was a need to standardise the form of coaches as much as possible, in order to ensure the most economic methods of production and use the same basic coach body for as many different vehicles as possible. At the same time it was desired to make use of the latest manufacturing techniques to produce vehicles of maximum strength and minimum weight. In the early 1950s current worldwide practice was studied, and in 1955 a collaboration agreement was made with the Swiss Car and Elevator Manufacturing Corporation of Zurich, and production was inaugurated later that year at the Integral Coach Factory, at Madras. The original intention was to produce only shells in this new plant, sending them to the various existing railway workshops for furnishing.

How enormously that original project of turning out 350 shells a year has been expanded was evident when I was privileged to make an inspection during my visit to Madras in 1975. At the outset I should mention that the collaboration agreement with the Swiss firm ended in 1961. Since then the ICF has been on its own—and to some purpose. First of all the basic design of the shell needs some explanation. The construction is entirely welded, and consists of three separate groups of fabrication; the underframe, the roof, and the side walls and end walls. Considerable saving of weight is effected by use of what is termed the 'stressed-skin' form of construction. The underframe consists of pressed steel channel sections welded together to give the floor the necessary resistance to crushing loads, and the complete welded assembly of floor, roof and side walls form in effect a hollow tube. Accuracy in construction is ensured by carrying out each stage of the fabrication in skilfully designed jigs, in which the members are held in precision while welding is in progress.

Although a great deal had to be done in the initial stages to train operators and get the planned flow-line of production swinging along, the original target of 350 unfurnished shells was surpassed within three years of inauguration, and two years later the output was up to 583 shells. Already however the original function of the factory was being extended, and many completely furnished coaches were being turned out. Using a minimum of basic shells a large variety of coaches was soon being produced ranging from electric multiple unit cars of all kinds, first and third class coaches for long distance trains, dining cars and luxury coaches for the air-conditioned express trains. The work was extended to metre gauge as well as broad gauge stock, and by the year 1970 the ICF was turning out 650 completely furnished coaches a year. These coaches are mounted on Indian Railway Standard 4-wheeled bogies, which give a very comfortable ride.

I have previously mentioned air conditioning. This was first introduced in India in 1952, and it proved a great boon, not only because of the climate, but also because any other system of ventilation inevitably draws dust into the vehicle. Only those with long experience of travel in India will appreciate what this means, and what a heavenly relief it is to ride in the modern coaches. Today air-conditioned accommodation rates as a special luxury class, and demands much higher fares than ordinary first class travel. On the special high speed express trains air-conditioned third class coaches are provided, at supplementary fares. The following table gives the inside temperatures maintained in air-conditioned coaches in different conditions of ambient temperature and humidity, ranging up to a maximum of 113°F. outside.

Outside temperature (°F.)	113	95	77	71½
Outside relative humidity (%)	25	50	92	70
Inside temperature (°F.)	86	77	71½	71½

Nevertheless, as I experienced during my own travels in India, it can be quite cold as well as very hot, and electric air heaters are provided for winter conditions.

It is of course not only the passengers that need 'air conditioning' in travelling in India. Rapid industrialisation and the growth of urban areas under successive five-year plans have led to a greatly increased demand for fresh fish, fruit and vegetables. The railways carry these over long distances, and there has been much development in production of refrigerated vans. The equipment has been designed to maintain temperature at exactly freezing point for 40 to 50 hours continuously. The vans are provided with an attendant's compartment in the centre, suitably insulated from the refrigerated compartments on either side, so that he does not get frozen!

At the name Varanasi, one thinks inevitably of elegant temples, of the sacred bathing ghats on the banks of the Ganga River, and the aura of Hindu history and customs; but although I was going there for a very different programme of sightseeing, it did at first seem that I had come to an unlikely place. To save nearly a day in travelling we had flown from Calcutta. The airport at Varanasi is some distance from the city, and in driving thence we passed convoys of camels, and in the city streets encountered elephants in service as pack animals. Was this indeed the place where one of the most modern locomotive building works in the world has been successfully established? Varanasi however is no more than a particularly vivid example of the astonishing contrasts that one meets so often in India. The manufacture of diesel locomotives on the outskirts of this most ancient and historic city is one of the later manifestations of the policy of self-reliance, undertaken when it was decided that diesel traction should gradually replace steam as the handmaiden of electricity.

While the Indian Railways had enjoyed the collaboration of the British Locomotive Manufacturers Association in setting up the great new works at Chittaranjan, and of Swiss expertise in production of the stressed-skin body shells at the Integral Coach Factory, it was to North America that India turned for assistance in the establishment of the Diesel Locomotive Works (DLW) with a collaboration agreement with ALCO, and its Canadian associate, the Montreal Locomotive Works. After worldwide study it had been the ALCO/MLW type of diesel electric locomotive that had been chosen as the future Indian standard, for both broad and metre gauge. The first one was completed at Varanasi in January 1964, and while naturally it took a little time to work up to a full production flow-line, by the year 1970 the Works was turning out a hundred locomotives every year. By that time the period of overseas collaboration was ended. The respective details of the main line broad and metre gauge types are shown in the following table, but it is important to add that the actual engines, although differently arranged, and of dissimilar power, have a maximum number of detail parts that are interchangeable.

Indian standard diesel-electric locomotives

	Broad Gauge	Metre Gauge
Class	'WDM-2'	'YDM-4'
Power (h.p.)	2400/2600	1200/1350
Engine	16-cyl. V-type	6-cyl. in line
Axle load tons	18·8	11·48
Total weight tons	112·8	68·88
Max. speed m.p.h.	75	60

In addition to the above the Diesel Locomotive Works is also producing shunting locomotives, class 'WDS-6', with an engine horsepower similar to that of the metre gauge main line locomotive, but geared to move a 4000-ton train from rest. These locomotives are being produced also for the Government owned steel plants in various parts of India. The wheel arrangement of all three types of diesel in production at Varanasi is Co-Co.

One of the most interesting recent developments in the long distance passenger service on Indian railways has been the move towards considerably higher speeds. The Research Design and

Standards Organisation (RDSO) acting as technical consultants to the Indian Railways was assigned a project to attain service speeds of 100 m.p.h. in passenger traffic, and 60 m.p.h. for goods, with an intermediate target of 75 m.p.h. for passenger trains. Hitherto the maxima generally accepted had been 60 m.p.h. for passenger and 45 m.p.h. for goods. Speeding up of service involves every single discipline in the field of railway engineering, and RDSO, with its magnificently equipped laboratories at Lucknow and its team of specialist professional engineers, was well equipped to make the necessary studies in track, locomotive and vehicle riding, and fatigue effects. Fortunately the history of engineering performance on the two routes chosen for the first introduction of higher speed trains was well documented, so that the staff of RDSO were able to study the areas of potential weakness, both in rolling stock and track. By June 1968 RDSO was able to recommend to the Indian Railway Board that an increase of speed to a maximum of 75 m.p.h. on the former East Indian main line between New Delhi and Howrah was practicable, without any large-scale capital investment on track, signalling, or bridges, by using existing locomotives and coaches.

High speed test runs were carried out with an American built diesel-electric locomotive of class 'WDM-4', similar in general characteristics to the indigenous 'WDM-2' built at Varanasi, and a train of ten coaches built at ICF, Madras. It was realised that a basic requirement for high speed running was a first class standard of track maintenance, and observations in the track recording car formed an important part of the test running. As a result the practice of 'measured shovel packing', as developed on the British railways between the two World Wars, was introduced to provide greater precision in maintenance of a good 'top' and correct super-elevation on curves. The ultrasonic testing of both axles and rails was introduced on the track between Allahabad and Mughal Sarai, and on the critical section between Kanpur and Tundla, both of which had proved vulnerable to rail failures in the past.

At New Delhi station one evening I had an opportunity for a walk through 'The Rajdhani Express', the first of the new higher speed trains introduced as from March 1969, on the run to Howrah. It covers the 895 miles in 16 hr. 35 min. at an overall average of

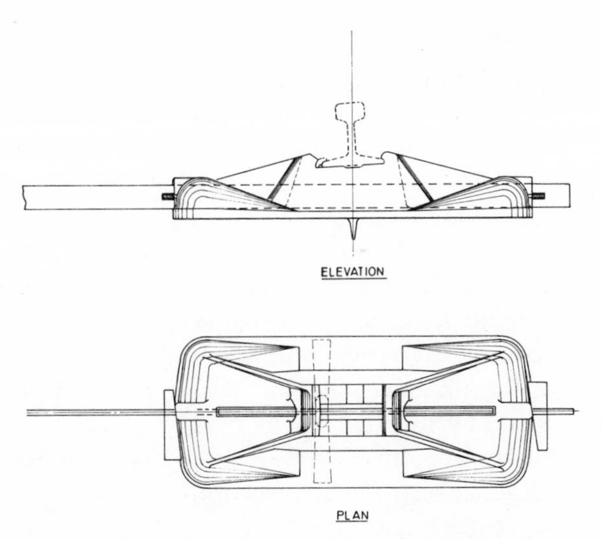

19. Modern Indian permanent way: cast iron supports under each rail

53·7 m.p.h. The train is air conditioned throughout, and a typical formation consists of five chair-cars, sitting three on one side of the central gangway and two on the other side; a sleeper coach; a pantry car, which also includes a pleasant lounge for sleeper coach passengers; and two power generating cars, which both include luggage compartments. Tickets for this luxury train include all meals, served airline style at one's seat, and include evening tea, dinner, morning tea and breakfast. The departure times are 6.15 p.m. from New Delhi and 5.10 p.m. from Howrah. On the westbound run the intermediate stops are at Dhanbad Junction, Mughal Sarai and Kanpur, and the overall time is 16 hr. 55 min. The eastbound run is non-stop between New Delhi and Kanpur, 267 miles in 268 minutes—one of the fastest in India, while the even faster continuation non-stop from Mughal Sarai to Dhanbad, over the heavy gradients of the Grand Chord Line, is 249 miles in the level 4 hr.—62·3 m.p.h.—a splendid piece of modern express train running. Reference to the timetable diagram on page 91 will show that the eastbound 'Rajdhani', leaving Mughal Sarai on time at 3.15 a.m. passed Gaya Junction 127 miles in 113 minutes from the start. The heavy climbing however, with about 10 miles at 1 in 90 occurs east of Gaya Junction.

Much research has been devoted towards improvement of the track. A high proportion of the earlier mileage was laid in the British style, including a subsequent changeover from timber to steel sleepers. But as in other disciplines Indian studies since Independence have been worldwide, and particular attention became centred upon the French practice of having concrete block supports under each rail, connected by steel ties. From this practice, Indian Railways have developed and standardised a design consisting of a cast iron support under each rail, connected, as in French concrete sleeper design, by steel ties. The complete arrangement is shown on the accompanying drawing, with the mild steel tie bar passing through both support plates, and secured by four tapered cotters.

The rapid increase in traffic in many parts of India has made essential the elimination of many sections of line which, though adequate in earlier days, had now become bottlenecks. One notable example was the lengthy single-line bridge of the former Bengal Nagpur Railway over the Godavari delta near Rajahmundry, now part of the South Central Railway. This forms part of the main line between Calcutta and Madras, and in the developing conditions it became essential to remove the single-line section. In view of the success of combined rail and road bridges elsewhere in India the railways, jointly with the Government of the State of Andhra Pradesh, decided on a new bridge that would carry a single line of railway on the bottom deck and a double lane roadway to National Highway standards on the top deck. As such it became the longest bridge of its kind in all Asia, with a total length of nearly two miles. Construction of the bridge itself was carried out by the railways, while the State Government built the road approaches.

The alignment was fixed about two-thirds of a mile downstream from the older railway bridge, for various environmental reasons, and this involved some highly interesting problems, due to the vast expanse of water that had to be crossed. It was difficult to make a precise survey for locating the piers to support no less than 27 spans. The foundations of the piers are on massive concrete wells sunk to a depth of about 100 ft. below low water, and for sinking these wells a base had to be created in the water course by forming artificial islands, in depths ranging from 10 to 40 ft. These 'islands' were used as working platforms on which cranes and other equipment could be erected. The Godavari delta is however particularly susceptible to heavy flooding in the monsoon season, and all constructional work had to be done during the intervening dry period. Some careful planning of the work programme had to be made, because all heavy machinery had to be withdrawn from the 'islands' before the onset of the next flood. The foundation work was completed in five working seasons.

The superstructure of the bridge consists of steel girders built up in the form of K-trusses, notable in that none but Indian-produced steel was used. They were erected by the cantilever method, thus enabling the work to continue round the year, without interruption by floods. In this method one end of the girder is anchored to the girder of the previous span, and the structure was built out piece by piece by a 'creeper' crane, moving forward on the top boom as the work proceeded. One of the most unusual features was the inclusion of several spans at one end on a curve. This splendid piece of precision civil engineering was opened for traffic on November 20, 1974, by the President of India.

Proceeding north from Rajahmundry and entering the territory of the South Eastern Railway one soon reaches the junction of Kottavalasa, a point of great significance in the development of the Indian railways, namely the building of a 'belt conveyor' type of railway to handle one particular form of freight traffic. In 1960, to provide for an export of 4 million tons of iron ore per year to Japan, a railway was driven through the hitherto impenetrable forests of Dandakaranya. It is strange to associate a land so famed in Hindu mythology with anything so ultra-modern as a 'belt conveyor' railway; extending for 278 miles from the main line junction of Kottavalasa to Kirandul—from the initials of its starting and ending stations the K-K Line, this line was driven through a wild and remote country that needed 61 tunnels, 87 major bridges, and reached the record altitude, for an Indian broad gauge line, of 3270 ft. above sea level. There is much severe grading at 1 in 60, 1 in 80, and 1 in 100, and the incessant curvature to lessen construction costs and find *any* kind of way through the tumbled ranges of the Eastern Ghats, resulted in the actual length of line of 278 miles, whereas the straight distance between the two 'Ks' is only about 135 miles.

The line was opened for traffic in November 1968, with diesel traction, using three 'WDM' locomotives in multiple, on the heaviest trains. But already the traffic is likely to exceed considerably the four million tons of iron ore annually for which the line was originally built, and plans are well advanced to convert the line to a.c. electric traction, at the Indian standard system of 25 KV at 50 cycles per section, to permit operation of trains having a trailing load of about 9000 tons. A depot capable of accommodating and servicing 100 electric locomotives is planned for Waltair, on the main line near Kottavalasa; but the rugged nature of the country, susceptible to the loosening of large masses of soft hill slopes and heavy boulders during the monsoon period, needs exceptional vigilance, particularly when overhead electric traction supply has been installed, to maintain the steady outward flow of iron ore, throughout each year.

When I was in India in 1975 I learned of another entirely new line in the south, this time on the metre gauge, being built to connect Hassan in the plateau area, with the new major port of New Mangalore on the west coast. Hassan is in the metre gauge network of the former Southern Mahratta Railway, and the new line 117 miles long, cuts through the mountainous and forest-clad range of the Western Ghats at a point some 350 miles south of the famous pioneer crossings of the range by the G.I.P.R. more than a hundred years earlier. My only sight of this new railway was from the air, when flying from Bombay to Cochin; but from what my friends of the Southern Railway told me I gather that its construction has been one of the most difficult tasks for Indian civil engineering forces since Independence, particularly as the work was pushed ahead through all seasons (regardless of the great heat of the south, and tremendous tropical rains) by teams of men far removed from all the comforts of modern civilisation and in a countryside teeming with wild life. Unlike the early construction days on the G.I.P.R. the health of the work forces remained good—a tribute to modern medical science, and the care taken by Medical Officers, pharmacists and other supporting staff.

Mention of my flight from Bombay to Cochin forms a prelude to my last chapter about India, which I have kept for some personal experiences and pleasant memories.

CHAPTER ELEVEN

India—a January tour

Towards evening on a Sunday of such warm and gracious sunshine that it was hard for an Englishman to believe it was January, I took a flight from New Delhi to Bombay. I was starting out on a tour that was to take me all round India. Many of the fine new works that I visited and the installations that I saw in action have been described in earlier chapters, in the context of the great plan of modernisation in which the Indian Railways are engrossed; but in recalling that pleasant flight to Bombay and what followed it there are many points on which I have not yet touched. And although the Railways of India form such a vast subject, and would need many volumes to treat comprehensively, not to say exhaustively, some further items within my own observation may help to fill in just a few of the gaps. If this chapter is a little more personal than some of the preceding ones, it is because I should like to convey something of the intense friendliness and eagerness to help that I found everywhere on the Indian Railways.

Representatives of the Central and Western Railways met us on arrival in Bombay and although the hour was late, they drove with us to the home of our hosts to arrange how my next days should be spent. As these two railwaymen discussed, most diplomatically, how my time should be divided, I sensed that something of the age-old rivalry between the G.I.P. and the B.B. & C.I. Railways lingered in their modern successors and here, as everywhere else in India, there was as great an eagerness to hear from me the latest railway news from Great Britain, the continent of Europe and North America, as to 'put across', with immense enthusiasm, their own latest achievements. It was a surprise to me to learn that night that I was to lecture on 'World Railways' to the Institute of Rail Transport during my brief stay in Bombay! The following morning was a very special occasion for the Western Railway, and we arrived at Churchgate station just as the inward suburban rush was working up to its maximum intensity. I had been in India long enough not to be unduly surprised at the packed electric trains, and the clusters of passengers hanging in groups around every open door of every coach; but this, as they proceeded to explain to me was a rush-hour with a difference.

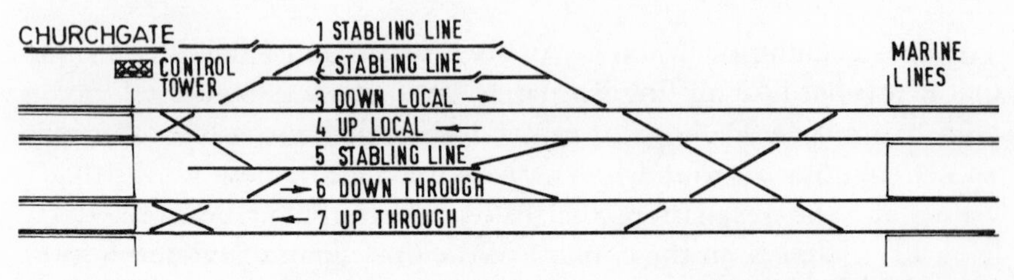

20. Track layout approaching Churchgate terminus, Bombay

Over the weekend the final stage of the quadrupling of the suburban lines from Grant Road into the Churchgate terminus had been completed. The civil engineering work carrying the line on viaducts through a crowded area of the city had been at times as intricate as a surgical operation, with precision-planned stage work to keep the tremendous volume of suburban traffic flowing freely and punctually despite all the piece-by-piece alterations to track and signalling. This Monday morning, when I watched the incoming trains from concourse, control room and signal box, was the consummation of the years of expert engineering and traffic planning. In Churchgate station there are only four tracks, but on each of these there are platform faces on both sides; so that when a crowded train arrives it can be unloaded in roughly half the normal time, by the passengers literally pouring out from both sides simultaneously. With each train bringing in roughly 4000 passengers—yes, *four thousand!*—and the timetable not allowing any train to occupy a platform road for more than four minutes, some pretty snappy movement was required. The accompanying sketch map shows the track layout and signalling in the approaches to Churchgate.

My days in Bombay were very full. In Chapter Nine I have told of the G.I.P.R. electrification, and the operation on the Bhor Ghat, but one evening when Jack Brown and I were sitting in the lounge of the sumptuous Taj Mahal Hotel, it occurred to us that among the numerous visitors and tourists awaiting their transport for a night out 'on the town' our assignment must have been one of the strangest. We were waiting for the Western Railway to take us out to Bandra Marshalling Yard. Had they known all our fellow 'loungers' must surely have rubbed their eyes with incredulity. But there was no other time to see this interesting place, and a marshalling yard is often as busy around the witching hour as at any other time of the day. Bandra, on the main line to Baroda and the north, is on the mainland just north of the Mahim River bridge that separates Bombay Island in this area. The yard is double-ended, with reception and sorting sidings each in one 'balloon' on either side of a symmetrically graded hump. The yard was busy enough in the night, because all movement to and from the main line has to be made in non-peak hours of the intense electric suburban service. I was interested to see that Canadian-built 'X-Dominion' 2–8–2 steam locomotives were being used for humping.

After Bombay my next call was at Cochin, 675 miles to the south, where I was welcomed by the local officers of the Southern Railway. Long before the aircraft touched down I could see we were flying over a densely tropical country, and we arrived in a land of intensely green palm trees, coastal lagoons and all the warmth and colour of a region only 10 deg. north of the Equator. Cochin Harbour is the southern terminus of the broad gauge line that comes southwestwards across the toe of the peninsula from Madras, and a number of British-built 'XD' class 2–8–2 locomotives in the orange and black livery of the Southern Railway were on shed. The immediate feature of interest however was the metre gauge line that follows the coast south to Trivandrum, which was in process of conversion to broad gauge. When my friends at Railway Board Headquarters in New Delhi had put this section of line into my itinerary, I was delighted at the opportunity of seeing something of the far-south, but I certainly did not then appreciate the reasons for the gauge conversion.

This section of line, and the northward continuation of the broad gauge line from Cochin almost to Mangalore, lies in the State of Kerala. Although this is one of the smallest states, it has the highest density of population in the whole of India, and the capacity of the metre gauge railway to Trivandrum had reached saturation point. From the splendid viewpoint of an officers' saloon, attached to the rear of a passenger train I enjoyed an unrivalled view of the line, the countryside, and of the works in progress for conversion of the gauge. My impression from the air of an intensely tropical vegetation was amply confirmed on this run. Except at the several river crossings we were running continuously through forests of palm trees, always beneath a cloudless sky. The preparation for conversion included widening of the formation and putting in the longer sleepers necessary for the 5 ft. 6 in. gauge, more closely spaced than hitherto, to carry the heavier loads. When the time comes for the change there will be no case of slewing existing rails across; the new ones will already be in place outside the present rails, on the same sleepers.

Bridges were being renewed, and at certain river crossings the new girders were already alongside, for rolling across when the time came. The photographs reproduced on plate 14 show clearly the method used for re-girdering in one case, with temporary gantries erected over the piers, enabling the old girders to be hoisted up and placed on rail-borne bogies, before the new girders were lowered into position. It was dark before we reached Trivandrum, and I was able to enjoy the leisure of a hot tropical evening at a beach hotel at Kovalum, 8 miles to the south. My railway friends regretted that time did not allow us to make the road journey to Cape Comorin, the southernmost tip of India, a further 70 miles to the south; but in my railway and scenic sightseeing I had reached something like satiety that day, and there was much more to come in the morning. In making a scenic diversion on the way from Kovalum back to Trivandrum my host told me of their hopes that following the gauge widening this section of line south of Cochin might even be electrified, such is the potential build-up of traffic. In the meantime we walked round the metre gauge steam locomotive yard, photographing the 'YG' 2–8–2 locomotives, and visiting the site of the new freight marshalling yard that is to be built.

I would have lingered for days in the tropical warmth and incredibly clear atmosphere of this southern end of Kerala, but engagements awaited me in Madras, and once again I had to take to the air to keep my schedule. An old friend, Mr. S. M. Gauri Shanker, Chief Signal and Telecommunications Engineer, was one of those who welcomed me at Southern Railway headquarters, and it was with particular interest that I went to see the route-relay interlocking plant at the metre gauge station of Egmore, where the control panel is one recently manufactured in the new signal works at Podanur, referred to in an earlier chapter. Surpassing all, however, in the sphere of signal and telecommunications on the Southern Railway is the remarkable microwave radio network, covering 11 key points on the Southern and South Central Railways, as shown on the accompanying sketch map. At a time when the frequency and speeds of trains have increased, and there are yet great distances between centres of population—with jungle and unprotected land, susceptibility to vagaries in the weather, and exposure to anti-social

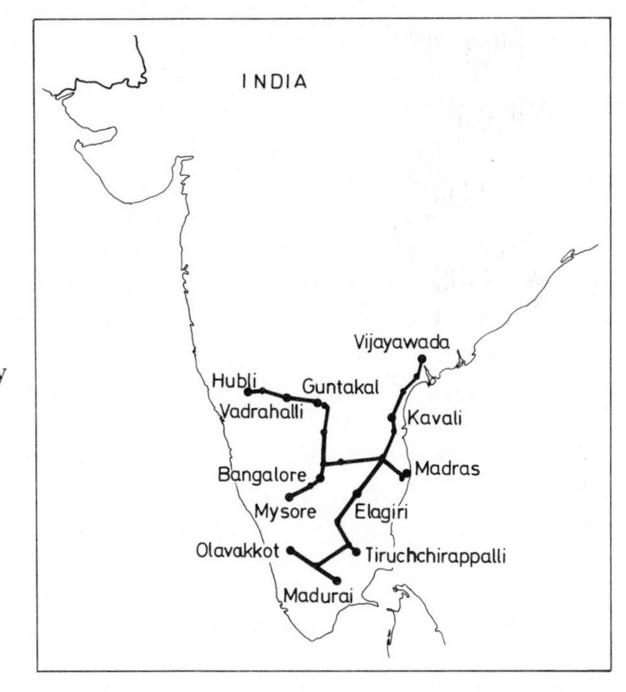

21. Microwave Radio Network, Southern Railway

elements—the change from landbased telephone and telegraph wires to microwave radio communication is a great step forward.

I was actually prepared in some small way for what I was to see in Madras, for Mr. V. Raghunathan, Deputy Signal and Telecommunications Engineer–Microwave was one of those who met me at Cochin, and in the brief time I had there he handed me a brochure to ensure that I did a little 'homework' before arriving in Madras. It was one of the many charming little courtesies that I enjoyed from railway officers on my travels in India. He explained to me that since Microwave resembles light wave and virtually travels in a straight line, advantage was taken of the mountainous terrain traversed by the Southern Railway to derive the most economical spacing of repeater stations consistent with efficiency. This was no mean task. An elaborate and comprehensive Microwave survey had to be undertaken before the most suitable sites could be selected—virtually hundreds of locations well off the lines of railway had to be surveyed and all sorts of ingenious methods adopted in order to ensure the existence of line-of-sight conditions, including flashing lights by night and reflection of the sun rays by day through oscillating mirrors carried aloft by hydrogen balloons. As a result, it was possible to establish microwave repeating stations over extended distances, so much so that the link between the two hill stations at Yelagiri and Tirupathi covers a distance of 87 miles and is possibly one of the longest static spans over which such line-of-sight microwave communication has been established. It is a most impressive example of modern telecommunication engineering.

I could write much more on a personal note of the pleasant days I spent in Madras, of the warm hospitality I received from the General Manager of the Southern Railway, Mr. G. S. A. Saldanha, of rides on the metre gauge electric commuter trains, of the C.T.C. signalling, while I have already written at some length of the work of the Integral Coach Factory. So I must take flight once again, this time for Calcutta. I do not think I have yet quite got over my astonishment at this amazing city! I have written earlier about the more technical aspects of the working at Howrah, but to see it one has to cross the Hooghly, and when shortly after nine o'clock one morning my friends of the Eastern Railway called for me, it was among the whirling crescendo of incoming commuter traffic that our car made its way across the great bridge, which I so vividly remember being pre-erected in the yard of the Cleveland Bridge and Engineering Company, beside the London and North Eastern main line at Darlington, in 1939. In the forecourt of the station the scene was indescribable. From overnight long-distance expresses a vast throng waited for taxis; the hand-drawn rickshaws of Calcutta were taking hundreds away, and at intervals a positive torrent of pedestrians surged out of the station. Inside, the concourse, which in its layout and structure might have been that of Waterloo or Glasgow Central, was dotted with the usual groups of squatters.

The transport problem within the city of Calcutta itself is somewhat reminiscent of Melbourne, Australia, in that efficiently-run electric railways bring in the commuters in their hundreds of thousands and discharge them at no more than two principal stations. And at Calcutta the situation is aggravated in that one of the two stations is on the far side of the Hooghly River. Now, however, work has been started on the bold project of an underground railway, starting from an exchange station with the former Eastern Bengal main line at Dum Dum Junction, and running under the very heart of the city for ten miles to a terminus near the park lands at the south end, Tollyganz. The philosophy behind this route planning is to distribute incoming commuters at a number of stations adjacent to their places of work instead of discharging them in a torrent, as now, at the Sealdah terminus. At the same time a second line is in contemplation, connecting by a line beneath the Hooghly the two great main line termini of Sealdah and Howrah. Near the latter there is proposed a surface connection with the Eastern Railway main line, so that incoming commuter trains could be run direct on to the underground, as is now being provided for in Melbourne. I was taken to see the constructional works near Dum Dum, where the new line on a descending gradient was approaching the stage where traffic diversion in the Belgachia Road was becoming necessary, to permit 'cut and cover' work for the underground tunnel to be started.

While in Calcutta I was very kindly received by the General Managers of the Eastern Railway at Howrah, and of the South

Eastern Railway at the former Bengal Nagpur headquarters at Garden Reach. We talked of many things, and I was interested to find that the memories of the old railway companies of India were not forgotten and that the decorative coats of arms of these adorned their office walls. As to coats of arms in general those of the East Indian and of the G.I.P.R. reveal their English origin in their inclusion of the arms of the City of London on their shields, while the six 'originals' of the Dalhousie plan, are all surmounted by the Imperial Crown. Five railways include either locomotives or trains in their devices, while elephants also figure prominently. The exception to this is the very colourful crest of the Bengal Nagpur of which the central figure is a tiger.

One is made aware of the earlier days of the Indian railways on visiting the steam locomotive repair shops at Lucknow. But this bustling city, in which historic memories are mingled with some of the most highly sophisticated railway engineering I have ever seen, was not one of those that I came to by air. I spent the best part of a day on the footplate of the diesel locomotive working the Amritsar Mail from Varanasi, down the main line of the former Oudh and Rohilkund Railway, and it was an absorbing experience. The locomotive was one of the American-built 'WDM-4' class, and on this mainly straight and level line we were running at 60 to 65 m.p.h. wherever possible. While all the incidentals of express travel were present, including token exchanging of the Neale's ball type at full speed, what interested me intensely was the relatively sparse population of the countryside compared to what I had seen earlier in the round trip down to Kerala. At the stations where we stopped, of course, the whole place was swarming with people, but the open country between was as quiet as the most rural of English shires.

One of my principal points of call in Lucknow was the magnificent establishment of the RDSO of whose work I have written in the preceding chapter, and on the following morning I was taken to the steam locomotive works. There one is not allowed to forget that this was once the mechanical engineering headquarters of the Oudh and Rohilkund Railway, although that highly individual concern was absorbed into the East Indian as long ago as 1925. Here again in the offices one saw coats of arms on the walls: the O. & R., the E.I.R., and the present Indian Railways' emblems alongside. At Lucknow two truly delightful relics of the earliest days have been preserved. On a pedestal in the locomotive works, and beautifully restored to its original condition, is a 'B' class 0–6–0 tender engine, one of 84 introduced between 1871 and 1878. The livery is a handsome purple-brown with plenty of polished brasswork. In the carriage works is a companion 4-wheeler, in crimson-lake with white sun-shades, and bearing the crest of the O. & R. This consists of the letters ORR intertwined, surrounded by multipointed ornamentation, and surmounted by the Crown. Lucknow now comes within the Northern Railway, and among a number of the modern standard Indian types were some of the sturdy old 0–6–0 tender engines.

From Lucknow the main line of the O. & R. continued northeastwards through Bareilly to Moradabad, where it forked, one line continuing towards the North West Frontier and the other turning west to make a triple-junction at Ghaziabad with the main line of the East Indian from Kanpur, and the old Scinde, Punjab and Delhi, later to become the North Western. It was over the metals of the last mentioned company that trains of both East Indian and the Oudh and Rohilkund entered Delhi. I went out to see the big steam running shed at Ghaziabad, where most of the engines on parade were the standard 'WG' 2–8–2s. The shed itself is picturesque with tall pointed arches over each of the roads that in shape reminded one of the arches of Shakespeare's Cliff Tunnel, near Dover. I was interested to see that one of the 'WG' engines on shed had been fitted with a Giesl oblong ejector.

Among railway lovers the 1970s will always be remembered as the decade when there was a general manifestation of awareness of the priceless historical heritage that existed in railway relics and the planning, if not actual opening, of great national museums of transport. No country is richer than India in memorials to the past, and in October 1971 the President laid the foundation stone of the Transport Museum in New Delhi. The museum is planned to display historic locomotives and coaches in the environment of their age of action, and in the genial company of the curator Mr. Ram Kumar I was taken to see progress in building on the site. Apart from such treasures as the little 2–2–2 outside cylinder tank engine

'Express' of the East Indian dating from 1854, many locomotives have been saved for preservation, and great care is being taken in restoration to reproduce once again their original liveries. What is important is that the size of the museum site and its presently planned layout will permit progressive expansion of the railway section. The full-sized exhibits will be supplemented by static and working models, photographs and a wealth of documents of historic importance. As in the recently opened new British National Railway Museum at York, the site at New Delhi has excellent rail access.

My railway friends in India had saved for the culmination of my visit a trip that in its many-sided interest had all the unique fascination that can be conjured up by the single word 'India'. I was to ride the engine of the 'Taj Express' from New Delhi to Agra, and then cast aside railways for the best part of a day and see, in a single coach tour, the wonders of that ancient city and its surroundings. I do not know if I can claim distinction in being the first tourist ever to set out to see the Taj Mahal clad in a boiler suit! But I was riding coal-fired steam, and beneath those dungarees were light clothes suitable to the warmth of the day. We had a choicely ornamental 'WP' class 'Pacific' of the Central Railway, the zonal colours of which are leaf green. The engine was beautifully turned out and in the cab above the firebox was a delicately cut silhouette in brass of the Taj Mahal itself. We broke no speed records on that three hour run, not that the timetable required it; but the big engine bowled comfortably along at 60 m.p.h., with the two young firemen taking turns to satisfy her healthy appetite for coal.

The railway geography of Agra is quite complicated, with lines of the G.I.P.R. on which I had come from Delhi, the B.B. & C.I.R. and the East Indian all coming into the city. Their relative positions can be seen from the sketch map. But what are railways in Agra! The road tour on which I was booked was skilfully timed. It brought us to the Fort in mid-afternoon, and from the battlements there we looked out down the course of the River Jumna to one of the most famous tourist sights in the whole world, the 'Taj': dazzling white, irresistibly alluring. I could hardly wait until it was time for our coach to take us there. This is no place to record one's impressions of that incredible building. All I will say is that I was not disappointed.

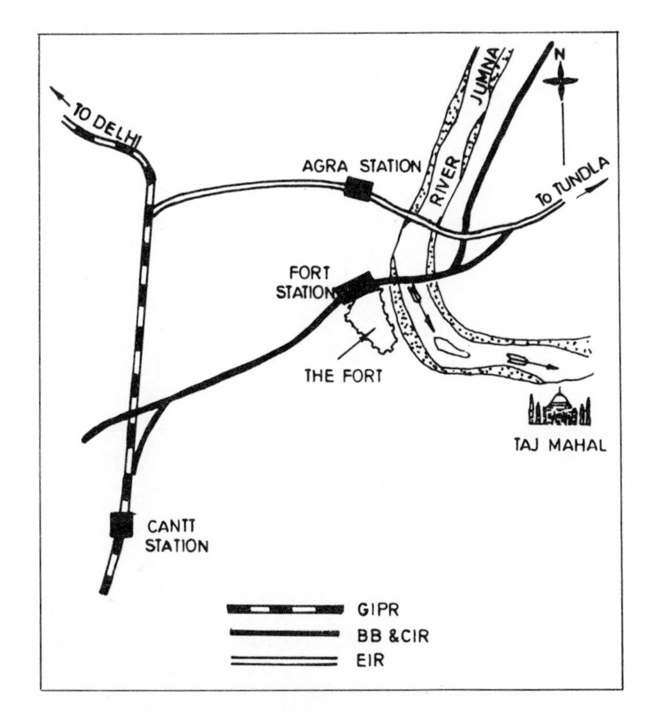

22. Railway connections in Agra

When we eventually got back to Agra Cantt station to catch the 'Taj Express' back to Delhi the kindly locomotive inspector asked if I would again like to ride on the footplate; but after the Taj itself the footplate would have been such a shattering return to mechanical things that I thanked him, and retired to the pleasance of an air-conditioned coach. With agreeable fellow travellers the three hour journey passed quickly, and my next 'hop', by air, was to Heathrow.

Part Two

South-East Asia

CHAPTER TWELVE

In the 'Land of the Yellow Robe'— The Royal State Railways of Thailand

During the Second World War nearly all the countries of South East Asia suffered very severely. Prolonged and fierce campaigns were fought in many of them, and when the tide of fortune in the war turned and the Japanese were in retreat, their lines of communication were remorselessly bombed and the local railways in consequence were badly smashed up. The Kingdom of Siam, by which name it is perhaps best known, would not in the ordinary way have been a belligerent in the war; for centuries the people have prided themselves on their complete independence. They were never aligned with any particular group of powers, either in the west, or the east. But in the attack upon Burma and the build-up for what the enemy hoped to be a full-scale invasion of India, Siam was a convenient base and it was over-run and occupied by the Japanese.

After the war, under the auspices of the United Nations, a Regional Council was set up called The Economic Commission for Asia and the Far East—E.C.A.F.E. This commission was naturally very much concerned with communications, as being a vital factor in the economic revival of the district, and a Transport and Railway Sub-Committee was set up. Having regard to the traditional neutrality of Thailand and appreciating that E.C.A.F.E. would be supported by all countries of the United Nations, including France, the U.S.A., Russia, and Japan, as well as the countries of the British Commonwealth, the city of Bangkok was a very appropriate place for the Headquarters.

After the retreat of the Japanese armies the victorious allied forces were able to lend immediate assistance towards the restoration of communications—rebuilding of bridges, relaying of permanent way and so on; but, as in Great Britain and elsewhere, the rolling stock and fixed equipment of the railways in South East Asia had become very much run down, and when traffic did revive, as it did remarkably quickly, the railways throughout the region were faced with carrying some of the heaviest traffic they had ever experienced, yet with worn out locomotives and rolling stock, and lineside equipment that had been no more than patched up after very considerable war damage.

A major subject of urgent discussion in the Railway Sub-Committee of E.C.A.F.E. was the means of increasing the capacity of single lines, and at the 7th meeting, which was held in Melbourne in 1962, the discussions on single-line working reached the stage of a strong plea being made for a text book embodying the fruits of experience in the various countries, and the British Delegation offered to undertake the preparation of this book.

About six months later, after certain negotiations had taken place in England I was asked to undertake the editorship, and when the script was finished I was invited to be a member of the British Delegation to the 8th meeting of the Sub-Committee, so that I could pilot that script through the conference.

I flew out to Bangkok at the end of October 1964, which was reputed to be the beginning of the cool season—that is, the general day temperature was between about 85 and 90°F. with 90 per cent. humidity. Statistics apart, and coming down to practical things, that meant about three shirts a day, and there was one memorable day when I actually used four! During the first week I hardly saw a train at all, but by Saturday afternoon we were free of the formal business of the conference and on the Monday set out on an inspection trip of the line.

* * * * * *

The first railway in Siam was built in 1892 on the 4 ft. 8½ in. gauge. This was very curious, since it is the only instance anywhere in India or South East Asia of the European standard gauge being used. The job of building the line was undertaken, under Government contract, by the British, French and Germans. Since they were all in competition with each other, the progress was very slow! The line ran northwards from Bangkok into the hilly country on the northern frontier, and some further northern and eastern extensions were all built to the European standard gauge. These lines radiated from a central station in the heart of the city of Bangkok on the left bank of the Chao Phya. This river is extremely wide where it passes through the city, in fact about twice the width of the Thames in central London, and for some time it provided a barrier between the railways on the left and the right bank.

The southern line which was commenced in 1900 started from a terminus station (Dhonburi) in the suburbs on the right bank of the river. This line was built to provide a link with the expanding system of the Federated Malay States and as this latter system was being built to metre gauge, the southern railway of Thailand was built likewise. Thus from the year 1900 onwards, Siam was all set for a battle of the gauges. There was however a battle of another kind over this southern line. There was great rivalry among the European powers to gain influence in Siam and strong pressure came from Germany to gain control. But there had been trouble in 1896 over one of the northern lines where there was a British contractor and a German director, and things hung fire until 1909 when a new treaty was made with the British, in which Siam waived her loosely-exercised suzerainty over four states in the south in return for a substantial British loan to build the railway. The four states were Perlis, Kedah, Kelantan and Trengganu, which henceforth became British Protectorates, and ultimately part of Malaya. The link with the Federated Malay States Railways at Padang Besar was made in 1917, and a metre gauge line completed between Bangkok and Singapore—a distance of some 640 miles.

After the First World War, however, the decision was taken to standardise metre gauge for the whole country. Plans were prepared for a combined road and rail bridge over the river just to the north of Bangkok, and from that time onwards the intention was to concentrate all the long distance traffic in the central station, even though it meant an extra ten miles on the journey from Bangkok to the south. I travelled over the whole of this line, and it was a truly absorbing experience. Apart from the French-built Beyer-Garratts of the 2–8–2 + 2–8–2 type which work on one of the hilly sections in the north, I saw almost every kind of motive power in action, as well as different stages of development in signalling and traffic control. At that particular time there were 298 steam locomotives, 88 diesels and 4 diesel railcar sets. There was considerable rivalry between the world powers for supply of new diesel locomotives—diesel-electrics from Japan and diesel-hydraulics from Germany; but as Achava Kunjara, the genial chief mechanical engineer explained to me, when we were footplate riding together, they would have to rely on steam 'for many long years'. Today, however, steam traction has ended in Thailand.

The line to the south runs through a strange and fascinating country. Seen from the air it looks as if it is completely flooded, such is the appearance of the interminable extent of the rice fields. Rice, southbound to Malaya, is one of the staple traffics of the railway, balancing which on the northbound run are carried rubber, coconuts, charcoal and lumber. The few passenger trains on the southern line are hauled by diesels, but the many freights I saw were all steam hauled. Except in the north where a few locomotives are oil-fired, wood is the standard fuel, and this poses some problems in rostering. The tenders stacked high with logs carry only enough for a run of 150 miles so that, unless supplies are available away from the depots, the workings have to be arranged so that the out-and-home run does not exceed the basic 150 miles. Actually however at many of the country stations I saw truck loads of logs from which engine crews in need could take a predatory fill-up. I gathered that this was quite common practice.

The oldest locomotives I saw were some of the familiar metre-gauge Indian 4–6–0s, built by the North British Locomotive Company, while another British-built freighter is the Nasmyth Wilson, 2–8–2. Both these types were used mainly for shunting and yard work, but Thai steam locomotives, whatever their duties, were in beautifully clean condition, in glossy black, with the oriental characters signifying RSR (Royal State Railways) on their tenders. The most recent acquisitions had come from Japan, of the 4–6–2 and 2–8–2 types, and these were far more handsome engines than any modern units that I saw later in Japan itself. The turn out of all of them was quite immaculate; I shall always regret that unwittingly

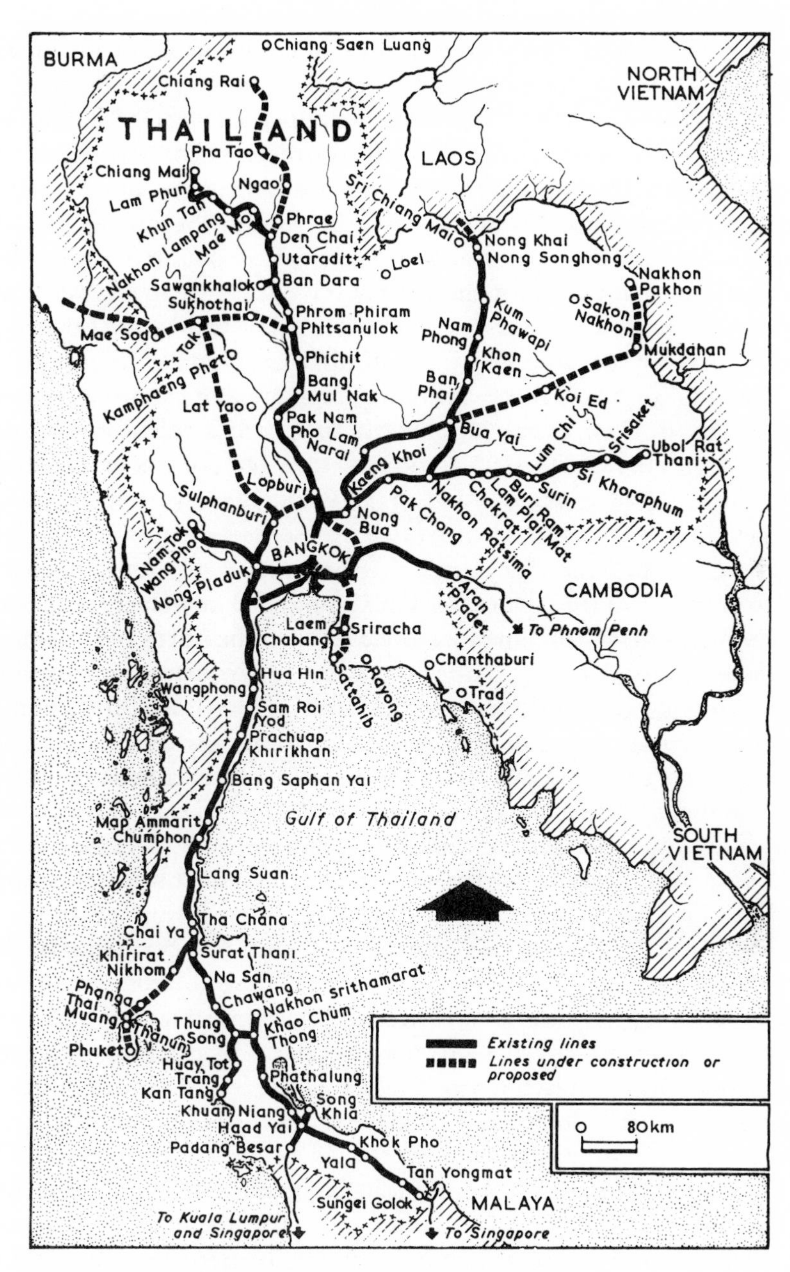

23. Map of the Royal State Railways of Thailand

I missed an opportunity of riding on the footplate of one of the 'Pacifics'.

The Garratts, of which there were eight in all, were designed for heavy load haulage on a section of the northern line where a gradient of 1 in 42 had to be mounted, with the heavy load of 530 tons. They were the most powerful of their type to run on the metre gauge in Asia, having a nominal tractive effort of 41,666 lb., which was greater than that of any of the Burma, or Assam Bengal types, even including the general service 'war' type. They had 17 in. by $21\frac{3}{4}$ in. cylinders, coupled wheels 3 ft. $5\frac{3}{8}$ in. diameter, and carried a boiler pressure of 185 lb. per sq. in. Their fuel bunker carried 5 tons of wood. Six of them were supplied in 1929, and a further two were added in 1936. It is good to know that one of them has been preserved, because when I was in Thailand they were being withdrawn, and their work taken over by diesels.

The Central station in Bangkok from which our journey to the south started, is a fine structure, with a single-span arched roof. After leaving the station, the line makes a circuit to the north of the city to cross the Rama VI bridge over the River Chao Phya. This bridge, like so many great bridges on the railways of Asia is designed to carry both road and rail traffic, though unlike many of its Indian counterparts road and rail are at the same level. Its construction was the result of King Maha Vajiravudha's decision in 1919, to unify the rail gauges on both sides of the River Chao Phya. It was built by Les Etablissements Dayde of Paris, and opened for traffic in January 1929. In the later stages of the Second World War it was a vital link in the supply line to the Japanese forces in Burma, and constantly under air attack. In February 1943 it was badly damaged, with the middle span crumbling into the river. After the war a contract for repair and reconstruction was awarded to the Cleveland Bridge and Engineering Company of Darlington, England, the builders of the great bridge over the Hooghly at Calcutta. The Rama VI bridge was re-opened to traffic in December 1953.

Mention of lines of communication in the Second World War takes us on to Nong Pladuk, junction for the notorious 'death railway' to the Burma frontier in the construction of which, thousands of lives were lost through the inhuman conditions under which slave and prisoner-of-war labour was used by the occupying enemy forces. The line runs beside the Kwai River (many will recall the dramatic film *The Bridge on the River Kwai*), but although in post-war years the line became something of an attraction for tourists, its flimsy trestles, viaducts and sinuous alignment together with the absence of any staple traffic, has caused a major portion of it to be closed down beyond Nam Tok. It is at Nong Pladuk that the main line, single-tracked throughout, turns through a right angle, and continues thence forward in a uniformly southerly direction.

I travelled for part of the way with Banyong Saralamp, the superintending engineer of the signal and telecommunications division, and at several stations where we stopped he took me to see the instruments in the station master's offices. Most of the signalling on the RSR consists of upper quadrant mechanical semaphores worked on the double-wire system. The stations are fully interlocked, and operation throughout the country is on the absolute block system. On the southern line over which we were travelling there were then 356 block sections, each with token block working. As in Indian practice the Neale's type of instrument is widely—though not exclusively, used. On 22 sections a system of tokenless block working had been introduced, by converting some of the existing Neale's instruments. The traditional methods of token working on single lines developed in Great Britain, and as adopted in many overseas countries provides a very high degree of security in operation, but it is apt to be slow in working at some crossing places where tokens have to be exchanged; and where lines are fully signalled in addition the safeguards of modern electrical methods have led to the development in many countries of tokenless block systems, with no lessening of security but a great improvement in operation. The engineers of the RSR had certainly achieved great success in their adaptation of the existing equipment. Banyong Saralamp told me that the installation of tokenless block beyond Pachi Junction was proceeding rapidly.

Train speeds on the RSR, even with express passenger trains, are not high. The line is not fenced, and while they do not meet the violent opposition of wild animals that occurs all too frequently on some tropical main lines in Africa there are occasional hazards. We were running along through a stretch of jungle, when the brakes were suddenly put on in full emergency, and we came to an abrupt stop. Looking out of the window I saw round a curve in the line a water buffalo lying on the track! The water buffalo despite its rather terrifying appearance—to European eyes at any rate!—is the most placid of animals, and when our train crew descended to remonstrate with the obstruction it got up slowly, and shambled off, entirely in its own time. In the early afternoon we came to Hua Hin, one of the most fashionable seaside resorts in the country, where the RSR operates a luxury hotel. Strangely the fine weather that had persisted during the week of conference had completely broken down, and the tropical beach, which in other circumstances could have been exotic to the last degree was cool, windy and forlorn.

After an evening of traditional Thai hospitality, I was glad of a sleeper that night, and after breakfast next morning we came to Thung Song Junction, 465 miles from Bangkok, and an important railway junction. The northern part of the narrow thousand-mile-long isthmus is divided in its exiguous width between Thailand and Burma, but abreast of Lang Suan, which we passed in the night, is the southernmost tip of Burma, and from Thung Song there goes an important branch to Kan Tang, a considerable port on the west coast. There are also railway repair shops at Thung Song, the only ones on the southern line south of Bangkok. Here, Achava Kunjara invited me to join him on the footplate of our German-built diesel-hydraulic locomotive. With freight trains some remarshalling is undertaken at Thung Song. The maximum load on level track is 55 4-wheeled wagons, but only 20 can be taken up the 1 in 50 gradient to the tunnel at the summit between Thung Song and Ronpibul, with one locomotive. There was no need for any load reduction on our own train. With eight coaches weighing about 240 tons our 1500 horse-power diesel made light of the 1 in 46–50 gradient, and sustained 34 m.p.h. Near the summit the line cuts through a hill range in a short tunnel, the only one on the southern line, and then made a regulation stop at the bank top, enforced with all trains, passenger and freight alike.

The diesel rode very quietly and smoothly, though of course the speeds were quite low. The maximum then on any part of the southern line was 56 m.p.h. Soon after restarting we came to Khao Chum Thong Junction, which in September and October each year is very busy with pilgrim traffic. It is the junction for Nakon Srithamarat where in the temple Wat Phra That is a shrine that houses Buddha's relic. Vast numbers of pilgrims come each year from all the Buddhist countries. The branch is only 22 miles long, but Nakon Srithamarat also lies on the main highway from north to south and this takes its share of the special traffic. The main line continues through very flat, smiling, rice producing country, and when we eventually came to Haad Yai, at 572 miles from Bangkok, the fine weather had returned. During our wait to examine traffic facilities, and such like, the sun beat down relentlessly. It was once a boom town profiting from the rapid development of the Malayan tin and rubber industries, but now it is of primary importance as a railway operational centre and main line junction. For while the main line turns to the south west, another important line running near to the east coast reaches the Malayan border at Sungei Golok, 133 miles farther on.

Haad Yai is an important locomotive centre, and many of the Japanese-built wood burning 4–6–2s and 2–8–2s were on shed. An early British-built 4–6–0 was busy shunting at the north end. Passenger traffic is considerable, and most of the long distance business on the southern line originates there, with a number of feeder services coming in from the branches. The countryside is quite densely populated. I saw from the train numerous closely packed villages, and both the people and their trade provide the railway with a substantial revenue. Although so much was told to us by our friends of the RSR I suppose it was no more than natural that they did not tell me that our train was being followed immediately by a 'Pacific' hauled ordinary passenger train, and that with the duration of formalities at the Malayan frontier station of Padang Besar there would have been ample time for me to have ridden on the footplate of that 'Pacific', and caught the express to the south. As it was I had plenty of time to take photographs of her after she had arrived, turned, and was ready to go back to Haad Yai.

The border is reached soon after Ban Tha Khoi, when a small white signboard at the lineside is passed, bearing the legend

SIAM/PERLIS, and the line enters one of the four states that became British Protectorates in 1909. Like most frontier stations Padang Besar was a scene of great animation. Apart from custom formalities, examinations and so on, locomotives were being changed, and a bright green diesel-electric of English Electric build, replaced the dark green German hydraulic, while the stopping train which had followed us in so closely, exchanged the Japanese-built engine for a British-built 3-cylinder 'Pacific' with Caprotti valve gear. We had not quite finished with the Royal State Railways of Thailand, for we continued in the Thai train for another 3¼ hours, to Prai, reached at 7.45 p.m. on a hot tropical evening.

CHAPTER THIRTEEN

The Malayan Railways

I travelled into Malaya on what is known as the Kedah Branch Line, which terminates on the waterfront at Prai; but before arriving there I had enjoyed talks with some Malayan railway officers, and read literature they gave me, and was becoming aware of the fascinating history of railway development in the peninsula. It is in every way a microcosm of the history of the country itself over the past hundred years.

Until the middle years of the nineteenth century Malaya as a country did not exist. There were the four British trading settlements on the Straits of Malacca—Penang, Province Wellesley, Malacca itself, and Singapore, and the native states. Some of these, as told in the previous chapter, were vaguely connected with Siam; in others the ruling sultans were autonomous. In a country like the Malay peninsula, then almost entirely covered by impenetrable tropical jungle, anything went. When Stamford Raffles first went to Singapore island in 1819 it was inhabited by a mere handful of Malayan fishermen; but he realised the immense potentialities of its geographical position, and persuaded the Sultan of Johore to cede it to Great Britain. In 1837 it became the capital of the Straits Settlements, collectively a British Crown Colony then under the administration of the India Office.

From the Straits Settlements began the development of world trade in the two indigenous riches of Malaya, rubber and tin, and because of the very small native population and their limited aptitude in those early days for industrial development there began a slow, but steady influx of immigrants, mostly Chinese and Indians. The Sultans of Perak, Pahang, Selangor, and Negri Sembilan were astute enough to realise that the development of trade through the Straits Settlements could be to their great advantage. Each of them asked for British advisers, and in 1874 they became virtually British Protectorates. At first the Sultan of Johore was of a more independent turn of mind, and he accepted a looser form of 'protection' in 1885. In 1895 the Federated Malay States, embodying all five, came into being. By then, with the Straits Settlements, the whole peninsula south of the then Siamese associated states of Perlis, Kedah, Kelantan and Trengganu was strongly under a unified British influence.

The railways began, like the states themselves, as so many independent concerns, though all of them were under the guidance of the Colonial Office in London. The first lines in Perak and Selangor were built in 1885, both of which were to bring goods from the interior down to the ports. Following the Indian decision for secondary lines during the time of Lord Mayo's Viceroyalty, the gauge was fixed from the outset at one metre, and there has been no further argument or deviation since. It was appreciated from the outset that the various state lines would be linked up before very long and, through the influence of the Colonial Office, a degree of equipment standardisation was established at an early date. The local conditions were—and still remain, exceptional. Including the four northern states which came under British protection in 1909 the area of the country is only slightly larger than that of England, and even today four-fifths of it is still covered by dense equatorial jungle. The climate is characterised by abundant rainfall, high humidity, and there is nothing that really could be called a 'cool' season. The temperature varies generally, throughout the year, between 70 and 90° F.

In these conditions, for the small pioneer traffics of Selangor and Perak there were introduced tiny little 4–4–0 tank engines, dainty little things that would have looked well, and completely in keeping, on rural English branch lines. To maintain them the Perak State Railway set up a small works at Ipoh, and in Selangor a similar establishment was set up at Kuala Lumpur, the capital city of the State. When the Federated Malay States Railway was formed, and the railway link between Perak and Selangor completed in 1903, Sentul, on the outskirts of Kuala Lumpur became the principal works of the organisation. The total locomotive stock of the two states was then 51, and it was augmented between 1905 and 1912 by 27 locomotives from the states to the south. As can be gathered from these small numbers traffic was still very light, though as will be told later, the first 'Pacifics' arrived from Great Britain in 1907.

The railways of Malaya were in the first place purely local trade links, but it is remarkable to record that within twenty years—1884–1903—a continuous line had been completed from Johore Bahru on the Johore Strait opposite to Singapore island, to Bukit Mertajam near to Prai, and the ferry crossing to Penang. The city of Kuala Lumpur lay almost exactly half way along this 480 miles of metre-gauge railway. The causeway across the Johore Strait, establishing a continuous line with Singapore was not completed until 1923. The straight line distance between the terminals of 1903 is about 350 miles, and the difference between this and the railway mileage of 480 gives some idea of the way in which the track was built, skirting rough country and at minimum cost. As a jungle railway it has always endured the attacks and obstructions of wild animals, and on more than one occasion charging elephants made 'mincemeat' of the early 4–4–0 tank engines. It was always said however that elephants under proper control made excellent shunting engines! The ruling gradients on the line do not exceed 1 in 100 except in the Taiping Pass, in North Perak, where the gradient is 1 in 80.

The first 4–6–0s to arrive in Malaya came from Kitsons of Leeds, in 1894. They were small, even for the metre gauge. The coupled wheels were only 3 ft. 3 in. diameter, and the bogie wheels looked like little castors. Imagine a 4–6–0 that weighed less than an L.N.W.R. 2–4–0 'Jumbo'—no connection with elephants this time!—for the Selangor 'D' class of 1894 weighed no more than 27½ tons, and their 4-wheeled tenders, stacked high with wood weighed only 14½ tons. From the experience with these little engines, and the larger 'E' class of the Perak State Railway, there evolved the first standard main line engine to operate in Malaya, the 'G' class 4–6–0, of which 34 were supplied by various British firms between 1899 and 1905. The first 21 were allocated variously to the Perak and Selangor Government Railway, and two later ones went to Malacca.

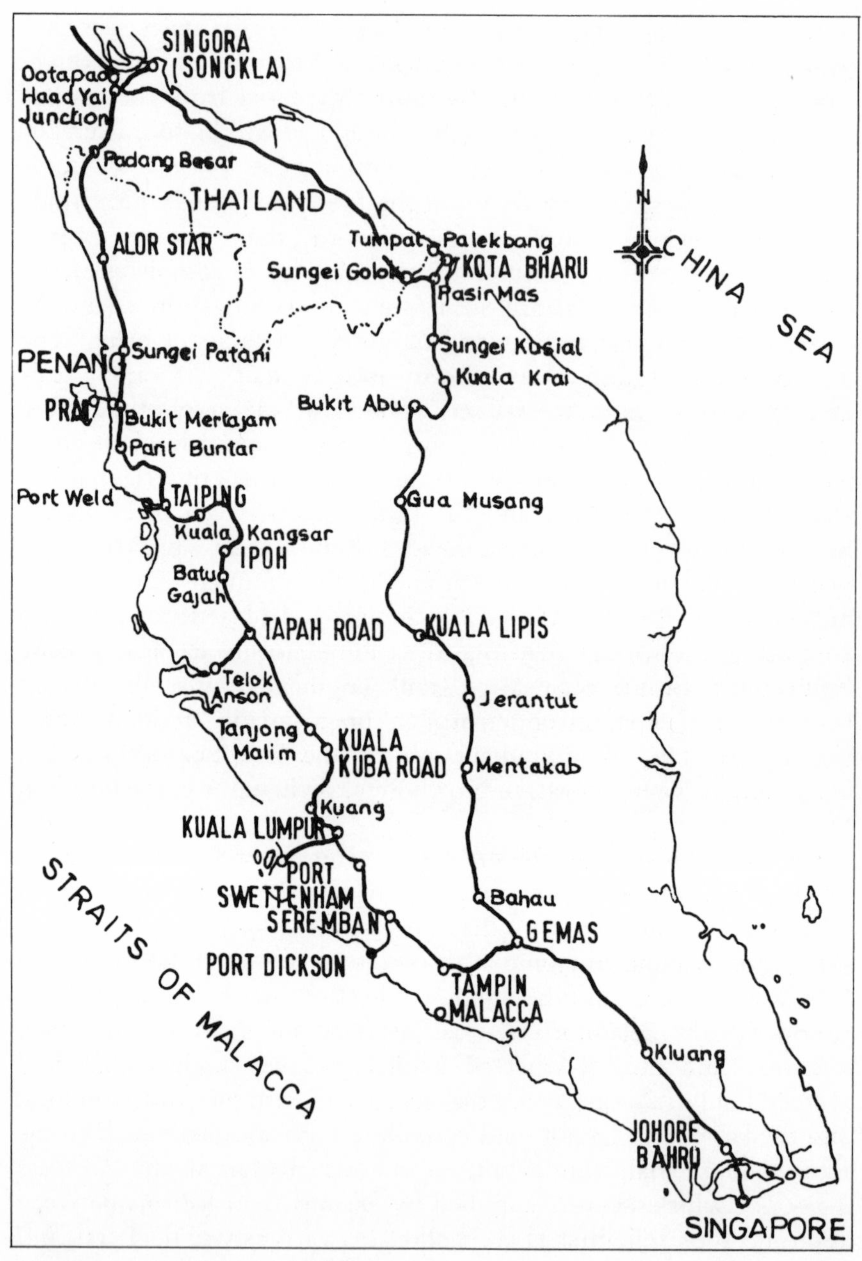

24. Map of the Malayan Railways

The 'G' class were very smart little engines, rather like a metre gauge 'Jones Goods' of the Highland Railway in Scotland, but distinguished by enormous headlamps which extended to the full height of their long chimneys. The engines of the Perak and Selangor railways were painted green, those of the former a light olive colour, and those of the latter a rather darker green. They were adorned with copper capped chimneys, and the dome covers were polished brass. In Johore, traditionally distinctive from the rest of Malaya at that time, the few locomotives on the State railway were painted in full Caledonian style, in the magnificent blue with crimson underframes.

The task of working these lines through the Malayan jungle was no sinecure, even though speeds were low, and trains were mostly short. The traffic working was organised in a blend of British and Indian practice with absolute block working throughout and single-line token working. As in the developing industries and trade of Malaya itself, so on the railways, there came that remarkable integration of several different races into a smoothly working unity. Indians and Chinese worked with the indigenous Malayans, under British guidance and leadership; but it was all the more remarkable that when Malaya attained full nationhood, and the oriental races were ready to take over complete management of the railway, that the co-operation between the diverse races continued rather than splitting into rival factions. When I was in Malaya myself the general manager was a Malayan, the chief traffic manager was a Chinese, and the chief mechanical engineer a Sikh—all absolutely first class railwaymen.

When the Federated Malay States Railways were established in 1903, Mr. G. C. Forbes was appointed locomotive superintendent of the combined organisation, and he planned and built the new central workshops at Sentul, where work started in 1906. In the meantime, to meet the increasing need for more powerful locomotives, he sponsored the design of the first 'Pacifics' of the 'H' class which took the road in 1907. A significant point about motive power on the F.M.S.R. was that it was based upon a single type of locomotive capable of running both passenger and goods trains. The freight traffic was not unduly heavy but was highly rated, and the stock employed was either vacuum braked, or piped through, and therefore could be run at roughly the same speed as the passenger and mail trains. The latter involved overnight journeys on both sections of the main line. Passengers would be travelling between Singapore and Kuala Lumpur on the one hand, or between Kuala Lumpur and Butterworth or Penang, and there was no point in running faster, which would result in undesirably early arrivals. So, from the 'G' class 4–6–0s, which were general service units, the power stepped up to the 'H' class 'Pacifics', of which there were 60 eventually.

The new engines were wholly British in design and appearance, with a complete absence of gadgets hung on outside. An unusual provision however for the year 1907 was the outside Walschaerts valve gear, actuating flat slide valves in a chest mounted above the cylinders on the running plate. The only oriental feature was the large cab, with deep overhanging sunshades. From the tractive point of view the new engines represented a considerable advance over the 'G' class 4–6–0s, though as may be gathered from the following table they were still quite modest sized locomotives. Six of them went new in 1908 to the Johore State Railway, and were duly painted in Caledonian blue, but were taken into the general stock of the F.M.S.R. in 1910–11. About that time the livery of Malayan locomotives was changed to unlined black, and the letters F.M.S.R. put on the tenders in yellow, shaded light blue.

F.M.S.R. early 6-coupled locomotives

Class	'G'	'H'
Type	4–6–0	4–6–2
Cylinders		
dia. in.	14½	15½
stroke in.	20	24
Coupled wheel dia. ft. in.	4–3½	4–6
Valve gear	Stephenson	Walschaerts
Total heating surface sq. ft.	736	1235
Grate area sq. ft.	13	18·5
Boiler pressure p.s.i.	150	180
Total weight of engine working order tons	29¾	47½
Tractive effort at 85% boiler pressure lb.	10,319	16,340

As introduced both classes were non-superheated. The earlier engines of the 'H' class had main frames only $\frac{7}{8}$ in. thick, and proved a little too light. Later engines had 1 in. thick frames, and it is to these that the weight of $47\frac{1}{2}$ tons refers. Those with $\frac{7}{8}$ in. frames weighed 45·9 tons. They were successful and long lived engines, and 11 out of the original 60 were still in existence after the Second World War. Most of them had been working in Siam during the Japanese occupation. They were originally all wood burners, though supplemented at times by coal imported from India.

The development of the 'Pacific' type of locomotive in Malaya was continuous and strong up to the outbreak of the Second World War. A super-heated version of the 'H' class was designed, and ten locomotives built by Kitsons of Leeds, in 1917; but such was the overall transport situation in Asia at that time in the First World War that six of these engines were commandeered for use in India, and allocated to the B.B. & C.I.R. Another 16 were built after the war by the North British Locomotive Company. To help out, the F.M.S.R. obtained 12 typically American 4–6–2s from Baldwins, but the true development of the Malayan 'Pacific' came in 1921, with the 'L', generally similar to the superheated 'H' but with much larger boilers. In 1924 G. C. Forbes (who had been locomotive superintendent since the inception of the F.M.S.R.) retired and was succeeded by A. W. Sutherland Graeme. Under his direction, to meet the need for still more powerful locomotives, were introduced the 'S' class 'Pacifics' with three cylinders, and the Gresley conjugated valve gear for actuating the valves of the middle cylinder. The first batch of these powerful engines was delivered in 1928, and a further group with rotary cam poppet valve gear took the road in 1931. The final development was the lightweight 'O' class of 1938, for use on lines where the maximum permitted axle load was $12\frac{3}{4}$ tons. A total of 28 had been built up to 1940, and a further 40 were added after the war. This was a very successful general purpose locomotive and saw steam out on the Malayan railways. Dimensional details of the 3-cylinder 'Pacifics' are given in the following table.

F.M.S.R. 3-cylinder 'Pacifics'

Class	S1/S2/S3	O1
Max. axle load, tons	16	12¾
Cylinders		
dia. in.	17	13
stroke in.	24	24
Coupled wheel dia. ft. in.	4–6	4–6
Total evaporative heating surface sq. ft.	1982	1109
Superheater sq. ft.	353	218
Grate area sq. ft.	35	27
Boiler pressure p.s.i.	180	250
Total weight of engine working tons	69·1	58
Tractive effort at 85% boiler pressure lb.	29,480	23,940

A passenger travelling on the F.M.S.R. would have seen little of its rolling stock and lineside equipment because the greater part of main line journeys was performed at night. The principal stations, however, were finely equipped, and at headquarters in Kuala Lumpur the station buildings are attractively designed with a profusion of minarets, oriental-styled windows and archways, with the general decor all in dazzling white. The terminus at Singapore is considerably less ornate, and during a brief stay at the hotel there I found the interior somewhat clinically austere. In these days, however, few tourists of the world-travel type would come to Singapore by train, so that the need for modern facilities does not arise at the station hotel. In recent years much has been done to encourage tourist travel by putting on day expresses on both the northern and southern sections of the line; but from the winter of 1941 for nearly 20 years Malaya and its railways were to endure a time of terrible disruption and enemy occupation; and after the war the disturbing time of ceaseless terrorist activities which were not finally overcome until 1960. The jungle through which so much of the line runs naturally afforded excellent cover for terrorist attacks.

During the re-occupation and eventual defeat of the enemy in 1945 the destruction of railway facilities, particularly at Sentul Works was infinitely more severe than during the Japanese invasion, and those who moved into Sentul had little more than a heap of smoking ruins on which to begin post-war reconstruction. In some ways it was fortunate that many Malayan locomotives had been transferred to Siam to asssist in the war traffic towards Burma, via the River Kwai line, and the consequent destruction was less than it might otherwise have been. But to get things going quickly an order for 40 additional 'O' class 'Pacifics' was awarded to the North British Locomotive Company. These were delivered in 1946–7. The shape of things to come was seen in 1949 when the first of these engines was converted to oil-burning. Wood as a locomotive fuel had been generally superseded by coal in the 1920s, although there had always been difficulties with this. Coal had been discovered in Malaya before the First World War, but it was of a quality that deteriorated rapidly when stored, and a supply of Indian coal had always to be kept for emergencies. But the existence of oilfields in other countries brought into the Federation of Malaysia, notably Borneo, made the introduction of oil firing an attractive proposition, and led eventually to the introduction of diesel traction.

In 1954 Mr. C. G. Harrison was appointed general manager, and was succeeded as chief mechanical engineer by Mr. A. J. Ball, who had been works manager at Sentul during the time of reconstruction after the war. Ball had been associated more than twenty years earlier, on the Buenos Aires Great Southern Railway, with some of the earliest developments ever in diesel traction, and his introduction of main line diesels in Malaya in 1957 was a model of careful engineering and administrative planning. While taking full advantage of the manufacturing expertise of the English Electric Company in its production of the standard 1500 horsepower design, careful consideration was given to the difficult physical characteristics of the line, particularly to its incessant curvature. Great attention was given to the design of the cast steel bogie frames to ensure good riding, and to restrict throw-over on the sharp curves. Even more important in some ways was the preparation of maintenance facilities for the new form of power at Sentul Works; to segregate diesel work completely from steam shops, and to train the staff comprehensively in the new disciplines needed.

It was originally planned to change over to diesel traction on the northern part of the main line between Kuala Lumpur and Prai, and a requirement for the new locomotives was to take a 450 ton train up the 1 in 80 gradient of the Taiping Pass without assistance. The first order was for 20 locomotives, and a further six were added subsequently. There was an amusing incident at the time of the introduction of the new power. There had been spells of locomotive naming on the F.M.S.R. between the two World Wars, but by the late 1940s these had all been removed. It had been suggested that the practice might be revived on the new diesels, and names of flowers of the Malayan countryside were chosen and applied. This led to a highly amusing cartoon in one of the newspapers, in which the crew of a diesel was being 'ribbed' by steam footplate men, and called 'pansies'!

The diesels went into service with practically nothing in the way of teething troubles, and by the year 1961 although there were only 26 diesels compared to 98 steam tender locomotives, the former were responsible for 34 per cent. of the total train mileage. Since that date, there has been a gradual changeover to diesel over the entire line; the 200 steam locomotives still in use being worked alongside the 130 diesel electrics and 67 diesel hydraulics.

Concurrently with the introduction of diesel-electric locomotives were some important developments in signalling, and a change from token to tokenless working on single lines. This involved the use of what is termed relay auto-block, and its operating fundamentals, including the important feature of tail-end checking by magnetic detectors, involved so many departures from existing procedures that an additional set of instructions was required to be added to the existing book of general rules and regulations. The advantages of tokenless block working on single lines have already been discussed in this book. In Malaya the provision of the tail-end magnet and detector for proving that the entire train had passed each check point was an additional refinement.

My journey south from Prai on the 'North Star' night express was an impressive experience. From the platforms at Prai there was an appealing night view of Penang, across the water. Much freight for Thailand is unloaded here, saving a long journey by sea round the toe of Malaya and into the Gulf of Siam. The freight goes straight up the Kedah branch line and on to the R.S.R. at Padang Besar. Soon the ferry arrived from Penang and there was a hectic rush for seats in the train for Kuala Lumpur. I was interested to find that we had a load of no fewer than 21 bogie coaches, with a single English Electric diesel locomotive. With a rake including several air-conditioned sleeping cars the load must have been considerably more than 600 tons, against the original design parameter of 450 tons. Yet the climb over the Taiping Pass was successfully made, and next morning we arrived in Kuala Lumpur slightly ahead of time. The air-conditioned sleeping cars were delightful to enter on a hot night, but were apt to become a little *too* airy as the night went on. In Kuala Lumpur, in addition to seeing Sentul Works there was time for a trip down the branch to Port Swettenham; then back to Kuala Lumpur for dinner, and the 'Southern Cross' night express to Singapore.

Part Three

Japan

CHAPTER FOURTEEN

Japan—the strange beginnings

In March 1898 *The Railway Magazine* published an article by a worldwide traveller, scholar and railway enthusiast, B. D. Timins, that opened thus:

> The words 'Japan' and 'railways' used in conjunction with one another strike anyone who has visited that charming country with a sense of incongruity. What should that placid little people know of the rattle and rush of an express train, typical as it is of the nerve-wasting haste with which we Westerners live our lives?—It is not within the scope of this article to discuss the merits of a so-called civilisation, nor the values of the benefits it is supposed to confer upon a people whose ethical, moral, social and political codes date from a time when all Western Europe was probably peopled by naked savages. But I cannot resist saying that when Japan finally exchanges her peaceful simplicity, her admiration for, and artistic appreciation of nature's beauties, and her contented national life for the storm, stress and hurry of that feverish existence known to the West, she will have given up the substance for the shadow.
>
> Happily for her, that day is not yet within measurable distance, and she remains in everything, whether borrowed from the West or not, Japanese. And especially does this remark apply to her railways. In them we shall find the national characteristics as truly exemplified as they are in her Shinto temples or her miniature pleasure grounds.

One feels that the author was rather over-playing the peaceloving, contented motif, seeing that when the first railway was built in 1872, the country had barely recovered from an exceedingly bloody revolution, and development was subsequently halted for six years—1876–1882—while the Government of the day was engaged in suppressing a rebellion by one of the most powerful of the old feudal clans. But these troubles were something akin to the Wars of the Roses in England, in that they concerned a few high-ranking families and their adherents. The rest of a very large population took little notice, unless a battle happened to be fought on their doorstep. It *was* a huge population too which, at the turn of the century, already exceeded forty million people.

Their early attitudes to trains, as noted by Timins, are worth recording in view of what has happened since. He writes:

> Though the Japanese are by no means a lazy or an idle race, and though they possess none of that apathetic indolence common to those Eastern races who dwell beneath a tropical sun, still all notion of speed, haste, or flurry are utterly foreign to their nature. Centuries of Western training will be necessary before a Japanese will be able to appreciate the significance of such a phrase as 'catching a train by the skin of one's teeth!' The native of Japan arrives at the station two or three hours before the train is due. If he be a rustic, or unused to travel, he will probably be making a point of taking up a strong position at the station the night before his prospective journey and camping on the platform . . .

One can smile at the suggestion of the expected centuries of training needed to urge the Japanese traveller to hurry; and I can well imagine that if Timins had been able to accompany me, exactly 75 years after his article was published, into the central control room of the New Tokaido line, and seen the indicating lights on the track diagram of train after train following each other at quarter hour intervals, all doing 130 m.p.h., it would have seemed strange and incredible to him.

The first steps towards a railway system in Japan came in 1869, when the Government of the day, rebuilding after the chaos of 1868 was anxious to improve communications. The aim was to link Tokyo with the ancient capital, Kyoto. It is however not generally realised to what extent Japanese railways owe their origin to the efforts made by Englishmen. In 1868 Sir Harry Parkes, then British Minister Plenipotentiary to Japan, strongly advised the Japanese Government to take in hand the construction of railways. In a letter dated Yedo, January 22, 1870, Sir Harry Parkes says:

The Japanese Government have been persuaded to undertake a railway between Yedo and Kioto—a grand work if properly carried out. They are going to construct the line themselves, with the aid of English engineers. To help them to make a start they borrow a million sterling.

Again, in a letter to the Earl of Clarendon, at the Foreign Office, dated Yedo, April 21, 1870, he says:

I have had frequent opportunities of discussing with the Mikado's Government the desirability of introducing railways and telegraphs into Japan . . . At the close of last year (1869) I was informed by the Government that they had resolved to construct a railway between Yedo and Kioto. Their difficulty in making a commencement lay in the want of funds, and this was met by an offer on the part of Mr. H. N. Lay, formerly of China, and who was then visiting Japan, to lend the Government £1,000,000 on the security of the projected line of railway and the Customs revenues. They accepted this offer, and Mr. Lay returned to England to raise the above sum and engage the necessary engineers.

Mr. H. N. Lay, mentioned in the letter, was an Englishman who was staying with the British Minister in 1869. Lay, who as stated was entrusted with the task of raising a loan, returned to England and engaged Mr. E. Morell as chief engineer, who arrived in Japan during the spring of 1870 to plot the path for the line.

The Japanese Government, however, disapproved of the methods adopted by Lay in obtaining the money in Britain, dissolved its contract and appointed the Oriental Bank to complete the financial arrangements and generally to supervise construction. As Morell, the engineer, was not associated with Lay except in a technical capacity, his appointment was confirmed and so he became the Father of Japanese Railways. Construction was commenced upon the 18-mile line between Tokyo and Yokohama, in 1870.

The gauge was fixed at 3 ft. 6 in., following practice in New Zealand and certain Australian states, rather than the metre gauge of the secondary lines in India. The first locomotive superintendent was Walter Mackersie Smith. On September 12, 1872 the ceremonial opening of the line took place in the presence of the Emperor of Japan. It was significant of the new era that was dawning that the

Emperor appeared for the first time ever in full State robes in front of a gathering that included many foreigners.

Although development was interrupted during the six troubled years from 1876 to 1882, work was subsequently pushed ahead, and a continuous line of railway was established from Kobe through Osaka and Kyoto to Tokyo in 1889. There was then no question of building a fast express route. Nothing was further from Japanese minds at that stage, and the line followed the route of the great Tokaido highway, skirting the shores of the Pacific Ocean for most of the way. The highway at that time was in fact little more than a track, and the railway followed a winding devious route where construction could be made at a minimum of expense. Most of it was single tracked, and the general running speeds were very low. Early locomotives came from Dübs and Co., Glasgow, and from Sharp Stewarts, and they were not called upon to run very hard. Some early 4–4–0s had a strong likeness to the 'Skye Bogies' of the Highland Railway in Scotland.

Travelling in those early days could be a diverting experience. The third and second class carriages had differing degrees of Spartan accommodation in which one saw Japanese partaking of the luxury of a luncheon box. Timins describes their contents thus:

> A portion of raw fish, some smoked rice, some greenlooking meaty substance and a few sugar sweetmeats represent to the Jap a pleasurable table such as the Savoy would be powerless to afford. All necessary items for the miniature *table d'hote* lie packed in these wonderful boxes, the whole being surmounted by two neatly tied chop-sticks!

The luncheon boxes of my own travels were more substantial, and usually half the total volume was solid rice. One does not have to travel far in Japan before realising the importance of green tea; and the early first class carriages were fully equipped for brewing this highly prized beverage. It seems to have been more potent in Timins's day to my own:

> We enter our first class carriage by a door at one end, and find that it is a sort of square-shaped saloon. The seats run round all four sides of the carriage. In the centre is a diminutive table, upon which reposes a tea service

properly furnished with all necessary requisites for brewing a cup of green tea *á la Japonaise.*

So inseparable an adjunct is this beverage to life in Japan that if we leave the tea-table untouched there will probably be very serious inquiries after our health upon reaching Tokio!

The tea itself is comparatively innocuous stuff when drunk in the very small quantities which a Japanese teacup holds, but it does not take very many such cups to render the traveller hopelessly inebriated. Not that a Jap will ever be seen in such a state! They are brought up to tea as Englishmen to meat, and though occasionally—very occasionally—the subtle *Sakki* proves too much for their natural and inherent sobriety, the spectacle of a drunken Jap is rare.

The carriages themselves were at first mostly four wheelers, but long bogie coaches had been introduced before the turn of the century. All were fitted with double roofs after the Australian style, with an air space between the outer and inner shell to provide some insulation against extremes of heat. When it came to long distance travel—or perhaps I should call it 'long duration' travel, since a trip over the entire main line from Kobe to Tokyo involved around twenty-four hours of jogging along at an overall average speed of about 15 m.p.h. with something like 50 intermediate stops—that would be on an 'express' train that omitted many of the smaller stations. On such odysseys the patient, stoical third-class passenger sat on bare boards, devoid of any upholstery. These might have been just tolerable on the Great Eastern suburban out of London, but not for 24 hours! Nevertheless the British influences were strong in many other directions. The stations had high platforms, avoiding the scramble up from rail level experienced so often overseas, and those in country districts were always smart, with attractively kept floral displays. The place names were displayed in English as well as in Japanese characters. But at the turn of the century, as Timins picturesquely describes it, Japan through her railways offered 'a new and surprising sensation to the jaded globe-trotter—that of being absolutely unable to hurry'.

CHAPTER FIFTEEN

Metamorphosis in thirty years

In whatever degree of placidity the Japanese railways may have opened for business that state did not last for long. The abolition of the foreign concession areas in the Treaty Ports in 1889, and the opening up of the whole country to foreign traders, acted as a great stimulus to national development and the railway system was expanded and improved accordingly. By the end of 1903 the route mileage had increased to over 4000, though at that time no more than a proportion was owned by the State. In 1881 a charter had been granted to the first private railway to be promoted, the Nippon, and from 1887 Japan had her 'Railway Mania', with many new schemes privately promoted. By the end of the century railways extended from end to end of the main island of Honshu, and there were developments in the northern island of Hokkaido and the southern island of Kyushu.

Even with the rapid increase in mileage that took place during the last ten years of the nineteenth century, foreign observers still did not see any great future for railway development in Japan, despite the high density of population. The physical conditions were certainly daunting to anyone used to the relatively flat country and stable geology of Great Britain and Western Europe. In Japan the central geographical feature of the main island of Honshu is a high and extremely rugged mountain range running almost without a break from north to south. It is volcanic, with the hazards and uncertainties that such conditions involve, and with the island itself relatively narrow it meant that the large population was concentrated into the coastal belts on both sides of the central range. Furthermore the group of islands is sufficiently far north for the mountains to experience heavy snowfall in the winter, and the numerous rivers, though not of any length are subject to violent flooding—not only in the spring from melting snow, but in the time of heavy autumn rains.

Before the end of the nineteenth century Japanese railway engineers had, in very full measure, experienced what nature could do to their fixed structures. In 1888 at Ogaki, northwest of Nagoya, the River Ibi burst its banks and a great torrent of water struck the railway embankment at right angles. It scoured out the bank itself and the ballast got underneath the sleepers, and for a distance of 200 yards turned the track completely upside down, the sleepers being on the top and the rails underneath! Seven years later, amid summer storms, a waterspout burst over the west coast line near Tsuruga. Landslides took vast quantities of rock and shale into the sea, carrying the railway with it, while the flood water rushed through the Yanagase tunnel with such violence as to uproot the permanent way *in the tunnel*, and swept it all out at the far end on the flood.

It certainly needed intrepidity from Japanese railway engineers to keep things going in the face of such early hazards; but far worse, of course, are the effects of earthquakes. There was a bad one in October 1891 in which the main line from Tokyo to Kobe suffered severely. A total of 63 bridges and 41 culverts were wrecked, and the line was shaken out of position in 45 other locations. One embankment sank 13 ft. These early experiences virtually dictated the civil engineering policy of the Japanese railways—the provision of structures that would stand the effects of earthquakes, not without damage for that would be impossible, but which would lend themselves to rapid repair and minimal environmental damage, or loss of life at the time of the actual earthquake shock. The outcome of such provisions proved of no small help at the time of the truly catastrophic visitation suffered by Japan in September 1923, to which more detailed reference is made later.

Despite the leisurely and hesitant beginnings the Japanese railway determined early upon a policy of 'do it yourself'. With the workshop facilities set up by W. M. Smith at Kobe, foreign advisers of the Imperial railways recommended that a start should be made on building locomotives in Japan. There was a second reason for doing this, apart from a policy of self-reliance. Government regulations had been made requiring delivery of locomotives within 12 months of the negotiation of a contract, including delivery time by sea, and while from early experience the Japanese had formed a strong preference for British locomotives, it was found difficult to comply with the new regulations and delivery was taken of many German and American designs. But so far as indigenous manufacture was concerned, the Japanese railways were fortunate in having as successor to W. M. Smith and manager at Kobe works, Richard Francis Trevithick who had much of his pioneer grandfather's dash and resource, and in 1893 he built the first locomotive to be constructed wholly in Japan. It was a handsome little 2–4–2 tank engine, completely British in appearance, with outside cylinders, inside Stephenson link motion, copper capped chimney and polished brass dome.

With locomotives imported from various countries there was considerable variety on the line during the early 1900s; the typical 'American' 4–4–0s, with bar frames, high raised running plates and large sand boxes on top of the boilers contrasted vividly with the neat 4–4–0s of Neilsons' build. The latter also had outside cylinders, placed rather high up to clear the outside frames of the bogie, and the running plate was inclined upwards from a point level with the leading coupled axle. At the rear end the frame was low down, and the upper part of the coupled wheels were hidden behind deep splashers, wholly in the current British style. There were several groups of these engines, built variously by Kitsons, Beyer Peacock, as well as Neilsons. Trevithick was 48 years of age when he built the first locomotive at Kobe, and he set the Japanese railways up on sound construction principles so that they were able to build a considerable proportion of their own locomotives, as well as maintain the stock in a high standard of repair. It was not until later that the Imperial railways developed a distinctive style in locomotive lineaments.

Japanese steam locomotives have always been coal burners, though from the economic point of view it is unfortunate that the large deposits exist only in the two outer islands of Kyushu and

Hokkaido. Originally supplies for the main centres of railway activity on Honshu had to be shipped to Yokohama, voyages of about 600 miles in each case. The coal is soft and smoky, but leaves little ash. When locomotives are being heavily fired it produces some magnificent photographic effects, if the wind is in the right direction; but one day when I was out on the line near Sapporo in the island of Hokkaido, some locomotives were producing effects that reminded one of the smoke screens laid by warships at sea!

Although the original stations were of neat design, and those in the country surrounded by close fencing, the stations in the cities were at first undistinguished architecturally. In view of the natural hazards of which I have already written it would in any case have been unwise to indulge in grandiose terminals like some of those on the continent of Europe, or adornments like the Doric Arch at Euston. The stations in cities like Yokohama, Kyoto, and Tokyo at first resembled the more work-a-day buildings that characterised the early periods of the American and Canadian railways. It was not until the magnificent central station at Tokyo was built, during the period 1908–14, that Japan possessed a station to compete with the greatest in other countries, and then it was certainly the largest and finest in the Far East. The architectural style was curiously however that of the French Renaissance period. How this style came to be chosen I cannot say. The traffic facilities have constantly been overhauled and modernised, the latest changes being made to accommodate the 4 ft. 8½ in. gauge tracks of the New Tokaido Line.

In early days the Japanese railways were operated with a minimum of signalling equipment, and little in the way of interlocking. Lower quadrant semaphores were used, mostly of the early British type working in a slot in the post, with the lamp and coloured spectacle glasses lower down the post to provide easy access for maintenance. From the outset however a high standard of operating discipline was established, and although appliances for reducing risks were few, so also were the number of accidents. There has always been a high sense of public responsibility towards the railways, even at times of the greatest overcrowding; and especially now, when speeds have increased enormously from the maximum of 25 m.p.h. at which trains trundled along at the turn of the century.

As the system developed, connecting lines had to be constructed through mountain passes giving access to the west coast, and some very fine examples of railway civil engineering are to be seen. Tunnels are numerous, but viaducts bridging deep ravines, and carrying lines across tidal estuaries involved much difficult and distinctive work. By long tradition the Japanese are highly skilled in the use of timber, and while no permanent structures of the trestle type have been built, most elaborate temporary false work has been erected, where large span steel girder bridges were used. Instead of building girders out cantilever-wise, or nosing them longitudinally into place, the temporary false-work was of such strength as to allow complete building up of the permanent steel members on its topmost surface.

On the coastal stretches there are many fine bridges over rivers debouching into the sea. These are usually of the Warren girder type, supported on massive masonry piers. The bridge is often extended on either side beyond the normal channels of the rivers to act as a safeguard in times of flood, when otherwise the approach embankments could be washed out. From the earliest days although the tempo of railway operating was leisurely the engineering was quite first class, and this was of the greatest benefit when activities were stepped up, and maximum speeds increased first to 45 and then, on certain sections, to 60 m.p.h. The growth of the system was very rapid, particularly after the co-ordination that followed the Railway Nationalisation Law, enacted in 1906. In the following year 17 private companies were purchased by the Government, and the mileage of the State-owned railways increased to 4371. By the year 1923 another 2000 miles of route had been added, and the total for the whole empire had increased to about 7900.

In no way had the advance of the Japanese railway been more clearly manifested than in all the incidental courtesies of travel. It was particularly gratifying to British visitors to find the station names rendered in English characters; but the timetables and all notices were printed in English, and on express trains—and by 1923 they were moving much faster!—there was always a train boy, who helped passengers in and out of carriages, lifted luggage to and from the racks, would dust a gentleman's hat, and so on. Not content with this, and other little courtesies for which the train boys expected no reward, the Imperial Government Railways of Japan, to give the organisation its full title, provided each express with a chief steward—what the French might call a *chef du train*—who always spoke fluent English and was at everyone's service with the traditional Japanese charm of manner. The coaching stock on the long distance express trains was built more in the American style than the British, including the sleeping cars. In these latter the upper berths were lowered from the ceiling, and lower berths were formed from the day seats. One reclined longitudinally, and to provide some degree of privacy curtains were drawn to screen off the central gangway of the car. The comments of an English traveller of 1922 came vividly to mind once more when I flew from London to Tokyo. Of the railway sleepers he wrote: 'But for three things—the shortness of the berths, the undimmed light and the midnight conversation of insomniacs (which among Japanese travellers seem to number legion)—one might repose in peace'!

The dining cars, in which European meals were served, were beautifully appointed, and there was a similarity to the practice existing for many years on some of the leading American railways, in that the catering was provided under contract by certain hotels and restaurants. Similar arrangements applied to the buffets at some of the large city stations. Allowing for the prevalent rate of exchange the prices, for table d'hôte meals, were much the same as one would have expected to pay on the leading British railways, and with immaculate service. If one ventured to try a Japanese-style meal it would certainly be an experience, both in the *décor* of the refreshment car and for one's digestion. There was little variation in menu, which usually consisted of fish soup, boiled rice, raw fish, pickled radish and assorted rolled seaweed. One sat on a revolving wooden stool, at a polished wooden shelf fixed to the side of the car, and looked out through the window at the passing scene.

The height of luxury on the Japanese railways was the Tokyo-Shimonoseki Limited, running from Tokyo to the southernmost railway point on the island of Honshu. Curiously enough at that time it appears to have been used mainly by passengers travelling to and from China, to which the journey then had to be made via Korea and

Manchuria. In these days of jet-air services one is apt to forget how difficult and lengthy journeys were no more than 50 years ago. I became aware of this when travelling from Bangkok to Singapore by train. It is true that for observational purposes I made certain stop-overs and took three days to get there; but with excellent connections the fastest service takes two days, whereas I flew back to Bangkok in a mere two hours. In Japan, 50 years ago, the Tokyo-Shimonoseki Limited covered the distance of 705 miles in 25 hours, an overall average of 28 m.p.h. On the easier stretches the start-to-stop averages were around 34 m.p.h. One of the most appreciated features of this train was the observation car with open verandah at the rear. Plate 31a depicts a famous posed photograph of the period showing passengers enjoying the view of the sacred mountain Fuji San, as the train rolls sedately along. The 'bullet trains' of the New Tokaido Line pass through the same country (plate 31b), but at 130 m.p.h. no one would dream of trying to take the air at the tail end!

By the early 1920s Japanese locomotives had taken on a very definite character of their own. The 'C 51' 'Pacific' type introduced for the express trains in 1919 was one of the most distinctive of the entire stud in the period between the two World Wars, and more than 300 were eventually built. Though the running plate, raised high over the coupled wheels, detracted slightly from their appearance they were otherwise most handsomely styled, with a shapely cast iron chimney, sweeping curves to the main frames at the front end and a minimum of external gadgets. The sand box on the boiler top was not unsightly, and contrary to usual practice was placed behind the steam dome. I was able to see one of these historic locomotives in the live-steam museum at Kyoto during my own travels in Japan. The companion freight engine to the 'C 51', was the 'D 50' 2–8–2 introduced in 1923, but a very powerful 2–8–0, the '9600' class first appeared in 1913. These all had what became the standard Japanese locomotive 'look', until 1928, when a new type of express passenger locomotive was introduced. The two 8-coupled freight types had the following dimensions:

(*a*) French-built Beyer-Garratt 2–8–2 + 2–8–2 formerly used in North Eastern Thailand on the Hill section

PLATE 17 Royal State Railways of Thailand

(*b*) American-built 1320 b.h.p. Co-Co diesel electric locomotive—in 1964 the most powerful locomotive in Thailand

(*c*) A Japanese-built 'Pacific' at Padang Besar, ready to work a northbound train from the frontier station with the Malayan Railways

(*a*) Bangkok main station, express for the south headed by German-built diesel hydraulic locomotive No. 3027

PLATE 18

(*b*) A characteristic station scene in Thailand: squatters on the line outside Bangkok terminus

(*c*) A Japanese-built 'Pacific' engine, with tender stacked with wood logs, at Haad Yai Junction, ready to work south to the Malayan frontier

(*a*) Burma Railways: an 0–6–6–0 Mallet compound, built in 1909 by N.B.L. Co. Ltd.

PLATE 19 British locomotives in South East Asia

(*b*) A Beyer–Garratt 2–8–0 + 0–8–2, built in 1924 for the Lashio Line, Burma Railways

(*c*) Malayan Railways 'Pacific' locomotive built in 1928, by N.B.L. Co. Ltd.

(*d*) Malayan Railways: the final type of steam passenger locomotive, 3-cylinder 'Pacific' of '564' class with Caprotti valve gear built in 1946, at the Queens Park Works, N.B.L. Co. Ltd.

PLATE 20
Malayan Railways

(*a*) One of the English-Electric built diesel electric locomotives at the spectacular station of Kuala Lumpur

(*b*) The station hotel, Kuala Lumpur, as seen from the main station office buildings

A woodblock print reproduction of a view on the first railway in Japan, dated 1872, showing the Vulcan Foundry tank engine

(*a*) (above) 2–4–2 tank engine No. 233, built in Japan in 1902, now in the museum at Osaka. This engine is of the same type as Trevithick's first locomotive of 1893
(*b*) (right) A Kitson 0–6–0 tank engine of 1896, also at the Osaka museum

(*c*) (left) The live-steam roundhouse museum at Kyoto, with the 4–6–4 'C62–2' and the 2–8–2 'D50–140' in steam

PLATE 23 Japanese stations

(*a*) Part of the impressive façade at Tokyo
(*b*) Hakodate, on the island of Hokkaido, with the train for Sapporo ready to leave

PLATE 24

(*a*) (above) The impressive front end of the 'D50–140' in the live-steam museum at Kyoto

(*b*) (right) The Royal engine, 4–6–2 No. C57–117 at Miyazaki, with decorations. Standing in front, left to right, are the Running Foreman, H. Uematsu and the author

(*a*) 2–6–0 No. 8360, a design of 1914, in the museum at Kyoto

PLATE 25

(*b*) Power in the yard at Miyazaki: a 'C57' 'Pacific', No. 115 in the foreground, and a 'D51' 2–8–2 beyond

(*a*) Local passenger train, approaching Miyazaki from the south, hauled by a 'C57' 'Pacific'

PLATE 26

(*b*) Interlocking frame on the platform of a country station in Kyushu: note the English-looking semaphore signals

(*a*) Freight train, southbound from Miyazaki at Kiyotake, hauled by the Royal engine No. C57–117

PLATE 27

(*b*) Northbound passenger train for Tokyo, on the Kyushu Line approaching Tano, hauled by a diesel electric locomotive No. DF 5056

PLATE 28

(*a*) A 2–6–2 of class '58' on the Sem-mo Line, north end of Hokkaido, between Kitahama and Namakoshimizu

(*b*) Another class '58' in wintry weather, climbing between Dogosan and Bingo-Ochiai

(*c*) Double-headed freight train from Sapporo to the Muroran Line passing Eniwa, with the station-master, on right of picture, taking the salute

PLATE 29 Japanese electric locomotives

(*a*) One of the first British-built (English Electric) freight locomotives of 1923, 1836 horsepower

(*b*) At Tokyo: on left 'EF 58' class, 2550 horsepower and 'EF 65', 3315 horsepower electric locomotives

(*c*) One of the 'EH 10' 'double' locomotives of 3390 horsepower

(*a*) The central control room at Tokyo

PLATE 30 The New Tokaido Line

(*b*) The servicing depot for the high-speed trains, at Tokyo

PLATE 31 (*a*) Passing Mount Fuji, old style, on the observation car platform of the Tokyo–Shimonoseki train de luxe

(*b*) Passing Mount Fuji, new style, at 130 m.p.h. by one of the Shinkansen 'bullet' trains

(*a*) 'Hikari' train on the New Tokaido Line leaving Kyoto for Tokyo: a view of the rear end

PLATE 32

(*b*) In the driver's cab of a 'Hikari', with the speedometer needle showing 205 km./h. (128 m.p.h.)

Class Type Year introduced	'9600' 2–8–0 1913	'D 50' 2–8–2 1923
Cylinders		
dia. in.	20	$22\frac{1}{2}$
stroke in.	24	26
Coupled wheel dia. ft. in.	4–1	4–8
Boiler pressure p.s.i.	180	180
Total weight of engine, working order tons	59·4	78·1
Tractive effort at 85% boiler pressure lb.	29,700	35,900

It was in 1928 that the celebrated 'C 53' class of 'Pacific' was introduced, with three cylinders and the Gresley conjugated valve gear. These fine engines, the most powerful passenger type in Japan, were put on to the express trains on the Tokaido–Sanyo line to Shimonoseki, and did excellent work, although not superseding the popular 'C 51' 2-cylinder 'Pacifics'. Comparative dimensions of the two classes were:

Class	'C 51'	'C 53'
Cylinders		
number	2	3
dia. in.	$20\frac{3}{4}$	$17\frac{3}{4}$
stroke in.	26	26
Coupled wheel dia. ft. in.	5–9	5–9
Total evaporative heating surface sq. ft.	1495	1829
Superheater sq. ft.	427	668
Grate area sq. ft.	27·2	35
Boiler pressure p.s.i.	180	199
Tractive effort at 85% boiler pressure lb.	25,400	30,000

Around 1930 the fastest train on the Tokaido Line was the 'Swallow', covering the 373·5 miles between Tokyo and Kobe in 9 hours, at an average of 41·5 m.p.h. inclusive of eight stops. The fastest lap was from Shiznoka to Nagoya, 115·4 miles in 151 minutes, 45·8 m.p.h.

This train was worked by the 'C 51' class engines. On the complete run from Tokyo to Shimonoseki, by two named trains 'The Fuji' and 'The Cherry Flowers', the time had been reduced to 19 hr. 50 min. with 22 intermediate stops, an overall average of 35 m.p.h. These figures are enough to show how the Japanese railways had changed from their leisurely beginnings, seeing that on the sharply curved 3 ft. 6 in. gauge line speed was limited to 60 m.p.h.

The great earthquake of September 1923 had been a terrible setback to railway development, quite apart from the fearful loss of life that ensued. The shock itself was bad enough, but in the Yokohama and Tokyo districts it was followed by a tidal wave, and then a fire the like of which has never been known before or since, and which consumed the greater part of Tokyo itself. The Imperial Railways lost the whole of the headquarters offices, 11 district offices and workshops, and 46 stations seriously damaged or wiped out; while 33 locomotives, 486 passenger carriages and 1249 freight vehicles were rendered unusable. Six passenger trains were wrecked, with 129 killed and 90 injured; 73 employees were killed at their posts, while no less than 10,018 had their homes destroyed, or seriously damaged by fire. The destruction to track, bridges and tunnels was incalculable. The work of the rescue and repair squads, aided by the Engineers Corps of the Japanese Army was instant and purposeful. A foreign correspondent wrote:

> Temporary bridges have been built to take the place of broken structures. They have been constructed of railway sleepers and beams of wood bolted together. The train goes gingerly over these, while planks and trestles groan and grumble, and a great trembling seizes the entire frame work. The wheels of the train grind against the metals, and the nervous foreigner becomes alarmed.

But all was well, and recovery was amazingly swift.

CHAPTER SIXTEEN

Tokyo south to Aoidate

Of Japan so far I have been writing of past history, of the fascinating things told me by many new friends, of things read in the books they and others recommended. From now onwards it is personal experience, and in all my life I do not think I have ever started on a journey from England with a greater feeling of adventure—to fly over the North Pole. It is true that the great Jumbo Jet of Japan Air Lines was the very embodiment of smoothness and comfort; but as we climbed high from Heathrow and the familiar indented coastline first of England and then of Scotland passed below, there seemed something a little unreal in the sophisticated atmosphere inside that aircraft as we headed towards the icy wastes of the north. And with the smart little Japanese hostesses, with their charming manners and gay kimonos, flitting to and fro the icebound mountains of Greenland passed some 30,000 ft. below in stately procession. An hour or so later we passed near to the North Pole, and eventually came to that amazing staging point Anchorage, in Alaska.

The weather was brilliant. The ring of high mountains glistened white, while at this unique international airport, which has been aptly called the crossroads of the world, tiny little planes bound for remote places in Alaska itself came and went amid the great jet liners flying non-stop to Amsterdam, to Hamburg, to London, and like ourselves to Tokyo. And from the airport building, snug and warm from the tough conditions outside, with snow lying close to the runways, one looked out on to a landscape devoid of any habitation, clad with forests of hardy Arctic conifers. Next stop Tokyo; the adventure was soon to begin—before landing though there was the perplexity of time. We had left Heathrow at 14.00 hours on a March afternoon, and here, 9 hours later, the sun was still high in the sky. In fact it did not begin to get dark till we were nearing the shores of Japan. In those last hours of the journey, when I was beginning to get very tired, I went through my papers again, and thought with gratitude of all the pre-planning that had gone into my itinerary from my pen friends H. Uematsu and Y. Kawakami, who I was soon to meet personally, the Japan Tourist Office in London, and above all the International Department of the Japanese National Railway. The moment we touched down any feeling of tiredness was pushed aside in the maelstrom of arrival, the welcomes, and an hour or so of checking up on my programme which was to start promptly next morning.

Although the construction and subsequent prowess of the SHINKANSEN, or New Trunk Line, has tended to overshadow all other activities on the Japanese National Railways in the last twelve years, I am leaving my impressions of this to the last three chapters of this book, and will deal first with the very extensive 3 ft. 6 in. gauge network, and the way it has been developed. The original main line electrification in Japan was on the 1500 volts direct current system (as in India and France, and as chosen for future development in Great Britain), but as in all those countries the advantage of high voltage alternating current at commercial frequency was appreciated, and all recent work on the 3 ft. 6 in. gauge lines in Japan has been on 20,000 volts a.c. at 60 cycles per second. In Tokyo all electrified lines are on 1500 volts d.c., except for the Shinkansen Line, which is quite separate on the 4 ft. 8½ in. gauge. At the Old Tokaido Line depot I saw many types of electric locomotive. These are used mostly on freight, all of which is worked on the 3 ft. 6 in. gauge. Except for a few overnight sleeper car trains that are locomotive hauled, practically the whole of the passenger service is operated by multiple unit sets. These will be discussed as I came to travel by them in different parts of Japan.

The suburban services of Tokyo are perhaps the most widely known activity of the Japanese National Railways. It is of course no more than natural that journalists and other seekers after good 'copy' should seize upon the use of human pushers to assist in getting passengers into the trains quickly in the peak hours. There certainly are a tremendous number of commuters, and in Tokyo those who cannot get through the doors are left behind. There is no hanging on in clusters round an open door as in Bombay or Calcutta. The operation is extremely efficient, and an interesting feature that I have not seen elsewhere is the painting of trains for the different routes in distinctive colours. A regular traveller will know that, for example, a green train will take him to his home station. This, of course, imposes a degree of inflexibility upon the utilisation of the stock, if the occasion arises when there is a need to optimise mileage, as is done on the Southern Region suburban services in London.

So far as long distance passenger travel is concerned, the philosophy in Japan is to use the 'lightning' trains of the Shinkansen system as far as possible, and to provide good connections to more distant destinations by Limited Express Trains, multiple unit sets—electric or diesel—according to the equipment of the line concerned. My own first expedition was to Kyoto, to which I travelled by one of the 'Hikari', or lightning trains as a passenger. Although we covered the 212½ miles to the first stop at Nagoya in only fifteen seconds over the level two hours, an average of 106·3 m.p.h. from start-to-stop, the travelling did not really give the impression of high speed. What did impress me was the almost continuous building and industrialisation along the entire route. The afternoon was rather hazy and when we came to the classic vista of Mount Fuji San it was no more than vaguely seen. The 83¼ miles on to Kyoto were reeled off in 48¾ minutes, at an average of 102½ m.p.h., again from start-to-stop.

In the ancient city of Kyoto I switched my interest from the ultra-modern to the not-so-modern, because on the outskirts there is the utterly fascinating Umekoji steam locomotive museum. This, like the French railway museum at Mulhouse, is based on a roundhouse; but it is a large one, and all engines still capable of being steamed can be brought out of their stables into the open and on to the central turntable. A number of the smaller and older engines are static exhibits, but there is a magnificent collection of the more modern types that can be steamed ranging from the famous 'C 51' to the largest ever Japanese passenger locomotive, the 'C 62' 4–6–4, discussed in detail in Chapter Eighteen of this book. From one of the stalls in the roundhouse there is a back door that leads towards the main line, and it is through this door that the locomotives selected for steaming on a particular day are taken for a short demonstration run. I was also interested to find one of the 'C 53' 3-cylinder 'Pacifics' in the roundhouse, in working order. From Kyoto also I made a short trip to Osaka to see the magnificent transport museum, with its many models, and the preserved Trevithick 2–4–2 tank engine.

I must pass over for the present my experience of cab riding on one of the Hikari trains on the Shinkansen Line, and jump quickly to Okayama, whence in company with Mr. Tonahara of the J.N.R. I was taking the branch train to Uno and the ferry to Takamatsu on the island of Shikoku. It was only a short run down the branch, but the short train was packed and when we got to Uno there was a great dash for the ferry, by about a thousand people, that reminded me of the hurried changes from train to boat on the Firth of Clyde. It was a cloudy evening and dusk was falling early. Sure enough on arrival at Takamatsu there was another concerted rush to get off the boat. Later that evening from the hotel dining room there were glimpses of floodlit temples, and beyond the garish illuminated signs there was the estuary with ships coming and going, lights reflected in the still waters—some from huge Japanese lanterns. The ferry boats carry about 1800 passengers and 27 railway freight cars. At one time after the Second World War there were 24 private shipping companies entering Takamatsu; there was often racing between rivals, and some fatal collisions.

On the island of Shikoku the trains are all diesel worked. I saw the modern colour light signalling in Takamatsu station, and was interested to find that the control panel was of the 'One Control Switch' type, as used on some of the earlier panel installations in India. It had been intended that I should return to the mainland by hovercraft, but the morning had brought rain and fog; not only was the hovercraft flight cancelled, but the ferry crossing from Uno was advised 34 minutes late. My connection with the Limited Express train 'Tsamabe No. 3', which was to take me on to Shimonoseki seemed out of the question. Tonahara was already phoning Tokyo to get me a reservation on a later train. Fortunately, however, when the ferry 'Tosa Maru' did arrive it was carrying no freight vehicles, nor were any to be embarked, and we got away only 12 minutes late.

Despite the mist we made a rapid crossing, but even so it was still an almost foregone conclusion that we should fail to make the connection.

As we neared Okayama the loudspeaker on the train warned us that only three minutes would be available; and when 1200 Japanese are intent upon getting off the platform as quickly as they can, whether they have a connection to make or not, a past experience of Rugby Football is apt to come in useful. How Tonahara and I fought our way through the crowd, up one flight of steps, over a long overbridge, down another just as that imperious bell that heralds the immediate departure of a Japanese train started ringing, and how Tonahara hurled me and my luggage through the first available door with seconds to spare before the doors closed, is one of those epics that could enliven some future series in *The Railway Magazine* on *Railway Passengers' Practice and Performance*.

It was then 13.35 hours, and I had in front of me five hours of pleasant travel on the Sanyo Line—after I had found my reserved

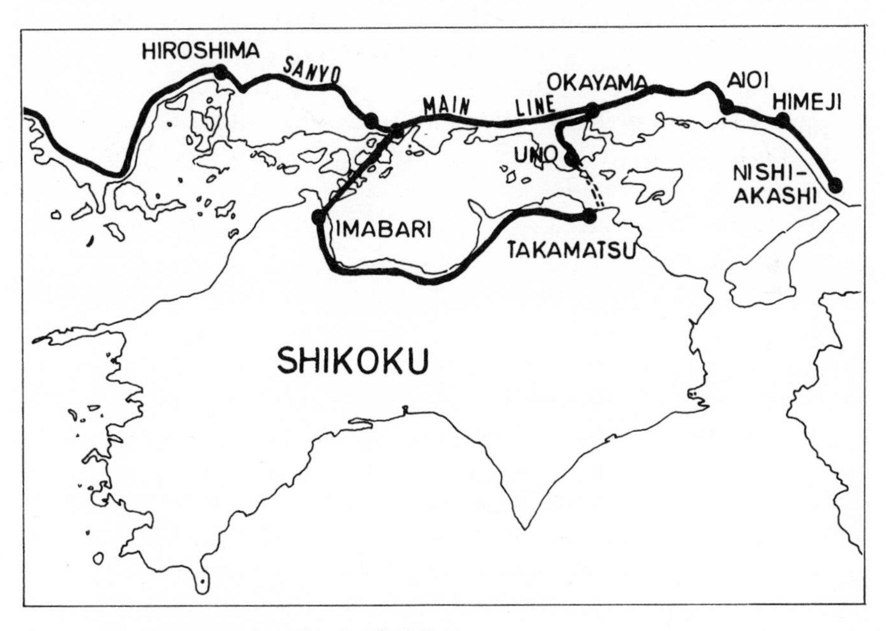

25. Connections to the island of Shikoku

seat, and recovered my breath. It was an interesting, and extraordinarily varied ride. It was my first experience of the 'Limited Express Trains' on the 3 ft. 6 in. gauge. The coach was roomy, very comfortable, and gave no suggestion of sub-standard gauge. We had plenty of fast running up to 75 m.p.h., but very smooth travelling on the curves. There was, at intervals, a pleasant trolley service of refreshments. For the most part the line runs near to the shores of the Inland Sea, and one is never long out of sight of intense industrialisation. While I was in Takamatsu I learned of the bridge that is planned to connect Shikoku with the mainland. This will start from Onomichi, where, as will be seen from the sketch map there is a chain of closely spaced islands across the sea. Beyond Onomichi where I saw enormous ships being built, the line turns inland for a while through mountainous country, where I saw the southward extension of the Shinkansen Line under construction. And so—to Hiroshima.

I must say I looked forward in somewhat awed curiosity to see this place, where one of the most significant pages in the whole history of mankind was written on that day in the summer of 1945; but apart from the name there is nothing to distinguish Hiroshima from all others in the chain of industrial centres on the Sanyo Line, so complete has been the rebuilding. Continuing round the coast we passed beside remote fishing coves of great beauty, to be followed soon by vast oil refineries, or shipyards. All the time the mountains of the inland range were getting lower in height, and after all the rain and fog over Shikoku the sun was setting in a cloudless sky. All the way there was evidence of the huge engineering works in connection with the Shinkansen extension and so, after passing beside marshalling yards and many electric locomotives, we drew into Shimonoseki at 18.31, just a minute early.

The southern island of Kyushu is separated from the mainland by no more than the narrow Kanmon Straits, which at one point are little more than 800 yards wide. From as long ago as 1896 a tunnel under the straits had been discussed, but it was not until 1936 that work was started, with two parallel bores. The first of these was opened in August 1942 and the second just two years later. Now the whole neighbourhood of the straits is under active development, and

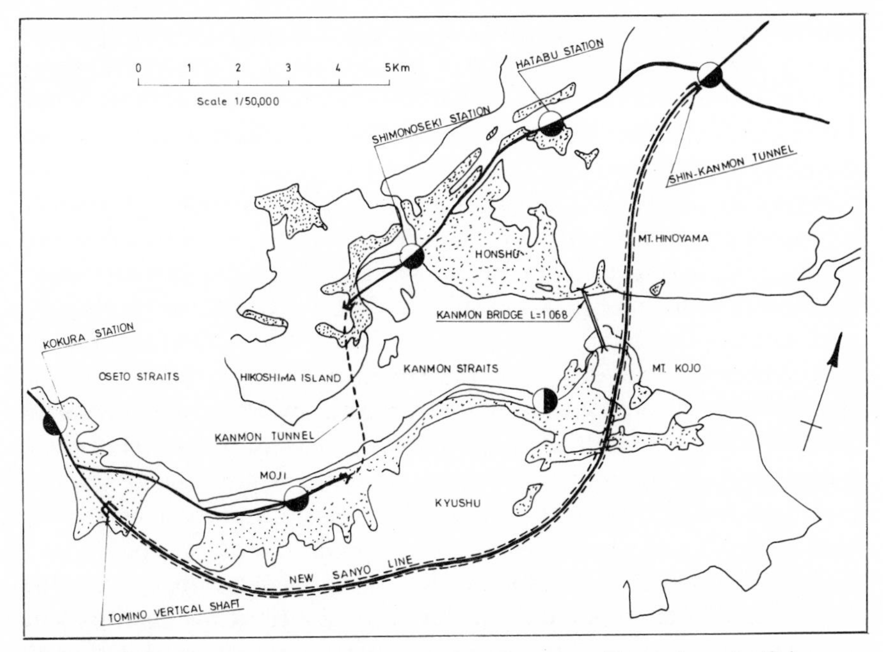

26. Map showing position of the existing Kanmon Tunnel, and of the new one, on the extension of the Shinkansen system towards Hakata

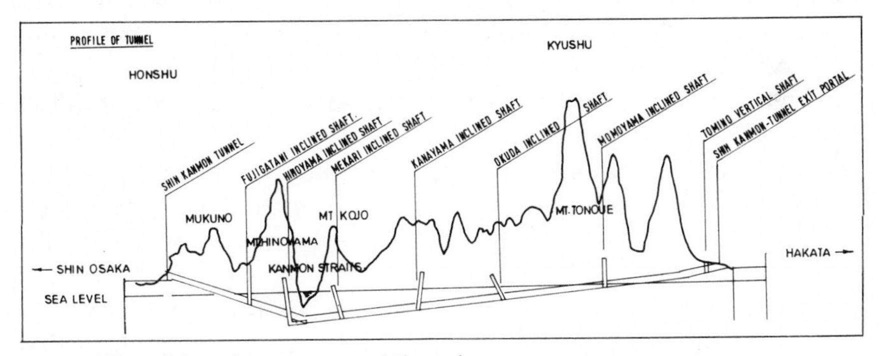

27. Profile of the Shin-Kanmon Tunnel

the accompanying map shows the present Kanmon Tunnel, through which our train was about to pass, and the route of the much longer tunnel of the New Sanyo Line of the Shinkansen extension, to which I was subsequently taken to see some of the works near the Kanmon highway bridge.

At the Kyushu end of the Kanmon Tunnel is the big railway centre of Moji, which at the time of my visit was in every way a general purpose locomotive depot, using steam, diesel and electric units. Then the numbers assigned were 36 steam, 15 diesel, and 85 electric, and this represents the largest accumulation of any locomotives throughout the 149 depots of the Japanese National Railways. The diesels at Moji are mostly with hydraulic drive, while the steam locomotives were of the modern 'D 51' class of 2–8–2 referred to particularly in Chapter Eighteen, and of the veteran '9600' class of 2–8–0 dating from 1913. Among the electric locomotives are the 'EF 30' series, which operate on the 1500 volt d.c. system of Honshu and the 20,000 volt a.c. system of Kyushu. There are also purely a.c. locomotives that work only in Kyushu. By the time this book is published it is expected that not only those stationed at Moji, but all other steam locomotives in Kyushu will have been replaced by diesels on the non-electrified sections.

I went on from Shimonoseki to Kumamoto by the Limited Express Train 'Tsubame No. 3', and to fit in with the closely dovetailed itinerary planned for my visit, it was necessary to cross the island of Kyushu from west to east by bus. It was no ordinary bus ride, and included three sections by aerial ropeway, and one lap in a different bus along the crater edge of an active volcano! It was in fact a run along part of the International sightseeing route crossing Kyushu from Nagasaki to Beppu. Unfortunately for sightseeing the weather was poor, and the spectacular Mount Aso was shrouded in mist, mixed with the issuing steam from the crater. Beppu, on the east coast, is a delightful place where I would have stayed several days longer than the one night allocated; because at last we were away from industrialisation, and the run down the coast to Miyazaki next day was in every way a 'rural ride'. I had already enjoyed the little ceremony that always accompanies the welcoming of a visitor in Japanese railway offices; and at Beppu the stationmaster's office was more like an English boardroom, with easy chairs round a central table, and green tea served within minutes of one's arrival. And Beppu was no great divisional centre, but a seaside resort of the size of Dawlish or Teignmouth.

My notes on the run down to Miyazaki in a diesel train are mostly those of the beautiful scenery, though the line was busy, and at the single line passing loops we frequently crossed other trains. At Usuki for example in the 12 minutes we were at rest, the northbound 'Phoenix Express' and the Limited Express 'Nichirin' going south went through and took the road ahead of us. Most of the country stations were very smart and clean, but of Saiki, I quote from my impromptu notes 'an old style station, like a scruffy English one'! South of this point there was an inland stretch through hilly country reminiscent of Switzerland, where our diesel train made rather heavy weather of the gradient; but from Nobeoka, where many 'D 51' class 2–8–2s were on the shed the line follows the coast, for a beautiful run of two hours. I noted a land entirely given over to rice growing, lonely shores with surf but no surfers, but best of all in view of the railway pleasures to come, a clear and brilliant sky.

We reached Miyazaki on time at 15.02 hours. Uematsu had flown from Tokyo to join in the party and such were the attractions in the locomotive yard as to cause my railway friends to forego the traditional green tea welcome. For there, in all her finery, stood the Japanese Royal Engine, the small 'Pacific' C57–117, still carrying the national flags and the gilded chrysanthemum insignia of the Emperor. The Royal Train had not long arrived, and the decorations had not been removed from the engine, so we were able to take photographs under almost ideal conditions. Apart from this piece of 'treasure trove' for a lover of locomotives, the small yard contained many other interesting examples, including the 'C 61' class small 4–6–4—small that is in comparison to the giant 'C 62' class that used to work in Hokkaido in their last days before withdrawal. Uematsu and I stayed that night at the Phoenix Hotel, which is on the bank of the River Oyoda and gave us opportunities for photographing trains on the viaduct from our bedroom windows.

Next morning I was booked out of Miyazaki on the footplate of the 10.23 hours southbound freight, and on arrival at the station we found it was to be worked by none other than No. C57–117, the 'Royal Engine' of the previous day. Although divested of the flags and other decorations she still looked very smart, and once we started I quickly sensed she was 'a real lady'—as the enginemen's term goes. Our load was not heavy—only 219 tons; but there were some stiff gradients to climb, as we made our way on single line into the hills. We were stopped at Kiyotake, to cross a passenger train, and then had some hard slogging up to Tano on a 1 in 60 gradient. I was going on to Aoidate, but with a kind thought for the enthusiast in me, my friends in the cab suggested that at Tano I should transfer to the 3-car diesel train which overtook us there, and then I should be able to photograph No. C57–117 climbing hard across a very picturesque viaduct. The working of the Royal engine was well known to several other enthusiasts, who were already at Aoidate and had their cameras set up. One of them had solved a great problem, by having two cameras mounted cheek by jowl on the same stand, and arranged for simultaneous release. So he could secure a record in both colour and black and white at the same time.

Aoidate is a delightful place, set deep amongst wooded hills. On this line there are prizes for the best kept stations, and all the small country ones are still open. Aoidate was a riot of flowers, even in April: sweet williams, cornflowers, pansies, wild violets, and azaleas already in full bloom. When I admired his display the station master said it was nothing, and thought I ought to return when the roses were at their best. We went into his office and drank green tea. He showed me the hand-drawn train diagram on the wall, and explained the working of the single line token instruments. But all too soon it was time to leave Aoidate. My railway journeys in Kyushu were one way only, and to keep up with my itinerary I had to get back to Osaka. The J.N.R. had very kindly laid on a car to take Uematsu and me back to Miyazaki; but we were not too hurried on this stage and were able to see and discuss various aspects of Japanese agriculture on the way. From Miyazaki I flew over the sea to Osaka in a smart Boeing 737 of All Nippon Airways, on which the hostess did the only Englishman on board the honour of repeating her various announcements in his language—very competently too.

CHAPTER SEVENTEEN

North to Hokkaido—the Hokuriku and Uetsu lines : the ferry

I spent a quiet Sunday morning in Osaka. It was very wet, and everybody seemed to be coming into town and walking under umbrellas. I had much to do in checking over my many notes, until it was time to meet Tonahara once again and take the Limited Express Train 'Raicho No. 7' for Kanazawa, up the west coast line, the Hokuriku. It was another of the pleasant multiple-unit electric trains, designed to operate on dual voltage. At first we were running over the old Tokaido Line on 1500 volts d.c., and fairly close to the Shinkansen Line; but then we came to Maibara. This is a major junction on the 3 ft. 6 in. gauge system, with the Hokuriku Line bearing away leftwards to reach the west coast and the Sea of Japan. But Maibara is of historic interest as the site of the first installation in Japan of power signalling, with electrically operated points, and the pistol-grip type of interlocking machine, imported from the U.S.A. in 1915. As in Great Britain relay interlocking began to supersede lever interlocking on the Japanese railways in the 1930s.

Since then, signalling in Japan has been developed to a high state of sophistication; the ultimate, so far, I shall describe when I come to the technical features of the Shinkansen system. On the 3 ft. 6 in. gauge lines colour light signalling has been developed from the simple three aspect 'stop', 'caution', 'proceed' indicated by a single red, yellow, or green light respectively to four, and even five aspects, when the signal sections are short, and additional indications have to be given to drivers. The fourth aspect used is 'yellow over green', which indicates 'run at reduced speed', while in the five aspect system, the fifth is 'yellow over yellow' which means run at restricted speed. In this respect it is quite different from the British

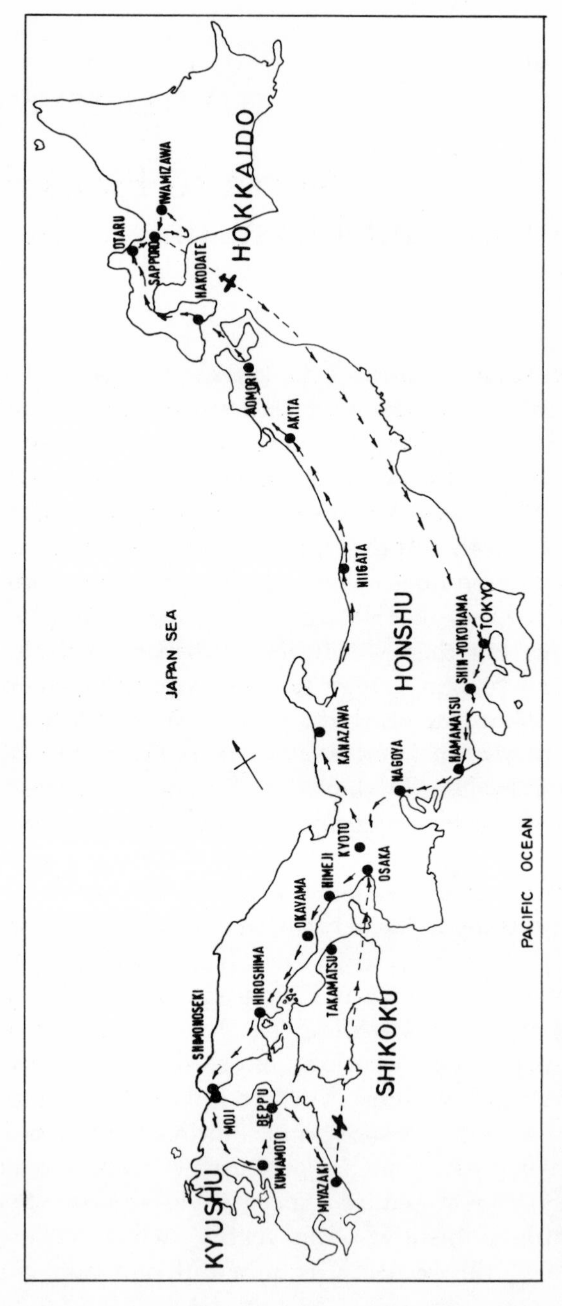

28. Author's route round Japan

'double-yellow', which in a four aspect system is the preliminary warning of a caution signal ahead. In Japan the 'double yellow' follows the single yellow 'caution', and indicates continue running at restricted speed.

At Maibara we were going to continue on a line electrified at 20,000 volts a.c. 60 cycles. On our train the changeover to our traction equipment was made while we stood in the station, and very briefly the lights in the carriages were extinguished. Then we set off again beside the large inland Lake Biwa, which looked rather forlorn on this wet afternoon. Through a wooded hill country there were many tunnels, and at Tsuruga the Obama Line from westwards along the coast trailed in. Just after this we came to the 8 mile-long Hokuriku Tunnel, one of the longest on the 3 ft. 6 in. gauge lines in Japan. We emerged into a very pretty glen, of quaint villages, high tumbled mountains, and everywhere the cherry blossom in all its beauty. To me it was all the more noticeable after the high industrialisation of the east coast of Honshu, and as we drew nearer to the coast, after passing the cultural centre of Fukui, there were miles upon miles of paddyfields so irrigated and saturated with water as to make one believe it was the rainy season. So in the early evening we came to Kanazawa, a city of some 370,000 inhabitants.

My railway friends were most anxious that there should be a break in my travelling before what they termed 'the long ride' of the following day, up the coast to Akita. I must admit that my recollections of Kanazawa are more of Japanese customs and hospitality than of railways: an initiation into the ancient 'tea ceremony', a tour of the city and its beautiful parks, and then a lunch, Japanese style, given by Mr. T. Yamazaki, the superintendent of the Kanazawa Operating Division. My friends were nothing if not alert to every chance of prolonging their welcome. I would not otherwise have mentioned that during the time of my visit there were disturbing labour troubles on the Japanese railways, including the all-too-familiar tactics of 'go slow'. We were to catch the Limited Express Train 'Hakucho', and during lunch close touch was being kept with the train running. When we were advised that it was 34 minutes late it was an excellent reason for prolonging the lunch party.

The 'long ride' turned out to be a good deal longer than expected, not as it transpired due to any 'go slow' activities, but due to a fire in some buildings adjacent to the line at Hoigawa and we stood for a solid hour at the previous station of Omi, while the fire was being brought under control. Apart from this it proved a very interesting run, for I saw many other sides of Japanese railway operating. The rural and agricultural countryside was backed to the east by the long chain of the Japanese Alps, at first no more than a hazy, snowy line in the distance, but when we came to the junction of Toyama snow was not something to be glimpsed far away. The Takayama main line which comes in from the south crosses Honshu from Nagoya and cuts through the high and difficult country of the Japan Alps National Park, which whatever pleasures it may provide for nature lovers often means tough work for railwaymen, and beside the yards of Toyama were many snow ploughs. There also is a large fully automated marshalling yard dealing with heavy freight traffic.

Beyond Toyama the mountain range comes close to the sea, and the railway is carried just inshore. There were many long tunnels, with very short open stretches between them, and even there the railway was often protected by avalanche shelters. It was on this section that we had the long wait for the fire hazard to be cleared. Unfortunately the stop was among the houses of Omi, and we did not have a very exciting prospect during the delay. Another hundred yards or so, and there would have been a lovely view over the sea. After the widespread rain of the previous day the weather was clear, and as we got under way again the sea and the mountains looked beautiful in the calm evening light. We were stopped again at Hoigawa, to be warned to go slowly past the site of the fire. But Hoigawa is also a point where the traction system changes back to 1500 volts d.c. The Oito Line from the south was one of those to be electrified earlier, and the coastal route is direct current onwards to Niigata. We then had a run just above the sea. The succession of long tunnels, with brief intermissions, reminded me of the Italian Mediterranean line south of Genoa. In one of these tunnels, the Kubiki, slab track is laid, as on the Shinkansen lines. Some of my English friends, attending talks I gave after my return from Japan, remarked on the possible amenity aspect of the Shinkansen extension south of Osaka, which will have a very large proportion of its mileage in tunnel. This will be nothing new to travellers in Japan. I should think that more than half the distance between Hoigawa and our next stop, Naoetsu is in tunnel.

Naoetsu is another important junction with a cross-country line, also electrified on 1500 volts d.c., and then we changed train crews. After this the coastal scenery underwent a change for a time, with level heathlands, short pines, and protective fences to stop sand drifting on to the railway. Then came another spell of the tunnel motif. In one brief opening there was a quaint fishing village; in another just enough room for a station, and yet again a sight of an old single-line tunnel nearer the sea, now abandoned, because of insufficient clearance for the overhead electric wires. Niigata is on the coast some distance away from the main line, and the train takes the branch at Nitsu to reach the terminus, before reversing direction again to rejoin the main line. We were due at Niigata at 17.28 hours, but because of the late start from Kanazawa, and the fire delay we were running about 1¾ hours late. It was also dark, and so my sightseeing came to an end.

Another 3¾ hours of travelling still remained before we should reach the ancient city of Akita, where I should meet the second of my Japanese pen friends, Y. Kawakami, and author of several fine railway books. But in the pleasant company of Mr. Y. Sakakibara of the international department of the Japanese National Railways the time passed pleasantly enough, discussing many aspects of railway working. He enlightened me on one thing, the Japanese practice of refunding fares in cases of late running. This is a very old tradition, and is applied when any train arrives at a destination or intermediate point more than one hour late. On the Shinkansen lines the margin is only half an hour. Thus when we arrived at Akita all passengers alighting made straight for the booking office. There was no argument or delay; the queue was dealt with as promptly and efficiently as the queue booking tickets at a London Underground station.

The following day there was a general strike of railwaymen, and all trains were at a standstill; but Kawakami and the railway management had between them organised a delightful day of non-railway sightseeing for me, except to visit a signal station south of Akita in what they call the 'sand forest', an area near to the sea, where the line has to be protected from sand drifting inland from the dunes. The prevailing winds, westerly from the Sea of Japan, are very strong, and the trees are all growing slantwise. Later in my visit to Akita I was taken to see the works at Tsuchizaki—a comprehensive plant inaugurated about eight years ago with about 250 men, it has now expanded its activities so as to need six times that number. Here major repairs are carried out on locomotives of all kinds, though when I was there the only steam engines were those awaiting scrapping. A large area is given over to the repair of freight cars, and a smaller one to passenger coaches. An interesting point I noticed was all the running gear, bogies and so on, are steam cleaned before any repairs are assessed. Situated in the country just outside Akita, a housing estate and recreation ground for the work people have been built adjacent to the works.

Leaving Akita I was continuing to the northernmost part of Honshu, prior to crossing by ferry to the island of Hokkaido. I was booked on the same train by which I had come north from Kanazawa, and Uematsu was travelling up from Tokyo to join me. But despite what those writers of 75 years ago said about the nature of the Japanese we had another case of catching a train by the skin of our teeth. The Limited Express Train 'Hakucho' arrived from the south on time; but on the OU main line by which Uematsu was travelling there had been a landslip in the mountains between Kita-Yamagata and Shinjo. The line was blocked, and traffic was being diverted by a more circuitous route to the east. His train made it—just!—and he arrived breathless with about a minute to spare before we started. A run of 2½ hours brought us to Aomori, the ferry terminal, just before midnight. The large ship of 8000 tons was very full, and fortunately after the rain, storms and high winds of the last few days, it was a clear night. Although I had a comfortable bunk one does not sleep much on these occasions, and a crossing of just under four hours' duration brought us to the large and picturesque port of Hakodate. From a small hotel where we spent the rest of the night I looked out over the harbour when a full moon added to the beauty of a calm and light-studded scene.

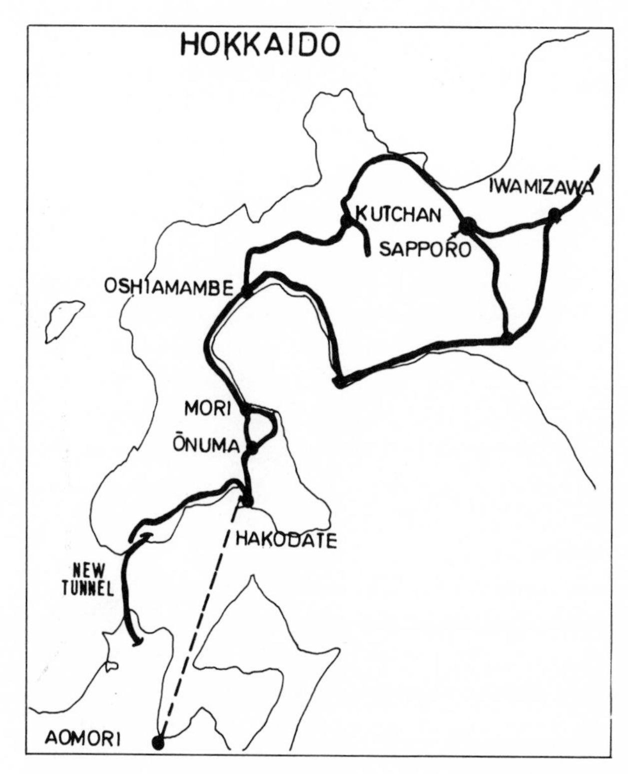

29. Site of the new undersea tunnel to Hokkaido

After breakfast our immediate concern was to see the workings for the great tunnel under the sea that will provide direct railway communication between Honshu and Hokkaido. The accompanying map shows the location of the tunnel in relation to the present ferry route from Aomori, and to reach the working site we had an interesting run down a branch line from Hakodate that runs along the shore of the Tsugarn Straits. The new tunnel is being built to carry both Shinkansen and 3 ft. 6 in. gauge traffic, and from the map it will be seen that when the Shinkansen line on to Hokkaido is built the connection from the tunnel to Hakodate will pass along roughly parallel to this existing line. The working shafts for the tunnel are set in mountainous country near the seashore, and the resident engineer, with the help of numerous diagrams made the plan of operations very clear.

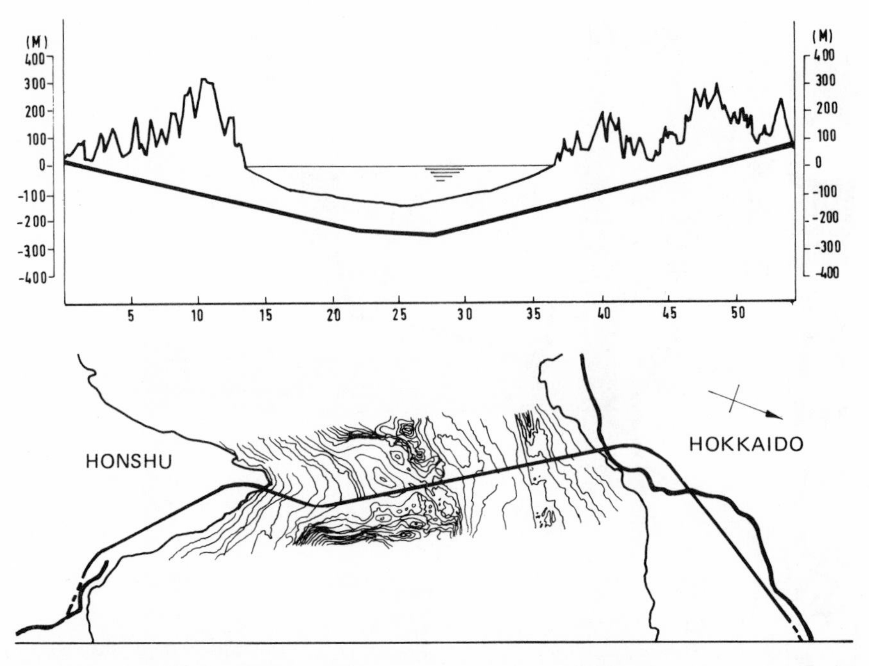

30. Cross-section and plan of the new tunnel to Hokkaido

The Seikan Tunnel, which is planned for completion in 1979 will be the longest undersea tunnel in the world, longer indeed than the projected tunnel under the English Channel. Its length from end to end will be no less than 33½ miles, and of this 14½ miles will be actually under the sea. The surveys indicated some exceptional difficulties, of which the most serious was the discovery of a vast fault on the sea bottom from which unlimited high pressure water will flow. For this reason it was considered necessary to site the roof of the tunnel about 110 yards below the level of the sea bed, at a depth of about 270 yards below sea level. It was this great depth in the centre that made the tunnel so much longer than the actual distance across the straits. The line is level only for about 2½ miles in mid-tunnel, and to reach the required depth there will be a descending gradient of 1 in 83½ for 13½ miles on the Honshu side and a similar gradient but 17½ miles long ascending on the Hokkaido end.

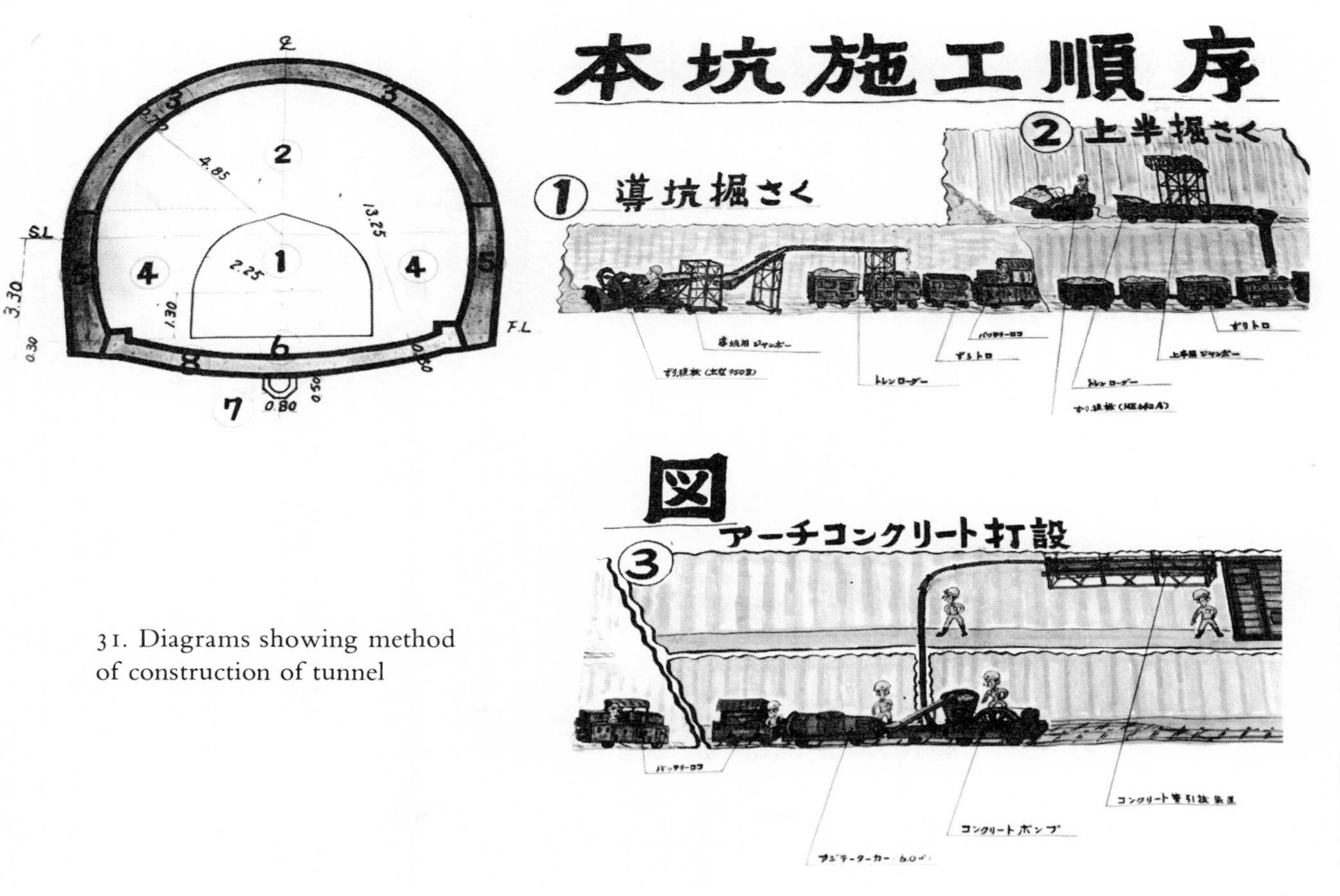

31. Diagrams showing method of construction of tunnel

The diagrams on pages 176–7 show the planned cross-section of the tunnel, with the main bore and the various subsidiary tunnels duly indicated. The one main tunnel will carry both 4 ft. 8½ in. and 3 ft. 6 in. gauge, but when I visited the site in 1973 it had not been decided whether to have one standard and one 3 ft. 6 in. gauge track, each quite independent of each other, or whether to lay in two mixed gauge lines.

Into the face of a steep hillside an inclined shaft had been driven to provide access to the workings. Along the line of the main tunnel the bottom drift method of tunnelling is being used, and Figure 31 shows the order of construction. The pilot tunnel 1, is driven first, to a distance of about one third of a mile ahead of the main working, to investigate rock conditions. Next the 'service' tunnel portion 2 is excavated, followed by 3, putting in the concrete for the arch. Then the lower shaft section 4 is excavated, and finally the side wall concrete put in. Additional pilot tunnels were driven, in various different cross-localities to test rock conditions, and these, together with the access and ventilating shafts have been finished by having the walls treated with spray concrete. The ingress of spring water has been overcome by grouting. It was certainly a privilege to visit this remarkable work, and to have the operations so lucidly explained, in English.

Next day the interest was concentrated on steam, while making our way to Sapporo, the capital city of Hokkaido. We spent some time out on the line photographing at the junction of Onuma, in a beautiful open countryside, with the volcano Komagatake forming an impressive background. I was interested in the extreme quietness of the big 2–8–2s while running at speed; in fact a 'D 52' approaching at about 40 m.p.h. came up so silently that Uematsu and I, happening to be looking the other way, nearly missed it. The country itself looked dried up, rather like the 'end of winter' aspect in South Africa. We took another steam hauled train, on a line that made an almost complete circuit of the volcano, seeing its queer spiky summits from many angles, and then coming to the sea again, and a run beside the shore to the important junction of Oshiamambe. We broke our journey here also to see the locomotives in the roundhouse. With the exception of one branch tank engine, all the power on parade was of the 'D 51' 2–8–2 class, the general work-horse of the Japanese steam lines at that time. No fewer than eight of them were on shed.

From Oshiamambe there are two routes to Sapporo. The modern diesel multiple unit expresses take the route along the southern coast, which I was to see later in my visit; but we were taking the route used in the heyday of steam, through very mountainous country to the north coast. It was here that the big 'C 62' class 4–6–4s did their last regular main line work, and in magnificent surroundings, very often working in pairs, they were a constant source of attraction to photographers. On the heavy gradients speeds were slow, and with a main road running alongside for much of the way, fast cars enabled the same train to be photographed two or three times. The only trouble was that so few Japanese own cars. The enthusiasts were, however, not to be deterred by this. They travelled to Oshiamambe and then chartered taxis. This was not the end of it, because the taxi-drivers became caught up in the excitement of this sport, bought cameras and joined in the fun!

At Kutchan, deep in the mountains, there is a locomotive depot, where many 'D 51' class were on shed, and some snow ploughs. In days when heavy passenger trains from Sapporo to Hakodate took this route, they took both water and more *coal* here before beginning the 1 in 40 ascent to Kamimena summit. There was more climbing for our train after Kutchan, and then down to the sea at Otaru, where a.c. electric traction begins. There is a big marshalling yard, and one of the 'C 62' 4–6–4 engines has been maintained here in working condition, and is sometimes used for summer excursions. From Otaru, which reminded me more of the teeming cities of Honshu, rather than of the more rural atmosphere of Hokkaido, we had a run along the coast before turning inland to reach Sapporo. Mr. Hata, Vice-President of J.N.R. in Hokkaido met us, and arrangements were quickly made for another day of steam on the morrow.

This time we went down the present main route towards Hakodate, to a junction with the Muroran Main Line, over which there is a heavy coal train traffic. The intersection includes a 'flyover', by which the southbound track from Sapporo crosses the main line. Here I saw, and photographed the 'D 51' class *in excelsis*, catching no fewer than 12 of them in full action. Another pleasant recollection of a long day on the line was of the invitation to join the country stationmaster at Eniwa, and his wife, for lunch, Japanese style. This day was fitly rounded off by a run on the footplate of a 'C 57' 4–6–2 hauling a local passenger train, which we joined at Numanohata and travelled on the Muroran Line to Iwamizawa. We were returning to Sapporo round two sides of a triangle, so that I could ride passenger over the first railway on Hokkaido, the section between Sapporo and Iwamizawa.

Sapporo was virtually the end of my journeyings by train in Japan, and although for historical sequences I have left other things to later chapters of this book, it was in many ways the climax of it all. My railway friends in Sapporo worked indefatigably to ensure that every minute of my time was filled to the best advantage. They took me to running sheds, to lineside locations, and to the Zoo, where on a cloudless Sunday afternoon all Sapporo, his wife and family were enjoying the spring weather—yet not warm enough to bring the cherry blossom out in these northern latitudes. The main object of this visit to the Zoo was not to see lions, tigers, elephants and such like, magnificent and well cared for specimens that they were, but to see a preserved 2–6–2 tank engine of Class 'C 12'. Judging by the crowds surrounding it, this exhibit is more popular than any of the large animals!

Another memorable occasion was a railway dinner party, Japanese style, thrown by Mr. Hata, at which I was quizzed on numerous details of British and other railway practices foreign to my hosts, while the geishas interspersed between the men around the table, sat wide-eyed in rapt, though doubtless quite uncomprehending attention.

CHAPTER EIGHTEEN

Modern Japanese steam locomotives

In my journeys round Japan I was fortunate in having many opportunities of seeing steam locomotives, both working and otherwise, and in this chapter I have brought together a synthesis of my notes—taken in the museums at Kyoto and Osaka; on the footplate; at the lineside; and even in the Zoo at Sapporo. Earlier in this book I have referred to the older designs, such as the 'C 51' 'Pacific', and its 3-cylinder successor the 'C 53'; now I am concerned with what could be termed the modern stud. Nevertheless, in using the word modern it must certainly be qualified. By the time this book is published there will be very few steam locomotives in regular operation in Japan—if any. When I made my own tour in 1973 most of the more spectacular sights had gone, such as the working of 'C 62' class 4–6–4s in pairs on the Hakodate–Sapporo expresses. But it was in forcing a way through the central mountain range of Honshu that Japanese steam was seen in its most thrilling aspects, from the viewpoint of an onlooker and photographer. There, many of the freights needed not to be double, but *triple headed*, and fortunately there were expert photographers to record those stirring sights.

The nationalisation of most of the Japanese railway, and the fact that in those islands there is a population nearly double that of Great Britain, have meant that while needing a lot of locomotives there was an opportunity for much standardisation; and in this chapter reference is mainly towards those classes, which at maximum strength mustered a hundred engines, or more. The 2–6–0 became a very popular type in Japan, and the '8620' class introduced in 1914, provided one of the earliest examples of mass standardisation, and eventually totalled 687 engines. They were neat, well proportioned machines, with 18½ in. by 24 in. cylinders, and construction of them continued until 1929. Until no more than a few years ago they were frequently used, in threes, on freight trains climbing the heavy gradients of the mountain passes through the central highlands of northern Honshu. As originally built the '8620' class had shapely cast iron chimneys, and a fine symmetry of line, but more recently aids to efficiency such as smoke-deflecting plates and plainer chimneys, have rather detracted from their appearance.

The 'C 50' class of 1929 was a direct development of the '8620', with a slightly shorter boiler, but higher boiler pressure. The running plate was raised higher, and stepped higher still over the leading coupled wheel and the motion to give easy access. This again was a numerous class, though after 1933, larger engines than a 2–6–0 were needed for main line mixed traffic work. The last Japanese engines of this type were the light branch 'C 56' class introduced in 1935. They had 15¾ in. by 24 in. cylinders, and a total engine wheelbase of 20 ft. 6 in. compared to the 23 ft. 6 in. of class 'C 50'. Their maximum axle load was much lower, and their total engine weight only 37·6, as against 53 tons. This made them a very handy little engine for areas where the axle-loading restrictions were severe. One of them has been preserved among the static exhibits in the steam roundhouse museum at Kyoto, but when I was in Japan a few of them were still working in the Miyazaki area, including one that had been specially cleaned up and burnished to act as pilot to the Royal Train. The basic dimensions of the three classes of 2–6–0s are shown in the following table:

Three varieties of Japanese 2–6–0

Class	Year first built	Cylinders dia. in.	Cylinders stroke in.	Coupled wheel dia. ft. in.	Boiler pressure p.s.i.	Number built
'8620'	1914	18½	24	5 3	180	687
'C 50'	1929	18½	24	5 3	200	158
'C 56'	1935	15¾	24	4 7¼	200	164

Derived from the 2–6–0s were two classes of tank engine of modern design. The 'C 11' is a powerful 2–6–4, introduced in 1932, which has some points of similarity to the 'C 50' 2–6–0, but with smaller cylinders and higher boiler pressure. I saw a number of these engines at work in different parts of Japan, one in particular, at Oshiamambe shed in Hokkaido. One of them also is among the static exhibits in the roundhouse museum near Kyoto. The smaller 'C 12', of the 2–6–2 type, is an exact tank engine equivalent of the 'C 56' tender engine, with the same layout of machinery. The only difference seemed to be that the tank engine did not carry smoke deflecting plates. It is one of this class that is preserved in the Zoo at Sapporo. It is sometimes said that imitation is the sincerest form of flattery, and in seeing these little Japanese tank engines, introduced in the 1930s I could not help thinking how much in general proportions, if not in their outward looks, they resembled the contemporary 2–6–4 and 2–6–2 tank engines of the London Midland and Scottish Railway.

In the 1930s also, Japan nearly, if not quite, became caught up in the streamlining craze, if I may be permitted to call it so. The fever was beginning to run high in Europe and the U.S.A., and the Japanese worked out streamlining proposals for the 'C 53' class of 3-cylinder express passenger 'Pacific' and one locomotive was altered thus, experimentally, in 1935. Although the first results were encouraging, test runs over the Old Tokaido Line between Hara and Suzukawa showed that the fuel economy obtained by the decreased air resistance was not sufficient to offset the higher maintenance charges. These arose from difficulty of access to the moving parts, and to the restriction of air flow over the various bearings—particularly the Gresley conjugated valve gear. In 1936 a second streamlined 'Pacific' was put into service. This was one of the 'C 55' class, with two cylinders only, 20 in. by 26 in. and 5 ft. 9 in. coupled wheels. On this engine, No. C 5521, the cowling extended over the locomotive and tender, but left the connecting and coupling rods open for inspection. The results again were negative, and no other locomotives of the class, or of any other 'J.N.R.' design, were streamlined.

These experiments with streamlining in Japan itself were no doubt influenced by developments on the South Manchurian Railway, that

32. Line drawings of famous Japanese steam locomotives:

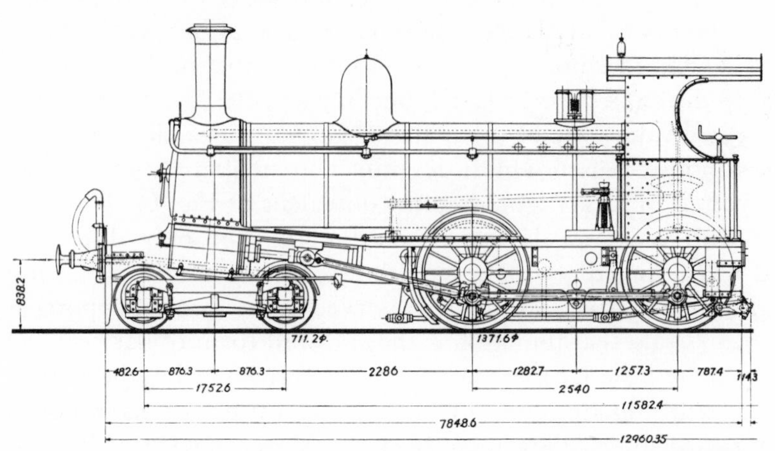

(*a*) The '5500' class 4–4–0 of 1893, built by Beyer, Peacock & Co.

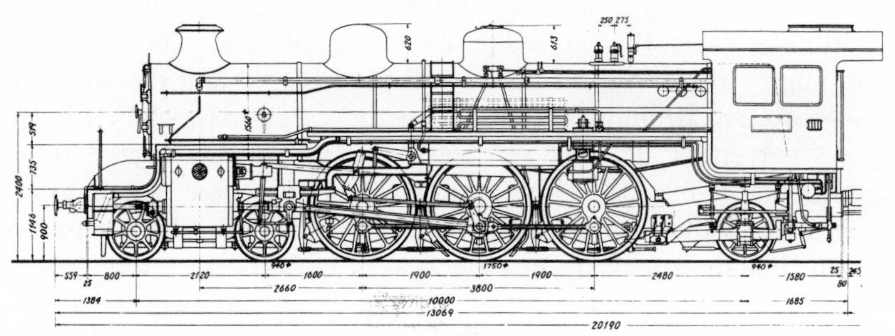

(*b*) The 'C51' class 'Pacific' of 1919

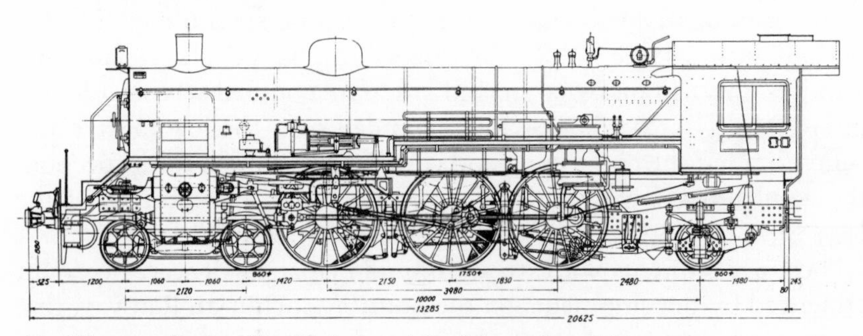

(*c*) The 3-cylinder 'Pacific' class 'C53' introduced in 1928

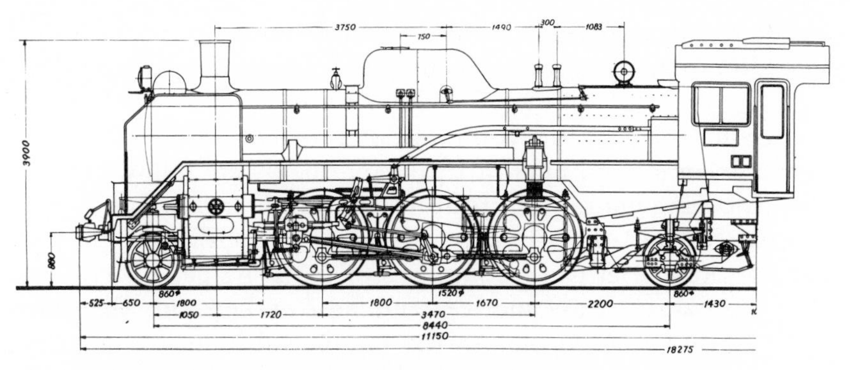

(*d*) The 'C58' class 2–6–2 introduced in 1938

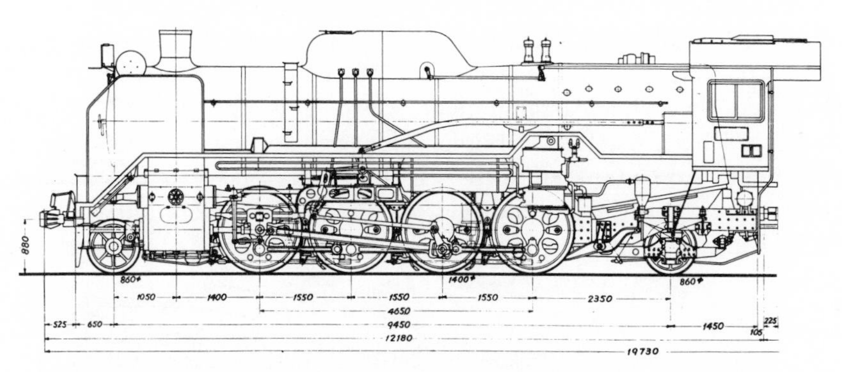

(*e*) The 'D51' class 2–8–2 introduced in 1938

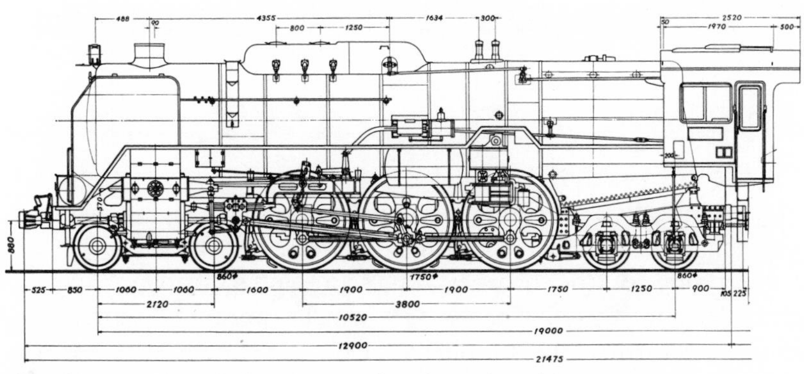

(*f*) The great 'C62' class 4–6–4, first introduced in 1948

came with more settled conditions in Manchukuo, since the ending of the Sino-Japanese war. There, the introduction of the 'Asia Express', running over the 436 miles between Dairen and Hsinking, was accompanied by the commissioning of two large streamlined 'Pacific' locomotives, built in Japan, and they were followed by an order for nine more. The so-called streamlining was not very attractive. It was largely a matter of encasement, rather like the style used on certain German locomotives of the same period. For very many years Japanese locomotives, and those of the South Manchuria Railway, had been uniformly black, but the streamlined engines for the 'Asia Express' were painted sky-blue all over, without any lining, the only relief being red connecting and coupling rods. But this colour scheme was nothing to what transpired when the South Manchuria Railway took delivery, from Japan, of an extraordinary, fully-streamlined 4–4–4 tank engine. When this locomotive was first proposed the wheel arrangement was 4–4–6, the rear end being supported by a 6-wheeled bogie. This was somewhat necessary as the bunker—on a tank engine—was designed to take 19 tons of coal: *nineteen tons*. But the locomotives, of which I believe only two were built, took the road as 4–4–4s, in an exotic livery of mauve and yellow.

Three Japanese 'Pacific' designs

Class	Year first introduced	Cylinders dia. in.	Cylinders stroke in.	Coupled wheel dia. ft. in.	Boiler pressure p.s.i.	Total number built
'C 51'	1919	20¾	26	5 9	185	289
'C 54'	1932	20	26	5 9	200	17
'C 55'	1935	20	26	5 9	200	62

In Japan itself there came two more 'Pacific' classes that were intermediate in their detail features between the classic 'C 51', and the beginning of the final era, as represented among passenger engines by the 'C 57'. The 'C 54', which appeared in 1932, represented a return to the simplicity of the 2-cylinder type, with all modern aids to good maintenance, in high raised running plates, ready accessibility of all working parts, and those doubtful adornments of the age, smoke-deflecting plates and stove pipe chimneys. The 'C 55' in its normal non-streamlined form introduced a feature that was to become standard in later Japanese practice, namely the enclosing of the steam dome and the sand box in a single casing. The comparative dimensions of these two new classes alongside those of the 'C 51' show the general trend of Japanese practice over some fifteen years.

I have referred in Chapter 15 to the numerous and powerful '9600' and 'D 50' classes of heavy freight engine. It is interesting to find that renderings in English and Japanese technical literature always refer to the class names of the various types rather than to their wheel arrangement, and the 'D 50' class are always referred to as 'Mikados', and the various 2–6–0 classes uniformly as 'Moguls'. There was a development of the 'D 50' in 1951. On certain routes the heavy axle loading of the trailing truck was found to be excessive, and a number of these engines were rebuilt with 4-wheeled trailing trucks changing them from the 2–8–2 to the 2–8–4 type, of which the American type name is 'Berkshire'. This was immediately adopted in Japan for the rebuilt engines, which became the 'D 60' class. The total numbers of these three powerful 8-coupled freighters were, '9600' class 775; 'D 50' class 380; 'D 60' class 71.

In 1936 one of the most important locomotive designs ever to be produced in Japan made its first appearance. This was the 'D 51' 2–8–2 freighter, the first of a stud eventually mustering 1116 locomotives. It will be appreciated that after the '9600' class of 2–8–0 all Japanese main line power for maximum duties had trailing trucks so as to permit of uninterrupted space at the rear end for a wide firebox. The grades of coal available required a large grate area, and the salient characteristics of the new engines compared to the 'D 50' were a larger grate, higher boiler pressure and reduced cylinder diameter. The boiler, firebox and smokebox were of similar design to those of the 'C 55' express passenger engine, but there were a number of detail features that were new. One of these was the use of Box-pok cast steel wheel centres, instead of the traditional spoked wheel, and a continuous casing from the chimney, rearwards to the steam dome and sandbox. Later batches of these engines varied in this latter respect. Those built from 1938 onwards had a simple combined casing over the dome and sandbox as on the 'C 55' 'Pacific', while those built during the time Japan was engaged in the Second World War had this combined casing with square instead of rounded ends, to simplify production. The basic dimensions of the 'D 51' are, cylinders 21⅝ in. diameter by 26 in. stroke; coupled wheel diameter 4 ft. 7 in. and boiler pressure 200 lb. per sq. in. The combined total heating surface is 2384 sq. ft. and the grate area 35½ sq. ft., and the total weight of engine only in working order 77·8 tons. It has proved an outstandingly successful design.

Two still bigger freight designs followed, from 1943. The first was also a 'Mikado', class 'D 52'. While the 'D 51' was the standard general purpose freight engine the need was felt for something still more powerful, and the 'D 52' represented an all-round enlargement. The cylinders were the same, and the running gear interchangeable; but the boiler pressure was stepped up to 228 lb. per sq. in., the grate area increased to 41½ sq. ft., and the total heating surface to 2650 sq. ft. The weight in working order of these large engines was 85·6 tons—a substantial proposition on the 3 ft. 6 in. gauge. The overall width was 9 ft. 6½ in. The design was introduced in 1943, and a total of 285 was built. As with the 'D 50' there was a 2–8–4 development, classed 'D 62'. The general dimensions were the same, except for the 4-wheeled trailing truck under the firebox. A total of 20 locomotives was modified in this way. It increased the weight of engine only to 87·9 tons.

From the 'D 51' 2–8–2 came the 'C 57' 'Pacific', in 1946. I found this design a fascinating study, particularly as I was privileged to make several trips on the footplate with engines of this class. It is essentially a light-weight job, with an engine weight in working order of no more than 67·5 tons. But from the tractive effort point of view it is a powerful engine, with cylinders 19¾ in. diameter by 26 in. stroke, coupled wheels of the usual Japanese passenger standard of 5 ft. 9 in., and a boiler pressure of 228 lb. per sq. in. From the viewpoint of mechanical design it is very much a utility product, with everything readily accessible, and easy for maintenance. The engines on which I rode steamed very freely, while being worked hard, at cut-offs up to 40 per cent with full regulator. The Royal

Engine, No. C 57,117 had the short German type of smoke deflecting plates, favoured in Kyushu, though other 'C 57' class that I saw there had the full depth type, having a large access hole just above the cylinder. I noticed a curious, though probably quite incidental detail variation on some of these engines. The Royal C 57,117 had a bogie on which the leading wheels were spoked and the trailing ones of the disc type, whereas on another engine of the same class in the yard at Miyazaki this variation in bogie wheels was reversed, with disc leaders.

At the same time as the 'C 57' class came out the Japanese National Railways introduced a larger variety of the same general type, with cylinders 20½ in. diameter, and a considerably larger boiler. Even so, the total engine weight of 79¾ tons was not heavy for a 'Pacific'. The practice of modifying the design by fitting a 4-wheel trailing truck, as in the development of the 'D 50' 'Mikado' was also followed in the case of the 'C 59', producing the first Japanese engine of the 'Hudson', or 4–6–4 type, and in this case designated 'C 60'. Reverting to the 'C 57' class I had another interesting run on the footplate while in Hokkaido. On a passenger train the speeds were higher, and with a train of 180 tons the engine ran freely on 20 per cent. cut-off at 55 m.p.h. The riding was quite smooth, with no more than a slight action off the motion.

In Hokkaido a number of engines, including No. C 57.38 on which I rode, had additional attachments at the tops of their chimneys which I had not seen elsewhere in Japan. Because of the soft, small coal a spark-arresting device is fitted. The top of the chimney is covered by a fan, which is caused to revolve by the action of the blast. It is covered by a net, while a tray is fitted round the top of the chimney in which cinders and small particles of unburnt coal are collected. From the footplate it was curious to see the fan at the chimney top revolving when the exhaust began to 'puff'. The friendly enginemen with whom I rode from Numanohata gave me their names, and it is a pleasure to include them here: Driver Nobuharu Nozaki, Fireman Saburo Yutani, and the Inspector, who was Vice-Manager of driver training at Muroran depot, Seiichi Morikawa. To conclude this reference to the 'C 57' engines, the basic dimensions together with those of the 'C 59' are tabulated:

Modern Japanese 'Pacifics'

Number Built	Class	Cylinders dia. in.	Cylinders stroke in.	Coupled wheel dia. ft. in.	Boiler pressure p.s.i.	Total heating surface sq. ft.	Grate area sq. ft.	Total engine wt. tons
201	'C 57'	19⅝	26	5 9	228	1820	27.3	67.5
173	'C 59'	20½	26	5 9	228	2610	35.3	79.75

Japanese partiality towards the 'Mogul' type in earlier years had its development, in the modern age that began in the late 1930s, in the production of a 2–6–2 tender engine for light general service. This wheel arrangement made possible the use of the wide firegrate standardised on the larger engines, though the 'C 58' class, as the new engines were designated, proved no counterpart to the introduction of the 2–6–2, or 'Prairie' type as a high-power mixed traffic unit, that on occasions, on the London and North Eastern Railway for example, deputised for an express passenger 'Pacific'. The Japanese 'C 58' had cylinders 18⅞ in. diameter by 24 in. stroke; coupled wheels 5 ft. 0 in. diameter; a total heating surface of only 1515 sq. ft., and a grate area of 23·2 sq. ft. The total weight of engine only was 58·7 tons. The design was a thoroughly successful one, and no fewer than 427 were built between 1938 and 1944.

The development of the 'C 59' class 'Pacific' into the 'C 60' 'Hudson', was the stepping stone towards the most powerful steam passenger locomotives to run in Japan, the 'C 62' class. Between these two came the intermediate 'C 61' class, built to provide a locomotive of 'Hudson' characteristics, with lighter axle loading. The 'C 62' in the stark functionalism of its appearance might have passed as pure American, with its Box-pok wheels, high running plate and everything hung on outside. But in the last days of steam in Japan these engines did a great job, and were as popular with their crews as with the enthusiasts who exposed such vast quantities of film on their comings and goings.

These big engines were capable of a great turn of speed, though in ordinary service this was not required of them. One of the 'C 62' class made the record speed, on the 3 ft. 6 in. gauge, of 80½ m.p.h.

Three Japanese 'Hudsons'

Class	Cylinders dia. in.	Cylinders stroke in.	Coupled wheel dia. ft. in.	Boiler pressure p.s.i.	Total heating surface sq. ft.	Grate area sq. ft.	Total engine wt. tons
'C 60'	20½	26	5 9	228	2610	35·3	82·9
'C 61'	19⅝	26	5 9	214	2390	35·3	79·5
'C 62'	20½	26	5 9	228	2640	41·5	88·8

Before concluding this chapter mention must be made of the giant 'E 10' tank engines, designed specially for work on heavy gradients. These were of the 2–10–4 type, and their 10-coupled wheels were only 4 ft. 1¼ in. diameter. The cylinders were 21⅝ in. diameter by 26 in. stroke, and the boiler pressure was 228 lb. per sq. in. The total weight in working order was 102 tons.

CHAPTER NINETEEN

Electric locomotive development

The general motive power policy of the Japanese National Railways is towards complete electrification. The intense industrialism of much of the country, the density of population, and a low proportion of traffic of all kinds using the motor highways (compared to that of other advanced nations of the world), all favour the gradual increase of the total mileage equipped for electric traction. So far as passenger traffic is concerned the aim is to convey as much as possible in multiple-unit trains, even those making long night journeys, and including coaches equipped as sleepers in their formation. But there is a further important factor that has stimulated the development of the electric locomotive. When the super-high-speed 4 ft. 8½ in. gauge line between Tokyo and Osaka was first conceived it was thought that the traffic would include a certain number of high-priority freight trains, possibly running at night; but for reasons that will be apparent from the concluding chapters of this book, the Shinkansen system is all-passenger, and the heavy and increasing traffic in freight has to be carried on the 3 ft. 6 in. gauge lines.

The volume of freight traffic had always been heaviest on the Old Tokaido and the Sanyo Lines, down the east coast connecting the great industrial centres of Tokyo, Nagoya, Osaka and Hiroshima, and this was naturally the first line to be electrified, and on the 1500 volt d.c. system. Even today, when the a.c. traction network is being steadily increased it is the d.c. locomotives on the Old Tokaido and Sanyo Lines that are still having to cope with the heaviest loading, and new d.c. locomotives were developed in the 1960s. Furthermore, the tempo of business has required higher freight train speeds in Japan, as in all other advanced countries, and the latest d.c.

locomotives introduced in 1966 were designed for maximum speeds up to 75 m.p.h. with freight trains on the 3 ft. 6 in. gauge.

The decision to adopt high voltage a.c. traction at commercial frequency, as in France and Great Britain, was not without difficulties of its own, quite apart from the problems of changeover at junction points with the 1500 volt d.c. system, because in Japan the commercial frequency of supply is not the same throughout the country. In some zones it is 50 cycles per second, and in others 60, and this involved further complication where through-running both of multiple-unit passenger trains and electric locomotives is concerned. The development of electric locomotive design has also had to be geared to the exceptional physical conditions existing on some of the mountain routes. While the great power that can be built into these locomotives, and the facility of being able to couple two or more in multiple for handling by a single crew, offers immense advantages over double-heading or triple heading with steam—however exciting the latter may have been to behold by enthusiasts and photographers!—it is not just a case of piling on the power and turning a few switches to apply it.

The working of electric locomotives on mountain gradients involves certain factors in design requiring the highest electrical engineering skill. There is the difficulty of wheel-slip, when rail conditions are bad; and while ample power can be provided to enable heavy trains to be hauled up the gradients, there is the equally vital matter of brake power to control them descending the opposite slopes. Then again the northern districts of Honshu and the whole island of Hokkaido have very heavy snowfalls in winter. So far electrification has not spread very far in Hokkaido, but the mountain routes of Honshu where the gradients are steepest are just the places where the snow conditions can be most trying, and the a.c. locomotives designed for working on these routes have various protective devices, such as housing all the 20,000 volt equipment inside in the machine room; fitting snow-proof covers over the electrical equipment; and using an internal circulation system for the cooling air. I should add that the actual traction motors are of the d.c. series type, supplied through a.c. to d.c. conversion equipment, according to circumstances.

During my visit to Japan I had two opportunities of studying electric locomotive practice; at the depot of the Old Tokaido Line in Tokyo, and at Moji in Kyushu. The conditions at each were somewhat different. In Tokyo the locomotives were entirely d.c. and the ones that I saw, and was able to climb aboard, were all of the B–B–B wheel arrangement, having three 2-axle bogies, with all axles powered. The latest class, for ordinary freight working was the 'EF 65', introduced in 1964 and of which more than 200 were then in service. These locomotives, with an all-up weight of 96 tons, have one-hour power rating of 3400 horsepower. A limited number of locomotives of the same electrical design are fitted with train heating apparatus to enable them to work passenger trains; these are classified 'EF 64'. While at the depot in Tokyo I saw some of the older 'EF 58' electric locomotives—the number following the 'EF' signifying the year of introduction—and also one of the 'double' 'EH 10' class. These large and powerful units were first introduced in 1954, when it became necessary to increase the speed of freight trains on the electrified sections of the Old Tokaido Line. Their dimensions and performance characteristics are interesting in view of what has been achieved since. The one-hour horsepower rating is 3350, at a speed of 30 m.p.h., and their maximum speed is 51½ m.p.h. Yet to achieve this, the 'double' assembly was needed, with the B–B+B–B wheel arrangement, and a weight of 123 tons.

The greatest interest, however, centres round the high speed 'EF 66' class. In the 'EF 60', which was the earlier version of the 'EF 64' and 'EF 65', the maximum speed was 60 m.p.h. This was increased to 70 m.p.h. in the latter two classes, but in the 'EF 66', which followed a prototype designated 'EF 90', not only was the maximum permissible speed increased to 75 m.p.h. but the one-hour horsepower rating was stepped up from 3400 to no less than 5200, for an increase in overall weight only from 96 to 100·8 tons. These locomotives are designed for use on lines with no more than moderate gradients, and the traction characteristics are arranged to provide a large power output at high speed. These provide for a sustained speed of 60 m.p.h. on level track, with a load of 1200 tons, and a speed of 43 m.p.h. up a gradient of 1 in 100 with the same load. The wheel arrangement is the same as that of the 'EF 65' class, and in view of the high power developed in relation to the weight careful attention has been given to the matter of weight-transfer, to counteract any likelihood of slipping. When taking up the load or climbing a gradient, some transfer of weight automatically takes place between the various axles, as it does in a steam locomotive in comparable conditions. On the 'EF 66' class, weight transfer between the axles is compensated for automatically by electrically lessening the torque exerted on the more lightly loaded axles, and transferring it to those more heavily loaded.

At Moji, as mentioned in an earlier chapter, one has the problem of change in traction system, with trains working through the Kanmon Tunnel from Kyushu to the 1500 volt d.c. electrified lines at Shimonoseki. When I visited the shed in 1973 there were 85 electric locomotives, 15 diesels, and 36 steam locomotives attached, and of the electrics 22 were of the dual voltage type. They could be readily distinguished by having body casings in stainless steel, ribbed like a Budd passenger car in North America. They were designed to work on the 1500 volt d.c. system, and the 20,000 volts a.c. at 60 cycles per second of Kyushu. For working only on the a.c. lines Moji depot had four types of main line electric locomotives designated 'ED 72', '73', '75' and '76'. All except the 'ED 76' are of the B–B–B wheel arrangement, with a one-hour horsepower rating of 2550, and a weight in working order of 65 to 67 tons. The electrical equipment, and the method of converting the a.c. current from the line into the d.c. required by the traction motors, varies in the different classes but generally they are similar from the viewpoint of utilisation. It should be explained that the retention of d.c. traction motors on a locomotive taking a.c. from the overhead line is almost worldwide practice, because of the far greater simplicity of control of d.c. motors and the suitability of their operating characteristics to railway traction.

The sixth class of electric locomotive stationed at Moji at the time of my visit, the 'ED 76', has a quite distinctive wheel arrangement, and was the starting point of a new development in electrical controls. As the electrified network spread there were routes converted on which the axle loading was less than on the principal main lines, and the 'ED 76' was the first design in which the traditional B–B–B wheel arrangement was replaced by two powered bogies, with a non-driving bogie in the centre. This was unique at the time in being equipped with air springs so that the axle load could be changed depending upon the loading permitted on the track and this arrangement was also applied to the later 'ED 78' class locomotive. In the case of the 'ED 76' the overall weight was heavier than that of the 'ED 75', 87 as against 67 tons, but the maximum axle load could be reduced to 15 instead of 16¾ if necessary. The 'ED 76' was one of the last class of Japanese a.c. electric locomotives to have the older form of power control of the traction motors; a stepping switch which cut out resistances sequentially, as the speed rose. A developing modern practice is to use an electronic regulating device called a thyristor, which has the advantage of providing a smooth adjustment of control, instead of in a series of steps. This lessons the chance of wheel slip.

An example of exceptional grading conditions in which the modern a.c. electric locomotives of Japan are used is that of the Fukubei Line, branching off the main line from Tokyo to Aoimori at Fukushima, amid the mountains of the Bandai-Asahi National Park, where there is a gradient of 1 in 30, extending for about 25 miles. Here the trains are powered by one 'ED 78' and one 'EF 71', coupled in multiple for control by one crew. The 'ED 78' has the non-driving air spung central bogie, whereas the 'EF 71' is a B–B–B. The combined one hour horsepower rating is 6200, with a total locomotive weight of 177 tons. Both classes have thyristor control, but equally important are the braking arrangements. The Japanese railways use the automatic air brake in a form derived from the Westinghouse, and for control of these heavy freight trains on the long descents, without the technical trouble of heated brake blocks and excessive wear, and the technical risk of the phenomenon known as 'brake fade', the locomotives of the 'ED 78' and 'EF 71' classes are equipped with regenerative braking. By this the traction motor action is reversed; they act as generators, and feed current back into the overhead line. It is the most effective brake yet devised.

There are certain main lines in Japan on which all three systems of traction are encountered. One of these is the line up the west coast from Maibara to Aoimori in the far north. This includes, in succession, a.c. at 60 cycles, then d.c., and eventually a.c. at 50 cycles;

and to meet such conditions J.N.R. have developed the 'EF 81' locomotive that can operate on all three. It is now considered that the 'ED 78', the 'EF 71' and the 'EF 81' are the standard a.c. locomotives for future production, though the technical development in certain directions is so rapid that one cannot say for how long so called standards will last, before being superseded by greater improvement. It is unlikely however that any development in electric locomotives for passenger service will take place, beyond the provision for train heating if necessary, on the 'EF 81' class. The general policy so far as passenger services are concerned is to provide fast and convenient connections with the Shinkansen network with the multiple-unit Limited Express Trains. The principal dimensions and performance data of the three types of locomotive being standardised for the present are shown below:

Recent Japanese electric locomotives

Class Wheel arrangement Traction system	'ED 78' B-2-B a.c. 50 cycles	'EF 71' B-B-B a.c. 50 cycles	'EF 81' B-B-B Triple current
One hour horsepower rating	2550	3620	3400*
at speed—m.p.h.	30½	28½	26
Maximum speed—m.p.h.	62	62	71
Weight—tons	81·5	96·0	100·8

* Working d.c.; 3189 horsepower working a.c.

CHAPTER TWENTY

Shinkansen—the mighty project

The areas lying along the Tokaido Line, from Tokyo to Osaka are the economic and cultural centres of the Japanese nation. About 40 per cent. of the total population and 70 per cent. of the industrial output are concentrated in this belt of country lying between the central mountain range and the sea. In the late 1930s, the 3 ft. 6 in. gauge Old Tokaido Line was carrying 25 per cent. of the total passenger and freight traffic of the Japanese National Railways, although its route mileage represented only 3 per cent. of the total network. The problem to be faced was, for how long could this old line stand the ever increasing traffic. Many improvements were made to increase the line capacity, until there were 120 passenger and 70 freight trains scheduled in each direction daily; but saturation point was very near. The very nature of the old line precluded anything in the way of substantial acceleration. In the late 1930s plans were discussed for an entirely new high speed line that would permit running between Tokyo and Osaka in 4½ hours, and between Tokyo and Shimonoseki in 9 hours. A project lasting 15 years was envisaged, from 1940 to 1954, and work had already begun when it had to be suspended because of the war.

The distance between Tokyo and Osaka by the Old Tokaido Line was more than 340 miles, so that a timing of 4½ hours was going to involve immeasurably faster running than anything previously attempted in Japan, an *average* of 75 m.p.h. Such a service target would have been impossible to achieve by a mere widening or quadrupling of the existing 3 ft. 6 in. gauge line, and so the momentous decision was taken to build the new line to the standard 4 ft. 8½ in. gauge, and construct it with an alignment that would permit of what was then considered exceptionally high speed running from end to end. No physical obstructions such as mountains, river valleys, or even cities lying on the route could be allowed to deflect the direct course of the line, and as the project began to take shape once again, after the end of the Second World War, the standard of passenger train speed on the new line was set at 125 m.p.h. to make possible an overall time between Tokyo and Osaka not of $4\frac{1}{2}$, but the even four hours. It is interesting to recall briefly the chronology of events up to the time when authorisation of the line was given by the Transportation Minister of the Japanese Government:

May 1956	Investigation Committee for enhancement of traffic on the Tokaido Line set up by J.N.R.
August 1957	Cabinet decision to set up J.N.R. trunk line investigating committee in the Ministry of Transportation.
April 1958	Construction standards committee set up by J.N.R.
July 1958	J.N.R. trunk line investigating committee reports to Ministry emphasizing need for new line.
August 1958	Aerial survey of route started.
March 1959	Appropriation for new line made in 1959 National budget.
April 13, 1959	Construction of new line approved.

No more than a week later on April 20, the ceremony called variously across the world as 'turning the first sod', 'cutting the first turf', or, in Japan 'ground breaking', was performed at the site of the east portal of the new Tanna Tunnel, destined to be the longest on the new route. Whereas the pre-war project was estimated to be spread over fifteen years, construction of the New Tokaido Line was pushed forward with such vigour that commercial service began on October 1, 1964. In that year the Olympic Games had been held in Tokyo, and in Bangkok I met some of those who had been present at and participated in the Games, and who had included rides on the new railway during their stay in Japan. Their impressions, mostly of a non-technical kind, were interesting to hear.

The boldness of the engineering work fully matched the epoch-marking nature of the entire conception. The contrast between this and the way the railway system of Japan was inaugurated in 1872 could not have been more profound. Nothing was allowed to stand in the way of a continuous high speed route. By elimination of the twists and turns of the Old Tokaido Line the distance from Tokyo to Osaka was reduced from 345 to 322 miles, and in this mileage only ten intermediate stations were provided. The original plan was to have a number of 'super' express trains stopping only at Nagoya and Kyoto, and making the run in the level four hours, and a number of Limited Express trains which would call at all ten intermediate stations, and make the overall journey in five hours. Even this longer time involved an average speed from end to end of 65 m.p.h. To enable this pattern of service to be set up all the intermediate stations were equipped with four tracks so that a 'super' express could pass ahead of a 'limited', while the latter was standing at a platform. The former became known as the 'Hikari', or 'lightning' trains, and the latter the 'Kodama', or the 'echo'. Although the new line was to be entirely separate and of a different gauge, the connecting pattern of train service with the old line made it necessary to locate the principal intermediate stations in close proximity to the existing ones—and this leads me on to the constructional features of the new railway.

To permit of uninterrupted high speed the line was laid out so that no curve had a radius of less than 2700 yards—in British railway track terminology, 123 chains. The only exceptions were within the city area of Tokyo, and in the vicinity of the major stations where speed would in any case be much reduced. An important and indeed vital feature was the elimination of all level crossings, and although much of the line runs through level districts it is carried for long distances on embankments 18 to 20 ft. in height, to carry it clear of intersecting highways. The embankments themselves have concrete retaining walls at the foot of the side slopes. In view of the anticipated intense utilisation of the line, very great care was taken in forming the embankments to obtain an adequate degree of compactness of the built-up earth formation. Stringent specifications were laid down to guard against the common weakness of mud-pumping at the surface, and unequal settlement between the embankment itself and the adjoining structures. The success with which this has been done was emphasised by the smoothness of the riding of the 'Hikari' trains in which I travelled, nine years after the inauguration of the service.

The areas served by the new line are the most highly developed in Japan, and while intermediately the line could be carried clear of urban and industrial conurbations, it had to pass through city areas at many points and on alignments permitting maximum speed running. These requirements were met by constructing the line on elevated track structures, consisting of continuous concrete rigid frames, with the rail level about 21 ft. above ground. These structures not only required a much narrower right-of-way for the line than would have been needed with embankments, but relatively narrow roads can pass beneath them, and the space under the track could be used for shops or other purposes. Recently however there has been a growing awareness and dissatisfaction among the public over the noise of passing trains on these elevated structures, and solid parapet walls instead of open railings have been added in certain areas.

There are 66 tunnels on the new line between Tokyo and Osaka and 12 of these are more than 1¼ miles long. All these have been built to a standard cross section, accommodating two tracks. Consideration had to be given to the aerodynamic effects of two trains passing in a tunnel, both travelling at maximum speed, and instead of the traditional spacing of 6 ft. between the nearest rails of opposing tracks (in Great Britain, the so-called 'six-footway'), in the tunnels of the New Tokaido Line the spacing was set at 9 ft. This track spacing has been made standard throughout the new system. The longest tunnel is the New Tanna, which runs parallel to and 50 yards apart from the old Tanna Tunnel. History was made for the second time at this location, because it was by opening the old Tanna Tunnel in 1925 that the circuitous and heavily graded original route of the Old Tokaido Line, via Gotemba, was avoided, and 1500 volt d.c. traction inaugurated through the then new tunnel. The new tunnel is only a few yards short of five miles long; whereas the original Tanna Tunnel took 16 years to build the new one was bored through in no more than three years.

There are some very long bridges on the new line, mostly crossing estuaries, and adjoining marsh land. The usual form of construction is a continuous Warren truss, made up of standard length spans, and erected cantilever fashion. The foundation supporting the truss portion varies according to the nature of the ground, or the river bed. In some cases there are reinforced concrete piers supported on pneumatic caissons, while in others the tubular supports are continued upwards to the underside of the girders. Some of these bridges are in localities of great natural beauty and care has been taken not to introduce any jarring note, seeing that high speed trains would be crossing the bridges at very frequent intervals throughout the day. It is perhaps significant that the longest bridge on the new line (and the longest in all Japan) is the Fujigawa, seven-eighths of a mile long, and having as its majestic background the sacred Mount Fuji.

The track is of massive construction. Except in certain locations to be mentioned later, the sleepers are of pre-stressed concrete with a depth of ballast 12 in. below the bottom surface of the sleeper. Crushed stones of definitely specified sizes are used, and compacting of the shoulder on either side is done by a special machine designed for the purpose. In certain tunnels and on concrete bridges what is termed 'slab-track' is used. In such locations there is no ballast at all, and the rail fastenings are attached to wooden blocks set in the concrete bed. The surface of these blocks is accurately finished to the specified height by a sleeper planing machine of the same type as used on certain steel girder bridges where wooden sleepers have to be used. On plain line, with normal ballasted track, a good 'top' is maintained by conventional track servicing machinery; but where the rail fastenings are made to wood, either transverse sleepers or blocks in ballast-less track, a pair of guide rails are laid down accurately at the specified height to carry the sleeper planing machine, which then trims all the sleepers to an equal and precise height suitable for carrying traffic at 125 m.p.h.

The only points and crossings are at the entrances and exits from the platform lines at intermediate stations, which non-stop trains have to negotiate at full speed. The turnouts are all equipped with what is known in Great Britain as swing-nosed crossings. The conventional form of switch layout used all over the world includes a short gap just before reaching the nose of the crossing. This is of no consequence where speeds are low, and the angle of the crossing is fairly acute; but where the turnout has to be negotiated at higher speeds and the angle of the crossing is slight, the gap between the nose and the wing rail is closed by making the nose movable, according to the setting of the points. This makes for very smooth running, when a train is turning into one of the platform tracks, at the maximum allowable speed for such movements of 44 m.p.h.

The system of electric traction chosen was alternating current, 25,000 volts single phase at commercial frequency, as was then being adopted in France and Great Britain for main line electrification schemes. One of the factors that led to this decision was the greatly increased amount of electrical power needed for the high speed trains. When the Shinkansen, or 'new lines' were at an advanced stage of planning the 'Hikari' super express trains were proposed to be of 12-car formation, and running at a maximum speed of 125 m.p.h. Now one of the Limited Express Trains on the Old Tokaido Line running at maximum speed, and consisting of 11 cars took 3000 kilowatts, or 4000 horsepower from the 1500 volt d.c. line. A 12-car 'Hikari' on the New Tokaido Line at 125 m.p.h. was estimated to take nearly *three times* as much power. It was considered, quite apart from any other considerations, that such a requirement *per train* could not economically be met by the 1500 volt d.c. system. A very lavish provision of a.c. electric power was made—far greater than enough to supply the needs of the train service as originally contemplated. This was fortunate beyond measure, for the public response to the new line demanded a rapid increase in the facilities originally provided.

The overhead contact line equipment was the subject of intensive preliminary research. At the outset it was realised that the ordinary method of suspending the overhead wire would not be satisfactory at speeds of 125 m.p.h., and more, because the pantograph would frequently break contact with the overhead line. As in Great Britain, when design work on the electrified line from Euston to the North was in progress, various types of suspension were tested. The Japanese engineers adopted the same form of suspension as used on the London Midland Region of British Railways, known as the 'compound catenary', though of course once the form of the suspension was decided in Japan ample clearance could be provided for it everywhere, as the whole line was new. (On the line from Euston to the North it was being applied to a railway built by Robert Stephenson in 1838, and special arrangements had to be made when passing under many over-bridges.) On the New Tokaido Line, from observation on the footplate of a 'Hikari' super-express train I can say that the overhead line suspension is remarkably accurate. When we met other trains in tunnel sections I could see that sparking from the contact line was negligible.

So, from the route, the bridges, the tunnels, the permanent way, and the overhead contact line we come to the trains themselves. There was no question of using locomotives. All trains are of the multiple-unit railcar type, and to ensure perfectly smooth running every axle is powered. The high tension a.c. current collected by the pantographs from the overhead line is stepped down, by main transformers, and then converted into direct current for the traction motors. The output of each motor at continuous rating is 250 horsepower, so that each car has a capacity of 1000 horsepower. When one recalls that the number of British steam locomotives called upon to develop 1000 horsepower continuously at the drawbar was very few, the power rating of these New Tokaido Line trains, with 1000 horsepower *for each car*, is seen to be colossal. The maximum speed originally provided for was 155 m.p.h., though this is not yet attained in regular service.

Both ends of each train are streamlined, to reduce air resistance. The nose is ball-shaped, and made of acrylic plastic, and at night it glimmers with light from the two headlights. Apart from the two ends, the coaches are close coupled, and give the impression of a continuous articulated unit. The original 12-car trains included first and second class accommodation with buffet cars, and had a total seating for 987 passengers. The first class cars had seats for four abreast, two each side of a centre aisle, while the 'seconds' had three seats on one side of the centre, and two on the other. They are fully air-conditioned, and are protected against the effect of a sudden rise of external air pressure, due to two trains passing while travelling at maximum speed.

In June 1962 test runs were commenced on a special section of the line, and in March of the following year the prototype train ran successfully at 159 m.p.h., but much had yet to be done before commercial service could be inaugurated. In July 1963 for nearly a fortnight, what were called 'human engineering' tests were carried out for the crew of a high speed train. In July 1964 track laying was completed over the entire route, and in August the first through test runs were made between Tokyo and Osaka; and when commercial service was started in October the schedule time for the 'Hikari' trains was the level four hours. Just over a year later, with full experience of operating on the line, both with the 'Hikari' and the 'Kodama' trains, the journey times were dramatically cut, to 3 hr. 10 min. for the 'Hikari' stopping only at Nagoya and Kyoto, and 4 hr. for the 'Kodama' trains. The 'Hikari' then had a sensational average, including the two stops, of 100 m.p.h. throughout. At that time the maximum service speed was 125 m.p.h.

When the line was first projected, it was intended that certain high speed freight trains might be run during the night hours; but as matters have eventuated, the popularity of the new service has been such that a great increase in density of traffic has been made, and the night hours are needed to be completely clear of trains to enable essential surveillance and maintenance to be carried out. When I was in Japan in 1973 work was well advanced on the southward extension from Okayama to Shimonoseki and Hakata, and when this is completed certain night passenger trains will be operated. Even by 1966 it had been decided that all trains would be made up to 16 cars, with seating accommodation for nearly 1400 passengers each. This 'strengthening' had been applied to all the 'Hikari' trains by 1973, though at that time some of the 'Kodama' were still made up to only 12 cars.

In Chapter Twelve of this book, I referred to my participation in the meeting of the Railway Sub-Committee of E.C.A.F.E. at Bangkok, in the autumn of 1964. Commercial service on the New Tokaido Line had only just begun, but I had an opportunity of talking to the Japanese delegates and studying the literature they had brought. I am afraid I did so, with feelings bordering a little upon disbelief, even though the full high speed service had not then commenced. But it was real enough, and its phenomenal success has been the catalyst towards super-high-speed railway projects in other countries. In 1973 I was to see for myself how it worked out in practice.

CHAPTER TWENTY ONE

Shinkansen—fulfilment and extension

For many years those of us who are professionally connected with signalling have discussed the possibilities of really long-range control: operating the traffic around Edinburgh, for example, from a panel in London. For an equal time it has generally been agreed that technically there were no longer any obstacles to such a procedure: the difficulties lay in the realms of railway operating circumstances and finance. But when I had the privilege of seeing the Shinkansen General Control Centre in Tokyo I quickly realised that there was our long-contemplated conception in actuality—an entire railway, and a very busy and fast running one at that, controlled technically and operationally from a single room. And its furthest extent was then well over 300 miles away. Everything from train running and the feeding of electrical power to the overhead line, to the scrutiny of track maintenance, is continuously monitored and supervised by senior officials working in close coordination with each other, in the same room.

It was in the late 1920s that the term Centralised Traffic Control—abbreviated to CTC—came into railway parlance, denoting an interesting and important development in American operating practice. Then the great majority of the transcontinental routes were not only single tracked, but worked on the telegraphic train order system. There were no signals in the ordinary sense. A driver's authority to proceed was a piece of paper with written instructions handed to him personally. It was slow and cumbersome in operation, while there was no overall 'picture' of train movements by which priorities for the different classes of train could be regulated to the best advantage. The installation of colour light signals controlled

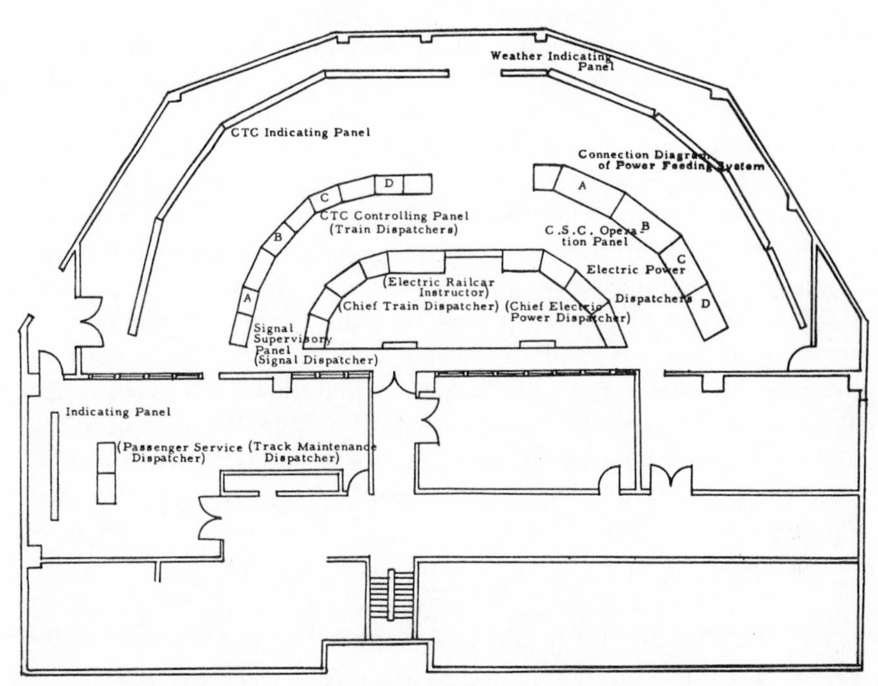

33. Layout of Central Control of Shinkansen Line at Tokyo

from a central divisional point worked like a charm, but it is important to recall that for more than twenty years after its first introduction, CTC was applied almost entirely to sparsely used, if vital, lengths of single-line railway where the total number of trains per day in each direction could be counted on the fingers of one hand. CTC on the Shinkansen system is certainly centralised traffic control, but on a fast moving line on which trains are following each other at less than 15 minute intervals on most sections, and travelling at 130 m.p.h.

The layout of the General Control Centre at Tokyo is shown on the accompanying diagram. It is the only place in the world that I know where the running of an entire railway can be watched, and on the CTC indicating panel which has five facets, the position of every train on the line is shown. These five facets have corresponding control desks at which the train dispatchers sit. When all is working punctually the operation is automatic, and the task of the dispatchers is that of constant scrutiny. At intermediate stations at which the 'Kodama' Limited Express Trains have to stop the route into the platform track is set automatically. Each train has its distinctive number, which is not only displayed on the indicating panel in the control centre as the train progresses, but is used in the automatic train control system for setting the route at the entrance to stations. If, however, a train is running late—a very rare occurrence on the Shinkansen system—the dispatcher has the facility of intervening, operating points at any intermediate station, and of talking to train crews on the radio telephone. When I visited the Control Centre the fifth facet and its associated dispatcher's desk, had just been added to cover the first extension of the line, southwards from Osaka to Okayama. The four desks on the original line cover the following stations:

A—Tokyo, Shin-Yokohama and Odawara.
B—Atami, Mishima, Shiznoka and Hamamatsu.
C—Toyahashi, Nagoya and Gifu-Hashima.
D—Maibara, Kyoto and Shin-Osaka.

The prefix 'shin' means new, and applied thus to Yokohama and Osaka denotes the new stations on the high-speed line, as distinct from the adjoining stations on the Old Tokaido Line.

I have many times watched trains running on the illuminated diagrams of busy signal boxes, and in both France and Great Britain have been able to make close estimates of the speed at which individual trains were travelling from observing the indication lights. At Tokyo, in doing likewise, and walking along the length of the panel, it was fascinating to realise the trains whose numbers were displayed were all sweeping along at 130 m.p.h. There was however one very important difference from any other panel I had previously seen: there were no lights to indicate the aspects showing in the signals along the line—for the simple reason that there are no signals at all! At first sight this may seem fantastic on a railway operating at such speeds and such density of traffic, but the line is equipped with a highly sophisticated system of automatic train control, and the only signals a driver sees are those on the dashboard of his own driving

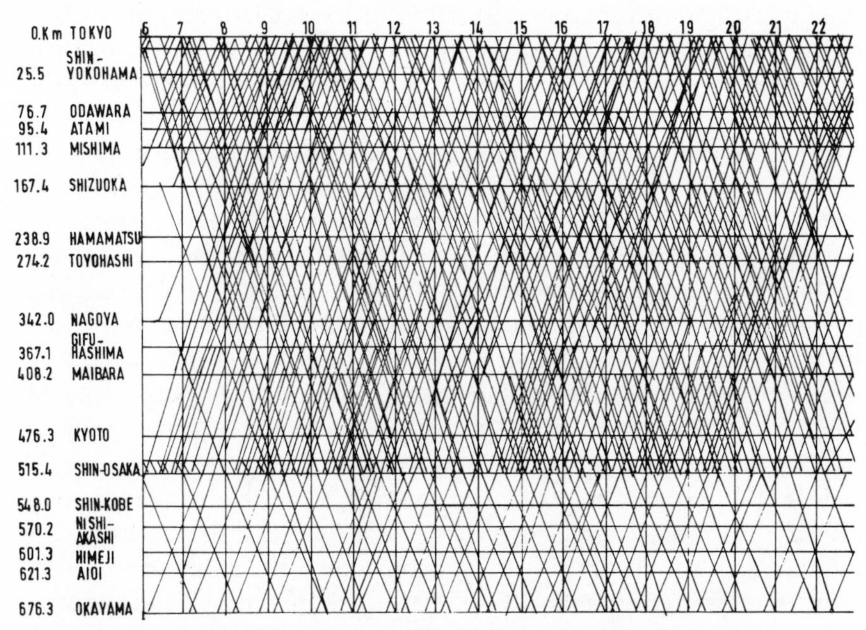

34. Timetable diagram of Shinkansen service between Tokyo and Okayama, 06.00–23.00 hours

cab on the train. This feature will be described more fully when I come to an actual run out on the line.

The second important part of the centralised control at Tokyo is that of the electric power supply. Over the length of the line, and of the Sanyo extension to Okayama, the public utility supply companies have distribution systems at voltages varying from 70,000 to 275,000 volts 3-phase a.c. and these supplies are transformed to single phase a.c. at 25,000 volts at the railway substations. These are located at 25 places between Tokyo and Osaka, on an average about 12–14 miles apart, because of the enormous demand for electrical power to operate the trains. The position of the power feeding connection diagram is shown on the layout of the control room on page 207. On that diagram the different power transmission supplies, the substations, the sectioning posts and the feeding system are shown in relation to the stations, while at the left hand end of the diagram there is a weather indication panel, especially to show the position of thunder storms or typhoons. For all the different activities the men in charge of the panels are known as 'dispatchers', and so far as the power feeding system is concerned the dispatcher with the aid of the connection diagram can at any minute visualise the situation over the entire Shinkansen, making himself acquainted with any significant changes in the weather and guaranteeing the safe operation of the electrical equipment. I may add that in the time I was in Japan the weather was generally good, apart from the occasional rainy day such as one would experience at home; so that no exceptional precautions had to be taken in running the Shinkansen, any more than any other part of J.N.R.

Before the extensive and illuminating tour of the General Control Centre was finished, I realised I was being given a most comprehensive survey of a complete railway system without seeing a single train! Having been concerned in the design of similar instruments for railways in remote parts of Africa and Australia, I was intensely interested in the diagram recorder, on which the running of every train is registered graphically. This feature of remote indication is initiated by the passage of trains over certain track circuits at the entrance to and exit from the stations, and it was absorbing to see the instant registering, on the chart of the recorder, of the movements of trains more than 300 miles away. But in contrast to the railways for which I did design work in earlier days, the Shinkansen diagram recorders were ticking away continuously.

On the following day we went out to the Tokyo car depot of Shinkansen, and I was able to see the trains and their equipment. As a Westinghouse man I was naturally very interested in the brakes, because when trains are following each other at such short intervals at 130 m.p.h. it is a prime necessity to be able to stop, when needed! At speeds exceeding 35 m.p.h. the braking is electro-dynamic, but as with the electro-pneumatic brake used on the London Underground railways and elsewhere, the trains are also equipped with the ordinary automatic air brake, which can be used over the entire speed range. There is no brake rigging as such, because the disc brake system is used, acting clasp-wise on both inside and outside discs on the rolled 'monobloc' wheels. The action of braking naturally polishes the discs, which have a striking appearance when seen from below in an inspection pit. Great care had to be taken in the design of the cars to reduce noise, since every axle in the train is powered. The air-conditioning had to be that of an aircraft rather than that of an ordinary train, and the interior of the cars made proof against the slightest surges of air pressure when two trains pass at full speed.

After my visits to the General Control Centre in Tokyo, and to the car sheds, the next thing was a trip on the line, as passenger. It was arranged for me to travel on 'Hikari' No. 89 leaving Tokyo at 15.30 hours, but one of my Japanese friends took me to the station some time before departure, so that I could see the arrangement for booking and seating passengers. Everyone has a numbered and reserved seat on Shinkansen. If no previous booking has been made, passengers have to queue up and are issued with tickets for the first train available. If there are no seats on the next departure there is a 'Hikari' every quarter of an hour from 6 a.m. till 9 p.m. so one has not long to wait. We went up to the platform about 40 minutes before departure time of my own train, and it was enthralling to watch the precise organisation that prevailed. The 15.00 hours 'Hikari' was at the platform from which we were booked to depart, but no passengers had so far been allowed to enter. The cleaners were still in possession. It was soon evident to me, however, that passenger movement had been streamlined as thoroughly as the trains themselves. The position of the doors of each car is marked on the platform, with numbers to correspond with the number on each passenger's ticket, and everyone was neatly queued up ready at the correct entrance place. It is a great boon to European travellers that despite their otherwise bewildering caligraphy the Japanese use our numerals.

The cleaners came out about 5 minutes before departure time, the doors were opened and everybody stepped smartly inside to continuous admonishings from the public address system telling all to hurry, and non-passengers seeing their friends off not to get left inside. The train left dead on time, with hardly a seat to spare, nearly 1400 passengers away on their dash to Osaka. Five minutes later, at the same platform, another one arrived, and promptly disgorged over 1000 passengers. It was all 'slick' and orderly: no rush, no pushing, just swift purposeful mass movement. In less than 5 minutes everyone was out, and an army of cleaners moved in. This was my train, and the cleaners had just a quarter of an hour to make it completely spick and span. While I was waiting, at the appointed place on the platform, I watched proceedings with the 'Hikari' scheduled to leave 15 minutes ahead of us. Its cleaners were not out until 15.12 hours, but in *three minutes* the 1200 or 1300 waiting people were in, and the train away on time. But before we left there was a 'Kodama' booked out at 15.25 from the platform where the 15.15 had just left. A 16-coach train of empty stock came in at 15.20, was loaded in 5 minutes and was away on time, just as the doors of our train were opening for us, and, needless to add now I suppose, we also left on time to cover the 213½ miles to Nagoya, our first stop, at an *average* speed of 106·7 m.p.h.! The tempo of things on the platform at Tokyo during the three-quarters of an hour while I was watching had been more like a London Underground station in the rush hour than the dispatching of 100 m.p.h. long-distance expresses. The calm and smoothness of the train once we were under way was something of an anticlimax.

With the line carried mostly on viaducts and away from immediate structures, one did not gain the impression of very fast running. It was extremely quiet in the coaches, and it was only when one came to compare time with distance that realisation came as to how fast we really were going. We were checked down to 40 m.p.h. for permanent way maintenance work between Shin-Yokohama and Odawara, and our time of 33¾ minutes for the 47·9 miles from Tokyo to the latter station was 1¾ minutes more than schedule; but the remaining 164·6 miles on to our first stop at Nagoya took only 86½ minutes, an average speed of 118 m.p.h. and we arrived 2 minutes early. Over the 47 miles from Shiznoka to Hamamatsu our 'flying' average was 128·3 m.p.h. After Atami we passed within sight of the beautiful Mount Fuji, but the day was warm and hazy and the sacred peak was not seen to the best advantage. It was however one of the few stretches on which one could get a broad view of the scenery. For the most part we were dashing in and out of tunnels, across busy industrial areas on viaducts, or running across fairly flat country. The central mountain range was no more than vaguely seen. I continued in this train to Kyoto, where I was spending a few days, and it only remains to add that we covered the 84 miles from Nagoya in 48¾ minutes, at an average speed of 103·7 m.p.h. start-to-stop. Inclusive of the stop at Nagoya we took only 171½ minutes to cover the 297½ miles from Tokyo to Kyoto—the average of 104·2 m.p.h. required from every 'Hikari', at 15 minute intervals throughout the day, in both directions of runnning. In speed this was equivalent to going from Euston to Carlisle in less than three hours.

A few days later I continued to what was then the furthest extent of the Shinkansen network, and also had the privilege of riding in the driver's cab. This section of 100½ miles, from Shin-Osaka to Okayama had been opened in March 1972, but although having a designed maximum speed of 160 m.p.h. against 130 m.p.h., on the New Tokaido section the actual working speed had not yet been increased to the higher figure. The train by which I travelled south from Kyoto was 'Hikari' as far as Shin-Osaka, and thereafter stopped at all intermediate stations. By this I should not give the impression of an old-style British 'parliamentary' because it was necessary to attain 130 m.p.h. on every intermediate section in order to keep time. From the cab I was able to take much more detailed measurements of the speed and our accelerations from rest than from the train. At the speed we were going between Tokyo and Nagoya for example it was difficult to sight the kilometre posts, and this was easy from the cab. The most interesting feature of course was the working of the automatic train control.

As mentioned earlier there are no lineside signals at all. This is not the first time that an important railway has been operated without lineside signals, because a busy freight section on the Pennsylvania Railroad in the U.S.A. was so equipped about 30 years ago. In that case, however, the indications given in the locomotive cabs were the standard aspects for 'stop', 'caution', and 'proceed' that were displayed by the lineside signals on other parts of the line. In contrast to this the cab indications on the Shinkansen trains tell the driver the *speed* at which he must travel. On the dashboard is a speedometer of the horizontal type, and train operation is regulated in five steps of speed, indicated by stencils on discs that are illuminated as appropriate. On open line when all is clear the disc showing 210 is illuminated, above the 210 km./h. mark on the speedometer scale.

The five steps are 210, 160, 110, 70, and 30 km./h. (130, 99, 68, 43½ and 18½ m.p.h.). All the driver is given is the illuminated number. The regulation of the speed is entirely in his hands, unless he should exceed the value indicated, when the brakes would be applied automatically.

The line is of course track circuited throughout and the automatic train control system is operated through an inductive link up between track and train. The utmost care was taken in designing the system to provide against any chance of failure, and in the 11 years in which the line has been operating, it has established a record of reliability second to none on the railways of the world. It is interesting to study the reactions on a train travelling at the maximum speed of 130 m.p.h. on approaching a location where the line was blocked, possibly by another train stopped in section. The signal sections are 3000 metres (roughly 1¾ miles) long, and the first warning that a stop might be necessary would come two sections previously, with the speed indicator changing from '210' to '160'. Immediate application of the brakes reduces the speed from 210 to 160 km./h. in half the length of a section, namely 1500 metres, after which the driver would continue at 160 or slightly less until the next check point. If a train had actually stopped in the section next but one ahead the automatic train control takes over, to stop the second train completely, short of the next check point, and at a safe distance from the obstruction.

Quite apart from a stop due to some obstruction on the line, the approach to stopping stations, which I saw from the driver's cab, is very strictly regulated, with enforced speed reductions, successively, to 160, 70, and then 30 km./h. Finally there comes an automatic brake application almost down to walking pace at the entrance to the platform. The driver must acknowledge this by pressing a button, upon which he regains personal control of the train. So far as the actual ride in the cab was concerned, our successive start-to-stop runs south of Shin-Osaka gave the following spectacular results, each including a maximum speed of 130 m.p.h. The riding was as near perfect as one could imagine, though the windscreen, when I entered the cab after the train had made the 'Hikari' run down from Tokyo, looked something like that of a car after a long fast spell on one of the

English motorways in high summer, when there are plenty of flies and other insects in the air.

Shin-Osaka to Okayama

Section	Distance miles	Time m s	Average speed m.p.h.
Shin-Osaka to Shin-Kobe	20·4	14 35	84·0
Shin-Kobe to Nishi-Akashi	13·9	10 47	77·3
Nishi-Akashi to Himeji	19·4	13 01	89·5
Himeji to Aioi	12·5	9 58	74·3
Aioi to Okayama	34·4	21 48	94·6

This line, known as the Sanyo-Shinkansen is the beginning of the extensive planned development of the high-speed national network, and the revised standards of construction and equipment, which will be applied to all subsequent work, are discussed in the concluding chapter.

CHAPTER TWENTY TWO

Nation-wide high-speed network

On May 18, 1970 the Japanese Parliament passed an act authorising the construction of nation-wide high-speed railways, the purpose of which was defined thus, in Article I of the Act:

> In view of the importance of the role played by a high-speed transportation system for the comprehensive and extensive development of the land, this Law shall be aimed at the construction of a nation-wide high-speed railway network for the purpose of promoting the growth of the national economy and the enlargement of the people's sphere of life.

The Tokaido Shinkansen had certainly been a phenomenal success in every way. The augmenting of train service and the strengthening of train formation were indications in themselves, and when I was in Japan in 1973 the all-the-year-round loading of the trains was 67 per cent. of full capacity—in other words an average of 950 people on every 16-car train, seven days a week, 365 days in the year. In development of the network J.N.R. have set their standards still higher, and these have already been incorporated in the first section of the Sanyo Shinkansen, over which I rode in the cab from Shin-Osaka to Okayama.

The new constructional standards arise from the decision to raise the maximum running speed from 130 to 160 m.p.h. and the factors shown in the table on page 217 are involved.

A radius of curvature of 2·5 *miles*, or 200 chains, would seem little removed from a straight track, and although the gradients themselves are steep when one has 16,000 horsepower available for a train of less than 1000 tons gross weight, such inclinations do not make a great deal of difference. The increase in the distance from centre to

Line	Tokaido Shinkansen	Sanyo Shinkansen
Designed max. speed	130 m.p.h.	160 m.p.h.
Minimum radius of curvature	1·56 miles	2·5 miles
Steepest gradient	1 in 50	1 in 67
Distance, centre to centre of tracks	13¾ ft.	14¼ ft.
Rail weight	130 lb. per yard	150 lb. per yard

centre of the track is to reduce still further the air resistance between two trains when passing at full speed; while the increase in rail weight is self-explanatory—for wear resisting, and increase in stability of the road. To obtain the alignment prescribed in the foregoing specification the extension of the Sanyo Shinkansen south of Okayama, which I saw under construction at many points, will have about 55 per cent. of its mileage (or 136 miles) in tunnel, making its way through the central mountain range of Honshu.

By the time this book is published the Sanyo Shinkansen will have been carried through to Shimonoseki, and under the Kanmon Straits to Hakata, on the island of Kyushu. Two new Shinkansen routes had already been decided upon north of Tokyo when I was in Japan, one running to Niigata, to be known as the Joetsu-Shinkansen, and a second running north-eastwards through Sandai to Morioka—the Tohoku-Shinkansen. At the same time further extensions had been projected, from Hakata south through Kyushu to Kagoshima, and an extension northward from Morioka to Aomori, and through the long Seikan undersea tunnel to the island of Hokkaido, and so to Sapporo. At the time of writing however it seems as though these further extensions may not be built as soon as was originally contemplated, because of the prevailing adverse economic conditions. The full extent of what is planned however can be studied from the accompanying map, and it provides a remarkable example of the faith that is put in railways in Japan, and the resurgence in railway traffic following the outstanding financial success of the Tokaido Shinkansen.

In view of the intense industrialisation of Japan the reader may well ask if the development of the Shinkansen network, as evidenced

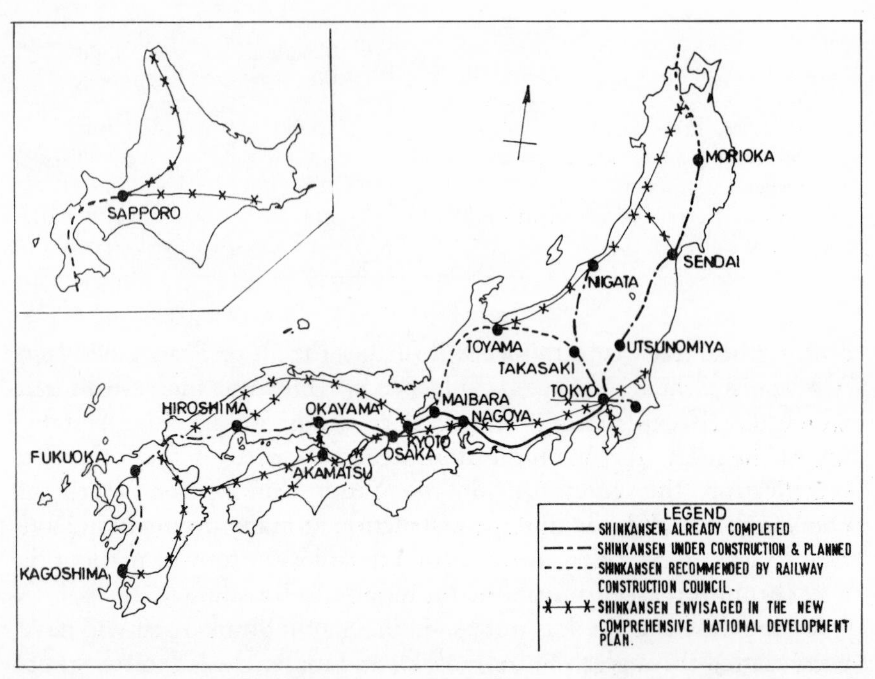

35. The nationwide Shinkansen network as now—and projected.

on the map, is to be devoted entirely to passenger traffic, as the Tokaido Line now is. The answer is almost certainly 'no'. The density of population, and the extent of industrial development is quite exceptional along the line Tokyo–Nagoya–Osaka–Hiroshima. No comparable situation at present exists along the proposed lines to the north. But the operational philosophy applied to the Tokaido-Shinkansen is readily applicable to the handling of a mixed traffic pattern of fast passenger and freight trains, and the possibility that freight will be conveyed faster than ever before in Japan, or anywhere else, would undoubtedly breed enhanced business. I have referred earlier to the construction of the undersea tunnel to Hokkaido. This project is well advanced, and will be available to improve north–south communication even before the Shinkansen Lines are extended north to feed into it.

In the meantime the original Shinkansen Line, between Tokyo and Shin-Osaka, inevitably the heaviest utilised railway in all Japan, is estimated to become completely saturated by 1980. Because of its original constructional standards it is limited to a maximum speed of 130 m.p.h. and this governs its total capacity. Looking ahead however, the Japanese National Railways are already thinking beyond a simple multiplication of facilities to meet the situation that is envisaged in 1980. Just as the Tokaido-Shinkansen provided a truly sensational acceleration between Tokyo and Osaka compared to the run of the Limited Express Trains on the 3 ft. 6 in. gauge Old Todaido Line—3 hr. 10 min. against 6 hr. 40 min.—they are planning a *really* high speed line, with a target time of exactly *one hour* between Tokyo and Osaka. Experiments have been in hand for some time with a car propelled by a 'linear motor', using the principle known as magnetic levitation. It was the basis of the now abandoned British project of the 'hover train'. The conception is that the second new line would be operated in this way to take the ultra-prestige traffic, leaving the original Tokaido-Shinkansen to cope with the tens of thousands of daily travellers who are not in *quite* such a hurry.

The prospect is quite fantastic, especially seeing how the Japanese railways began their business. In the years between 1872 and the turn of the century there had been no Brunel to declare impatiently that he would not argue with those who considered speed unnecessary. It was one of his major precepts that speed was an essential part of perfection in travelling; but one wonders if even he, the most far-seeing and venturesome of all the railway pioneers, ever looked forward to average speeds by land transport of more than 300 m.p.h.! It is an amazing thought, with which to leave this tour of railways in Asia and the Far East. For the traveller who just wants to get from A to B a train propelled by a linear motor will have much the same appeal as an aircraft, but will probably be less subject to delays. But for the person who enjoys travelling as such even the existing Shinkansen may well be getting a little too slick, and swift. It is enthralling if one should have the privilege of a driver's cab pass, and can see the incredible straightness of the line, carried regardless over hill, dale, and river estuary; straight as a die through rugged mountain ranges, and high above teeming cities; but only one, out of 1400 passengers can enjoy such a privilege. And even to a dyed-in-the-wool railway enthusiast a line on which 55 per cent. of the entire mileage is in tunnel has its disappointments, however often the speed may be sustained at 160 m.p.h.

This would nevertheless be a very one-sided note on which to leave the railways of Asia and the Far East. While it is upon Japan and its spectacular Shinkansen that these concluding chapters have focused attention, one can look back with interest and admiration for all that has gone before, not only in Japan but in the other countries of which I have written. Everywhere there is an organisation and a readiness to cope with the most violent manifestations of nature, with earthquakes, exceptional floods, such stark mountain routes as the Bolan and the Khyber passes, and pure jungle. One thing is nevertheless the same, and as unchanging, as on every railway I have ever visited, anywhere in the world. Whatever their race or creed, whatever their colour, whatever their political inclinations, railwaymen are the same the world over. If you are interested in their work, and they can sense quickly enough that you are, you are accepted at once—on locomotives, in signal boxes, workshops, and regaled with their own favourite beverages, from the hot, sweet tea of the British footplate, through all sorts of concoctions to the ceremonial green tea of Japan. I have many memories of it all on railways of Asia and the Far East.

Bibliography

Couplings to the Khyber. P. S. A. Berridge. David and Charles, 1968.
A Hundred Year History of the P. & O. Boyde Cable. Ivor Nicholson & Watson, 1937.
Indian Railway: A study in public utility administration. Amba Prasad. Asia Publishing House, Bombay, 1960.
Indian Railways 1853–1953: A Centenary history. Indian Railway Board, New Delhi, 1953.
Light Railways, in the United Kingdom, India and the Colonies. J. C. Mackay. Crosby, Lockwood & Son, 1896.
Permanent Way through the Khyber. Victor Bayley. The Beacon Library, 1939.
Railway Management in India. G. S. Khosla. Thacker & Co. Ltd., Bombay, 1972.

Burma. R. Talbot Kelly. A. & C. Black Ltd., 1905.
North British Locomotive Co. Ltd. Manufactures during the war 1914–1919. N.B.L. Co. Ltd., 1920.

Beautiful Steam: a pictorial record of Japanese trains at speed. H. Uematsu, 1972.
Centenary history of Japanese Railways 1872—1972 (in Japanese, with English picture titles). Japanese National Railways, 1972.
The Fascination of Steam Locomotives (pictures, with English titles). H. Uematsu and others. Yamakei Color Guide, 1973.

Periodicals:

The Railway Magazine. From 1897, London.
The Locomotive Magazine. From 1896, London.
The Railway Gazette. London.
Indian Railways. New Delhi.

Index